Palgrave Studies in European Union Politics

Series Editors
Michelle Egan
American University
Washington, USA

Neill Nugent
Manchester Metropolitan University
Manchester, UK

William E. Paterson
Aston University
Birmingham, UK

Following on the sustained success of the acclaimed European Union Series, which essentially publishes research-based textbooks, Palgrave Studies in European Union Politics publishes cutting edge research-driven monographs. The remit of the series is broadly defined, both in terms of subject and academic discipline. All topics of significance concerning the nature and operation of the European Union potentially fall within the scope of the series. The series is multidisciplinary to reflect the growing importance of the EU as a political, economic and social phenomenon. To submit a proposal, please contact Senior Editor Ambra Finotello ambra.finotello@palgrave.com.

More information about this series at
http://www.palgrave.com/gp/series/14629

Alexandra-Maria Bocse

International Networks, Advocacy and EU Energy Policy-Making

palgrave
macmillan

Alexandra-Maria Bocse
International Relations Department
London School of Economics and Political Science
London, UK

ISSN 2662-5873 ISSN 2662-5881 (electronic)
Palgrave Studies in European Union Politics
ISBN 978-3-030-49504-6 ISBN 978-3-030-49505-3 (eBook)
https://doi.org/10.1007/978-3-030-49505-3

Cover credit: Magic Lens / Shutterstock

This Palgrave Macmillan imprint is published by the registered company Springer Nature Switzerland AG.
The registered company address is: Gewerbestrasse 11, 6330 Cham, Switzerland

Acknowledgements

I want to thank Mette Eilstrup-Sangiovanni and Julie Smith for the support offered in the development of this research project. I owe gratitude to Joanna Depledge and Christoph Meyer for the great comments made on the manuscript. Special thanks go to Oliver Krentz for his availability to read my work and always provide a candid opinion.

I am grateful to Trinity College Cambridge and London School of Economics and Political Science for providing financial support for this research and its development into a book. I want to thank my colleagues at LSE for their advice and guidance in approaching the publishing world, particularly Karen Smith and Robert Falkner.

Above all, I thank my parents, Maria and Alexandru, for all their love and support. This book is dedicated to them.

Contents

List of Figures

List of Tables

CHAPTER 1

Introduction

Concerns related to the European energy supply security and climate change have moved energy policymaking to the centre of the European and international agenda in recent years. An impressive amount of academic literature has emerged around the EU-Russia energy relationship or the increasing role that EU institutions play in shaping European energy policy. However, the in-depth investigation of the EU policymaking environment that led to this book reveals that EU energy policy outcomes are most often the product of the interaction between the EU institutions, the EU Member States, and non-state actors based inside and outside the EU. These actors tend to form networks advocating for specific energy policy options. Consequently, this book proposes a policy network approach for investigating the expanding EU energy policy field. This volume focuses on advocacy coalitions, a type of policy networks (Eikeland 2011). The research that led to this book was triggered by two main research questions:

- *what shape does public-private interaction*[1] *take in the field of EU energy policy?*

[1] By public-private interaction this book understands the interaction between governmental and EU structures (on the one hand) and entities in the business (broadly defined) and civil society sectors (on the other hand).

A.-M. Bocse, *International Networks, Advocacy and EU Energy Policy-Making*, Palgrave Studies in European Union Politics,
https://doi.org/10.1007/978-3-030-49505-3_1

- *what explains the success of advocacy coalitions operating in the field of EU energy policy?*

The impact of interest groups has been only marginally covered by the advocacy literature, mainly because it is considered very difficult to assess (see Mahoney 2008; Dür 2008). This research attempts to remedy this by studying coalition impact. It advances and tests hypotheses with the aim of developing a theoretical model that can help us understand what factors determine the success of an advocacy coalition, as well as the way in which these factors interact in generating impact. In developing this theoretical model, the research draws on an original combination of policy networks/advocacy coalitions' literature, studies of framing, and social network theory.

The study concludes that the interplay among: informational and material resources; a broad, timely, and dynamic frame; and social structure accounts for the success of advocacy coalitions. The findings of this book depart from the focus placed in the literature on material resources when explaining the success of advocacy or lobby coalitions. Not only material power but also relational power and the interactions between different types of power are important in explaining the coalitions' success.

The volume is focused on networks working on two issues that have been central to EU energy policy debates over the last decade: fracking for domestic shale gas[2] and developing the Southern Gas Corridor, a pipeline system linking Europe with the gas-rich region of the Caspian Sea and eventually with the Middle East. This makes the book very appealing to both scholars and policy practitioners. Increasing the security of energy supply has been a priority of EU energy policy in recent years, alongside promoting sustainable energy.

The book covers an area and a range of actors that are due to play an important role in international energy policy and governance. In the EU and globally, energy policymaking is gaining importance relative to other policy fields. In addition, states alone cannot support the energy transition. Consequently, coalitions of intergovernmental organizations, states, NGOs, and corporations have emerged at regional and global levels. This

[2] Shale gas is natural gas found in natural underground rock fissures and rocks need to be broken open ('fractured' or 'fracked') to release the gas through a process known scientifically as 'hydraulic fracturing' and referred to in the policy circles in Brussels by using the more colloquial term 'fracking'.

book provides valuable theoretical and methodological tools for studying not only the international coalitions of today but also those of the future.

The Relevance of the Field of European Energy Policy

Energy policy experts based in Brussels indicate that, from the late 2000s, there was an increased interest in energy policymaking at the EU level. The 2009 Treaty of Lisbon places energy policy and specifically energy security policy formally in the EU area of competence (European Union Member States 2009a). The transfer of competences from the state to the European level in a particular policy field usually leads to the proliferation of interest group activity at the supranational, EU, level (Tenbücken 2002; Mazey and Richardson 2006). Consequently, the EU has become in recent years an attractive venue for corporations and industry associations, as well as for NGOs pursuing various energy policy interests. As an insider in Brussels energy policy circles explains, energy is an issue of interest for the EU institutions, Member States, and other Brussels-based stakeholders:

> the evolution of energy policy over the last five years has been very rapid. … When I first started here a decade ago energy policy was so minor and, you know, even when the new commissions came in, people were not really fighting to have the energy dossier and now it's a big one, it's an important one. (interview with representative of industry association 2014)

My own observation of the European institutions in 2012–2014 suggested that energy benefited from a lot of attention, despite being an area in which the EU did not have exclusive competence.

European energy policy is a particularly fruitful area for studying the impact of advocacy coalitions on policymaking. Several features of the European Union indicate that it is more open to the interaction with policy networks than a state government. European institutions often engage in stakeholder consultations that create opportunities for networks to approach the EU. The European Union institutional system is rather flat and based very much on a network model, which should make it very responsive to similar network-like structures (Rose 2000, p. 7). EU policy generally, and especially EU energy policy, appears to be prone to accommodating network-like structures of social interaction. EU and governmental officials rely upon the energy corporate and NGO sectors for technical information, energy policy implementation, investment in energy infrastructure, and so forth. Some of these private and NGO actors form policy networks and coalitions in the process of promoting a certain policy position.

Particularly, the book tackles policy relationships that are established between supranational institutions, national governments, and interest groups in the EU context in an area that is increasingly associated with that of high politics, that is, energy security policy (Eikeland 2011; Maltby 2013). In the EU context 'energy security' tends to be considered the equivalent of 'security of energy supply' (Escribano and Gracía-Verdugo 2012, p. 26). In addition to the availability of energy, the affordability of energy and using energy in a sustainable and environmental-friendly way have been growing dimensions of EU energy security over the last years (Goldthau and Sitter 2015, p. 7). Security of supply can be generated by increasing domestic production or by tapping into various external energy sources (European Commission 2013).

Case Study Selection

This research discusses the work of advocacy coalitions on two dimensions of European energy security policy, that is diversifying EU energy resources by increasing internal gas production through fracking for shale gas and facilitating EU access to the gas reserves of the Caspian region through the Southern Gas Corridor. Working on these two cases enabled me to study the work of contemporary social structures and to collect detailed and accurate information from advocacy coalition participants, especially on the social connections that they establish.[3] The two cases share the same temporal and broad legal and political contexts.

The research conducted on these two case studies is systematic and highlights processes of policy interaction in an area that benefits from increasing EU interest. The cases were selected given their centrality to the energy security policy debates taking place in Brussels in the last decade. Developing the Southern Gas Corridor benefited from increasing attention from policymakers after Russia limited gas delivery to Europe in 2009. Shale gas dominated the energy debates and energy events in

[3] In a few years' time, it is debatable if interviewees would be able to provide equally accurate information, as they might forget whom they interacted with, the details of the cases, and so forth.

Brussels as the shale gas revolution in the US made a massive contribution to the US domestic energy supply in the last decade. As one EU official noted, there are more conferences on fracking for shale gas in Brussels than exploratory drilling projects in Europe (interview with European Commission official, DG Energy 2013). This study will investigate particularly the coalitions emerging around the 'European Parliament resolution of 21 November 2012 on industrial, energy and other aspects of shale gas and oil' (European Parliament 2012a) initiated by the Parliament's Committee on Industry, Research and Energy (ITRE).

Case study research is particularly useful for investigating causal pathways, tackling causal complexity, and exploring areas in which data is limited (Gerring 2007), as is the case with the domain of EU energy policy. The in-depth investigation on the two cases allowed to process-trace the factors behind the success of the coalitions studied, as well as the interaction between these factors and their importance relative to each other. Process tracing enables the researcher 'to assess causality by recording each element of the causal chain' (Zürn 1998, p. 640) and by building 'a logical chain of evidence' (Betsill and Corell 2001, p. 77). European energy policy and especially policy outcomes studied here satisfy the criteria according to which a research topic needs to be important to the researcher, those researched (interviewed), and the broader public (Rubin and Rubin 2005, p. 48). Both fracking and the Southern Gas Corridor had the potential to radically change the EU energy security landscape. They also demand investments of billions of euro and might affect the quality of life of millions of Europeans.

This book focuses on coalitions operating in the gas sector. This is motivated by the EU's dependence on imported gas, as well as by specifics of the gas sector that make it more vulnerable to political developments.[4] Political analysis is a good tool for making sense of developments in this field. Gas is likely to play an important role in the EU energy mix as a transition fuel to a renewables-based energy system. The discovery and exploitation of shale gas reserves in North America and in the Eastern Mediterranean might extend the gas lifetime. Gas also has a reduced

[4] Buchan argues that energy security is not of equal concern in all energy sectors and that some might be more prone to energy insecurity. According to him, the gas sector which depends on foreign gas and is linked to fixed supply networks is more likely to raise energy security concerns, while the electricity sector is more concerned with network reliability and the consistency of renewable energy sources (Buchan 2010, p. 370).

carbon footprint compared to coal and it can help the EU meet its climate change commitments.

The existing literature on EU policy developments on fracking for shale gas is limited. There is an emerging body of literature on the regulatory framework in which fracking takes place in the EU and the US (Boersma and Johnson 2012; Tawonezvi 2017). Certain literature discusses the outcome of the EU level policy debates (Stokes 2014) rather than the process and coalitions that led to a certain policy outcome. Coalitions that emerged around fracking are, in general, underexplored. Some literature discusses advocacy coalitions involved in policy developments and debates in the EU (Bomberg 2017) or EU Member States (the study of Ingold et al. 2017). Bomberg (2017) explores in a comparative way the coalitions working on fracking in the EU and those in the US. However, her study is reliant mainly on media output and websites in identifying the coalition actors. This makes it more difficult to capture informal ties or ties on which information is not available publicly.

This will not be the first study conducted on the Southern Gas Corridor. However, it is to the best of my knowledge the most extensive academic study on the competition between the Nabucco Pipeline and the Trans Adriatic Pipeline (TAP), crucial to the opening of the Southern Gas Corridor. The competition ended in 2013 with the selection of TAP. Existing studies on the Southern Gas Corridor tend to focus on the preferences of governmental actors inside and outside the European Union and neglect non-state actors in explaining policy developments (such studies are the ones of Ahmadov 2010; Belova 2010; Sartori 2011, 2012; Mikhelidze 2013; Siddi 2019). This is the case despite the fact that previous studies of the involvement of energy corporations in energy developments show that energy corporations have economic leverage (decide on trade routes and pipelines, contract quantities of energy supplied, etc.), and are often able to lobby governments successfully (Jaffe et al. 2006). National and multinational companies play an important role in global and regional governance (Büthe and Mattli 2010; Ronit 2011). These would indicate that their preferences and actions should be included in any attempt to explain developments around the Southern Gas Corridor.

Theoretical Framework

This research draws on concepts such as 'advocacy coalitions', 'access goods', 'framing', and on social network theory. This subchapter will discuss these concepts, theories, and their connections, and use them to advance hypotheses that provide answers to the research questions. The first research question I advance is: ***what shape does public-private interaction take in the field of EU energy policy***? The mushrooming presence of energy interest groups in Brussels, as well as their presence in the Transparency Register,[5] would suggest that formal and informal contacts between energy interest groups and decision-makers do take place. However, as indicated also by other researchers (Kreutler 2014), few studies go beyond simply claiming interaction between energy stakeholders and decision-makers. Little is known about the nature of these contacts and their outcomes. Energy groups and organizations participate in policymaking, but participation does not necessarily mean influence or the exercise of power over policymakers (Mazey and Richardson 2006; Eikeland 2011).

The theoretical toolkit employed in this book expanded as empirical data collection progressed. The fieldwork for this research was informed by the literature on governance and especially governance exercised through networks (Rhodes 1997; Krahmann 2003b; Pollack 2010). 'Governance' in this book 'refers to self-organizing, interorganizational networks characterized by interdependence, resource exchange, rules of the game and significant autonomy from the state' (Rhodes 1997, p. 15). This book studies governance in relation to public policy and embraces a definition according to which governance: 'takes place through organized networks of public and private actors which "steer" public policy towards common ends' (Pollack 2010, p. 36).

Policy networks are defined as: 'sets of actors that share an interest in a specific issue area and are linked to each other through stable formal or informal relations' (Krahmann 2005, p. 25).[6] Lack of formalized hierarchy

[5] To increase the transparency of EU decision-making, the European Parliament and the European Commission introduced a Transparency Register. One can perform lobbying and advocacy functions without being registered. However, there are incentives for joining the Register, including physical access to the premises of the institutions. Acceding to the Register is a condition that needs to be fulfilled before requesting accreditation to the European Parliament (EP).

[6] Atkinson and Coleman (1992, pp. 157–159) provide a similar definition.

is supposed to define policy networks: 'a set of relatively stable relationships which are of non-hierarchical and interdependent nature linking a variety of actors, who share common interests' (Börzel 1998, p. 254). Resource exchanges are central to the networks' existence and activity (Bomberg 1998, p. 167). Advocacy coalitions are regarded as subspecies of policy networks (Eikeland 2011).[7]

The literature on policy networks has been successful in researching the impact of private actors on energy policymaking (Nilsson et al. 2009; Buchan 2010). The literature on security governance has analysed the role of non-state actors in shaping the field of military security, investigating, for instance, the role of private military companies (Krahmann 2005, 2010; Kinsey et al. 2009). A more comprehensive security agenda has given a mandate to a wider variety of actors to shape the field of security: 'to long-established actors in the defence industry have been added an increased number of charities, environmental organisations, human rights watchdogs, medical organisations and think-tanks' (Webber et al. 2004, p. 6). However, the role of energy companies, NGOs, and consultancies in shaping energy policy at the intersection with security policy has been overlooked. Studies on the role of corporations as energy security players are limited or outdated (Youngs conducted such a study on data previous to 2006 and published it in 2009). There is a need to further explore the way in which private actors behave when they shape areas crucial to EU energy security.

Following the actual empirical investigation of case studies, adjustments or additions in the theoretical framework are often required. The empirical data is meant to confirm or not hypotheses, but also generate new, sometimes unexpected knowledge (Rubin and Rubin 2005, p. 40). In the case of this study, the empirical investigation of European energy policy

[7] Policy networks can take different forms, depending on their characteristics. In addition to advocacy coalitions, they can take the shape of policy communities characterized by 'high interdependence, stable relationships, restricted membership, insulated from other networks' (Eikeland 2011, p. 246), or issue networks defined by 'limited interdependence, open membership, less stable relationships, less insulated from other networks' (Eikeland 2011, pp. 246–247). They can also be epistemic communities (Haas 1992a, b) if their main function is the transfer of expertise and knowledge. An epistemic community is defined as: 'a network of professionals with recognized expertise and competence in a particular domain and an authoritative claim to policy-relevant knowledge within that domain or issue-area' (Haas 1992a, p. 3). Keck and Sikkink (1998) discuss the role that 'transnational advocacy networks' of activists play in international politics. All these types draw on a network-like form of social organization.

networks revealed the polarization of different segments of the two networks. Each network included actors working on the same issue area, but their interests were opposed, and this led to the emergence of two coalitions advocating against each other. The 'advocacy coalition framework' (Sabatier 1988, 1998; Jenkins-Smith and Sabatier 1994) accommodates well such opposition that takes place between two structures that share the same policy subsystem; 'a subsystem consists of actors from a variety of public and private organizations who are actively concerned with a policy problem or issue, such as agriculture, and who regularly seek to influence public policy in that domain' (Sabatier 1998, p. 99). The advocacy coalition framework (ACF) assumes that, if certain interest groups mobilize, other interests will decide to become organized in order to counteract them (Mazey and Richardson 2006, p. 254). As is the case with the fracking for shale gas study presented in this book, one faction tends to represent economic interests and the other faction represents environmental interests (Sabatier and Brasher 1993; Jenkins-Smith and Sabatier 1994).[8] The ACF explains policy outcomes in complex multi-level subsystems and facilitates the understanding of policy changes in particular subsystems and domains, for instance, air pollution control, dangerous chemicals regulation, and so forth (Sabatier 1988, 1998; Jenkins-Smith and Sabatier 1994).

An advocacy coalition approach accommodates the presence of policy actors from different sectors, that is, companies, consultancies, NGOs, governmental officials, and so forth. The ACF regards governmental officials and legislators not only as entities that are the target of lobbying or advocacy, but also as actors in advocacy coalitions. This is also the case with the policy networks this research studies. Sabatier claims that actors in advocacy coalitions: '(a) share a set of normative and causal beliefs and (b) engage in a non-trivial degree of co-ordinated activity over time' (Sabatier 1998, p. 103). The main weakness of the frame identified by the literature is the emphasis that it places on beliefs (Rozbicka 2013). The

[8] Jenkins-Smith and Sabatier (1994) show that two different coalitions work on US automotive control: an environmental coalition (environmental and public health groups, officials in federal and state air pollution agencies, legislators, researchers and journalists) and an economic efficiency coalition (automobile manufacturers, petroleum companies, individuals in legislatures, research enterprises and media). Analysing the developments of the environmental policy concerning Lake Tahoe, Sabatier and Brasher (1993) showed that, over time, policy actors formed two major coalitions, that is an economic development/property rights coalition and an opposing environmental coalition.

framework needs to take into consideration the fact that actors build coalitions based not only on beliefs, but also on interests, interdependencies (Kenis and Schneider 1991; Börzel 1997; Rozbicka 2013) and regard for individual and organizational welfare (Schlager and Blomquist 1996). Sabatier responded to this criticism by defining beliefs broadly to include not only the aspirations of ideational groups, but also of material groups.[9] If beliefs are extended to include material goals, corporate actors operating in the energy field seeking to fulfil material objectives (for instance, maintain a certain level of profit or increase profit) can be considered members of advocacy coalitions. In addition, material interests of the energy industry are underpinned by ideological beliefs, for instance that economic growth can be fostered by competitiveness and limited state intervention. As will be shown later on, one of the arguments of the energy industry is that excessive regulation will prevent development of the shale gas sector in the EU and limit economic growth.

The advocacy coalition framework also assumes that there is a lack of trust between the coalitions opposing each other on the same policy issue. Members of different coalitions interpret pieces of information in different ways which leads to in-group cohesion and generates mistrust in relation to other coalitions that might draw different conclusions from the same data (Sabatier 1998). Sabatier argues that it is easy in high-conflict situations for one coalition to see an opposing coalition as more malign and powerful than it probably is (Sabatier 1987, 1998). This explains why it is difficult for coalitions to resolve their differences and why mobility between coalitions tends to be reduced (Sabatier 1998, pp. 105, 106). Consequently, their membership is more likely to remain stable. Of course, like many assumptions that Jenkins-Smith and Sabatier advance as part of the framework, the assumptions presented here need to be tested on empirical data. As the empirical chapters of this book will show, mistrust indeed characterizes the relations of advocacy coalitions opposing each other both on the issue of fracking and on the Southern Gas Corridor.

This book also aims to *explain the success of advocacy coalitions operating in the field of EU energy policy*. Similarly to Mahoney, I define advocacy success as: 'whether advocates achieve their goals or not at the conclusion

[9] Building on existing literature (Jenkins-Smith and St. Clair 1993; Jenkins-Smith and Sabatier 1994), he claims that: 'the most fundamental (and probably least changing) beliefs of material groups are not very abstract. Instead, they tend to be quite concrete: material self-interest, operationalized as profit or market share' (Sabatier 1998, p. 110).

of a policy debate' (Mahoney 2008, p. 183). Unlike other studies that invite associations and NGOs operating in EU energy policy to self-assess their influence when acting as a coalition (Kreutler 2014), my research will evaluate coalition success by contrasting its position with policy outcomes. Current scholarship supports hypotheses according to which advocacy coalitions are more likely to be successful:

- *If they possess and make good use of material and informational resources;*
- *If they develop a broad, timely, and dynamic frame;*
- *If they are well interconnected and include members who are central to the social structure (policy subsystem) working on a particular issue.*

Resources: Access and Influence

Resources are identified in the literature as contributing to the success of advocacy and lobby groups (Cress and Snow 1998; Bouwen 2002; Mahoney 2008). Access to material resources is considered to influence group success in shaping policy (Kohler-Koch 1994; Gerber 1999; Crombez 2002; Hall and Deardorff 2006). Possessing expertise and information is thought to be another important factor (Rozbicka 2013) and these constitute 'access goods' (Immergut 1992; Bouwen 2002). According to Mahoney (2008, p. 171), the benefit of pooling resources determines interest groups to form coalitions, especially on salient topics that are the object of a lot of public attention. However, several scholars pointed to the fact that existing advocacy coalition literature fails to explain how coalitions use resources and venues to shape policy (Weible and Sabatier 2007, p. 133; Kreutler 2014, p. 28). Building on existing literature on the role of resources in policymaking (Beyers 2004; Eising 2007), this research aims to analyse the use of material and especially informational resources in the work and successful advocacy of coalitions operating in the newer and underexplored area of EU energy policy.

The literature indicates that material resources positively impact the success of interest groups in the EU context. Eising (2007) shows that: 'a larger budget improves access to the EU institutions' (p. 339). EU associations that control large financial resources are more likely to come in weekly contact with the Commission than less-resourced associations (p. 353). A larger budget allows interest groups to employ permanent, specialized staff to conduct their campaigns (Knoke 1990, p. 76). Access to funding also allows to pay staff and researchers to conduct studies and can lead to a greater access to knowledge that can be passed on to policy-makers. That being said, there are also substantial amounts of research conducted by publicly funded institutes and universities and that is available freely to advocates (businesses or NGOs) to use.

This research will concentrate particularly on information and information exchanges. Information: 'is the most important resource to study in order to understand the exchange between business interests and the EU institutions' (Bouwen 2002, p. 369). The informational lobby is acknowledged as being the predominant type of lobby in Brussels, more important than political patronage or campaign contributions (Broscheid and Coen 2007, p. 347). In Brussels, interest groups influence decision-makers through informational services (Chalmers 2012). The European Commission has limited internal capacity to generate policy knowledge and a need to receive information from across different economic sectors and across its Member States (Mazey and Richardson 2006, p. 248). In order to fulfil its informational needs, the Commission often takes an active role in the development of transnational networks of experts and stakeholders (Princen 2011, p. 935; Maltby 2013, p. 436).

Interest group participation in the making of EU legislation enhances the quality of decisions by enabling the transfer of expertise to decision-makers (Greenwood 2007; Dür and Mateo 2012). The institutionalization of consultation with interest groups reduces the risk of policy disaster (Mazey and Richardson 2001, p. 72, 2006, p. 249). In addition, by engaging stakeholders, bureaucrats reduce opposition to their proposals in other venues and at later implementation stages and avoid being blamed for policy failure (Henderson 1977). Furthermore, through the information they provide, advocacy coalitions play an important role in linking and helping establish consensus between the EU institutions on certain policy aspects (Mazey and Richardson 2001, pp. 85, 92). Lobbyists act as carriers of ideas and understandings across various institutional venues (Dudley and Richardson 1998). The two case studies included in the book illustrate very well the benefits that EU officials find in interacting with energy corporations and NGOs.

A survey of the literature seems to indicate that opportunities for interaction between EU institutions and interest groups increase when it comes to highly technical areas and areas characterized by uncertainty. Broscheid and Coen (2007, p. 361) show that there is a positive correlation between the information demand on an issue and the volume of lobbying. Interest groups contribute information, especially on specific and technical issues, to the work of both the European Commission and the European Parliament (EP) (Mazey and Richardson 2006, pp. 256, 259, 261). In addition, Zito argues that the more complex and ambiguous the policy problems, the greater will be the role that experts play in EU policy (Zito 2001, p. 588). The extreme complexity of the energy policy field increases the dependence of EU institutions on private actors as information providers,[10] while the high economic stakes associated with energy policy constitute an important incentive for interest groups to supply information (Nilsson et al. 2009).

Under conditions of uncertainty, policymakers turn to experts for advice. The uncertainties faced by decision-makers are generated by the increasingly technical nature of issues entering the international agenda, for instance monetary, macro-economic, environmental, population, and health issues (Haas 1992a, p. 12). Energy exploitation, transport, and consumption can also be added to this list. Reducing uncertainty is an important goal for both policymakers and legislators. Similarly, the corporate sector is very interested in reducing uncertainty and engages in dialogue with governmental and supranational actors in order to address issues associated with potential public sector action that might have an impact on the business environment. Therefore, the information exchange on issues related to energy policy can be expected to be very intense.

Opposing advocacy coalitions cite scientific work in support of their arguments and the scientific evidence is sometimes contradictory. A more detailed discussion of this will take place in the chapters on the coalitions working on fracking. However, neither public servants nor researchers should be treated as neutral entities in the policymaking process. A wide range of literature indicates the lack of neutrality (Primack and von Hippel 1974; Knott and Miller 1987; Jenkins-Smith 1990; Barke and Jenkins-Smith 1993; Zafonte and Sabatier 1998).

The paragraphs above indicate that resources and especially information and knowledge exchanges play an important role in the work of advocacy coalitions operating in the EU context. Therefore, this section will advance the following hypotheses to be tested in relation to my two case studies.

Advocacy coalitions are more likely to be successful if they possess:

[10] A function scholarship associates to interest groups (Bouwen 2002, p. 369; Dür and Mateo 2012, p. 972) operating in the EU context.

- *informational resources of a technical nature*;
- *financial resources.*

Framing as a Source of Influence

The concept of framing will be used in this study to explain the process through which advocacy coalitions contributed to a change in understanding regarding the benefits of shale gas and of an alternative route for the Southern Gas Corridor, as well as a change in the broader understanding of what EU energy security entails. I argue that changing the understanding that decision-makers have on these issues shapes policy outcomes in these fields. Frames reshape the way policy actors consider policy problems and even 'bias' their response in tackling them (Dudley and Richardson 1999).

Framing entails: 'selecting, organising, interpreting, and making sense of a complex reality to provide guideposts for knowing, analysing, persuading, and acting' (Rein and Schön 1993, p. 146). The act of framing involves a narrative, one in which the accent falls on certain aspects of reality. This focus on certain aspects of reality is mentioned by Entman: 'to frame is to select some aspects of a perceived reality and make them more salient in a communicating text, in such a way as to promote a particular problem definition, causal interpretation, moral evaluation, and/or treatment recommendation' (Entman 1993, p. 52). A frame goes beyond being a mere argument as it provides a certain understanding of the world (Hänggli and Kriesi 2012).[11] Frames enable individuals, groups, and organizations to interpret the world around them (Gahan and Pekarek 2013).

As Oliver and Johnston (1999), Marx Ferree and Merrill (2000), and Vliegenthart and van Zoonen (2011) show, in the literature the distinction between frame and framing is often poorly made as many fail to differentiate between the content features ('frames') and the process and contextual features of building and receiving the frame ('framing') (Vliegenthart and van Zoonen 2011, p. 102). Framing is defined as a process through which a frame is built by taking into account a particular context and audience. The literature acknowledges that frames are multiple and can be oppositional, as well as being: 'part of a struggle for

[11] Nowadays, the concept of 'frame' is used to provide explanations all across the social sciences (Benford and Snow 2000). It is present in cognitive psychology, linguistics, media studies, and political science (Rein and Schön 1993; Triandafyllidou and Fotiou 1998).

meaning between different actors that have unequal material and symbolic resources' (Vliegenthart and van Zoonen 2011, p. 105). As discussed in more detail later in the book, in the cases of fracking and the Southern Gas Corridor coalitions advance frames that are in many respects oppositional.

This book will mostly engage with processes such as frame amplification and frame extension to which different coalition actors studied by this research resort in order to attract more support for their point of view and achieve desired policy outcomes. The literature on social movement organizations (SMOs) and especially the work in this field undertaken by Snow and Benford provide a lot of insight, transferable to advocacy coalitions, into frame construction and change.

Frame alignment processes are defined as: 'the linkage of individual and SMO interpretive orientations, such that some set of individual interests, values and beliefs and SMO activities, goals, and ideology are congruent and complementary' (Snow et al. 1986, p. 464). There are different types of alignment processes, frame amplification and frame extension being more relevant for this study. Frame amplification entails:

> the clarification and invigoration of an interpretive frame that bears on a particular issue, problem or set of events. Because the meaning of events and their connection to one's immediate life situation are often shrouded by indifference, deception or fabrication by others, and by ambiguity or uncertainty (Goffman 1974), support for and participation in movement activities is frequently contingent on the clarification and reinvigoration of an interpretive frame. (Snow et al. 1986, p. 469)[12]

Frame amplification can be used also to attract support for and participation in advocacy coalitions. Frame extension is a concept that helps us understand how lobbyists and advocates build a sufficiently broad frame. Through frame extension: 'an SMO may have to extend the boundaries of its primary framework so as to encompass interests or points of view that are incidental to its primary objectives but of considerable salience to

[12] Snow et al. also advance the concept of frame transformation, but I do not find it very different from the concept of frame amplification. Frame transformation: 'redefines activities, events, and biographies, that are already meaningful from the standpoint of some primary framework, in terms of another framework' (Snow et al. 1986, p. 474 drawing on Goffman 1974, pp. 43–44).

potential adherents' (Snow et al. 1986, p. 472). The social movement in this case is:

> portraying its objectives or activities as attending to or being congruent with the values or interests of potential adherents. The micromobilization task in such cases is the identification of individual or aggregate level values and interests and the alignment of them with participation in movement activities. (Snow et al. 1986, p. 472)

The ACF claims that coalition members need to be entrepreneurial in order to induce policy change by taking advantage of the changes in the policy context (Jenkins-Smith and Sabatier 1994). Changing policy requires: '(a) significant perturbations external to the subsystem (e.g. changes in socio-economic conditions, system-wide governing coalitions, or policy outputs from other subsystems) and (b) exploitation of those opportunities by the heretofore minority coalition within the subsystem' (Jenkins-Smith and Sabatier 1994, p. 179). External events will translate into policy change only if a coalition is willing and able to use them entrepreneurially (Radaelli 1999; Weible et al. 2009). External events are a necessary, but not sufficient cause for policy change (Sabatier 1998). In the case studies presented in this book, policy actors integrate arguments regarding external crises into their frame in order to attract support.

Counterframing or prognostic framing: 'typically includes refutations of the logic or efficacy of solutions advocated by opponents as well as a rationale for its own remedies' (Benford and Snow 2000, p. 617). Benford and Snow argue that: 'opposing framing activity can affect a movement's framings, on the one hand, by putting movement activists on the defensive, at least temporarily, and, on the other hand, by frequently forcing it to develop and elaborate prognoses more clearly than otherwise might have been the case' (ibid. 2000, p. 617). This seems to indicate that the frames are not developed in isolation, but shaped by what the opposing coalition says or might say. Actors have an incentive to refer to their opponents' frames if those frames are successful or they anticipate they will be successful (Hänggli and Kriesi 2012, pp. 262, 264, 275).

Based on the discussion in this section, I hypothesize that advocacy coalitions are more likely to succeed if they advance frames that:

- *are broad and resonate with many actors;*
- *respond to exogenous unfolding events;*
- *respond effectively to opposing frames.*

Can a frame prevail based only on its discursive merits or does it also matter who articulates it and where that actor stands in the policy subsystem? Benford and Snow claim that 'framing is a dynamic, ongoing process' which 'does not occur in a structural or cultural vacuum' (Benford and Snow 2000, p. 627). This study will build on such literature to argue that, when discussing the effectiveness of actors as information conveyors and framers, the position they occupy in broader social structures is highly relevant.[13] The next section will show how social network theory can help us understand the connection between the ability of an actor to promote a particular frame and its position in social structures.

Network Theory and Structure

Advocacy coalitions and policy subsystems are networked social structures characterized by informality. In order to explain the dynamics taking place at the level of the policy subsystem and the success of certain advocacy coalitions, I draw on network theory. Networks are thought to play an important role in the exchange of information and frame promotion. In trying to explain the success of certain actors in convincing other actors to embrace their point of view in the process of influencing EU policy and legislation, this research examines not only the power different members of coalitions have as a result of their attributes, but also the power they display as a result of their interaction with other members of the subsystem:

> a structural analysis of networks equates the power of a particular node[14] to its position in the network, defined by its persistent relationships with other nodes. Power is no longer derived solely or even primarily from individual attributes, such as material capabilities. (Hafner-Burton et al. 2009, p. 570)

[13] This is not to say that there is not also literature claiming that specific identity categories, such as race and class, play an important role in determining successful frames (Ernst 2009). Considering race and class would not make any difference here as the actors involved in the cases studied are white policy elites.

[14] In network studies, network members are referred to as 'nodes'. In social network analysis software they can be referred to as 'vertices' and connections between them as 'edges'. Connections between actors are also referred to as 'links' and 'ties' in this book.

If in the power-as-currency/attributional power approach the power of each actor is dependent on the possession of weapons, financial resources, personnel, and so forth, the relational approach to power assumes that the actor's position in the network shapes its power to influence decision-making (Krahmann 2003b). The concept of relational power rejects attempts to explain human behaviour as caused only by the categorical attributes of individual or collective actors and generates explanations that are based on the involvement of actors in structured social relations (Emirbayer and Goodwin 1994, p. 1414). For network theorists, relations among actors rather than the actors' interests, power, or ideology are causally significant (Goddard 2009, p. 254). Hafner-Burton et al. argue that structural relations are as important, if not more important, than the features of a network member in determining political outcomes (Hafner-Burton et al. 2009, p. 560).

This is not to say that resources, informational or material, do not matter. In the process of networking and network development there is often an interplay between attributional and relational power. Material resources can be used by certain actors to build social connections with other actors. This makes it difficult to measure the impact of relational power in isolation from attributional power. However, there are some ways to do so. For instance, the policy subsystem analysis and map included in this book capture attributional power that is already converted into relational power.

Highly interconnected networks are thought to support more efficiently flows of resources, policy ideas, and preferences in the networks (Krackhardt 1990; Faul 2013). Transposed to the field of advocacy coalitions, such an assumption would indicate that connectedness enables the coalition members to engage in information exchanges, pool their resources, and develop/change frames in order to achieve their advocacy goal. The closer these members are in the social space, the more likely they are to act jointly as successful advocates.

Policy success happens at the subsystem level so the research will examine the positions that key actors in each coalition occupy in the broader policy subsystem working on the issue. According to social network theory, the positions that actors occupy in the network are indicative of their power and influence in the network (Hafner-Burton et al. 2009). Nodes central to networks possess a greater amount of social capital (Hafner-Burton et al. 2009, p. 568). 'Social capital' is: 'the sum of resources, actual or virtual, that accrue to an individual or a group by virtue of possessing a durable network of more or less institutionalized relationships of mutual acquaintance and recognition' (Bourdieu and Wacquant 1992, p. 119). A high level of social capital is determined both by the number of links a network actor has with other network actors and by the capital (economic, cultural, or symbolic) that the latter possess (Bourdieu 1986, p. 249). Possessing a high number of connections (known in the network literature also as 'ties') is considered to be a source of power and influence in the network. As Carley argues, well-connected individuals 'are seen as having greater power in the organization to affect the flow of information and decisions' (Carley 2006, p. 58).

Actors that are well connected in the network are often referred to as hubs (Kahler 2009a). Previous research on transnational advocacy networks operating in the field of security showed that hubs play an important role in deciding what issue will be included on the network agenda (Carpenter 2011).[15] Carpenter claims hubs play an important role in shaping understandings and in setting the agenda within the broader social network as contagion effects are noticeable in the network when hubs adopt new issues. This is consistent with claims advanced by Goddard according to which political entrepreneurs are more likely to come from the interstices of networks as this enables them to set connections between different ideas and discourses (Goddard 2009). Lake and Wong (2009) also argue organizations central to a transnational advocacy network set conditions of network participation and decide on the messages to be passed through the network. This would suggest that these hubs play an important role in the circulation of information in the policy subsystem and can contribute significantly to the way understandings of an issue are developed at the level of coalitions (if they are central to these coalitions) and policy subsystems (if they are central to these subsystems).

From network theory, this research will draw upon the concept of 'brokerage' which helps explain why certain actors in coalitions are more likely to influence policymaking on the issue area of shale gas, as well as the Southern Gas Corridor. Brokers are a type of network hubs. Given their role as connectors between actors that would otherwise be isolated, brokers 'provide shortcuts in network typology, allowing for new ideas to spread faster than would otherwise be possible' (Kenney 2009, p. 95). Brokerage is an efficient way of reducing network segmentation (Diani

[15] Carpenter 2011 makes this argument in her study of the advocacy networks demanding the banning of land mines, blinding lasers, depleted uranium munitions, and autonomous weapons.

2003).[16] They play an important role in facilitating information flows within the network (Kenney et al. 2012, p. 740). Brokers have a privileged position in policy subsystems and policy networks they are part of.

The presence of brokers has implications for our understanding of advocacy networks as it shows that they are not flat structures, but that certain actors can dominate the network, generating a degree of hierarchy in its structure. The pathways between nodes peripheral to the network pass through the hubs (Carpenter 2011). There is an expectation that policy subsystem members that are well connected to other members and benefit from a central position in the subsystem will impact more on the information exchange and framing processes.

The hypotheses that this section advances are that advocacy coalitions are more likely to be successful if:

- *they are well interconnected*;
- *they include nodes central to a policy subsystem.*

This research contributes to the nascent literature on the relation between the position actors occupy in a network and their impact. The Advocacy Coalition Framework literature has recently called for drawing more upon network theory to explain the interdependencies between actors in coalitions (Rozbicka 2013, p. 849). Social network analysis will help detect the central actors in the policy subsystems. The next section includes details of this data analysis method, as well as the other data collection and analysis methods used in this book.

Research Methods

The hypotheses advanced in the previous section are tested by using mixed methods of data collection and analysis. For increased accuracy, in studying the coalitions, this research resorts to triangulation, meaning that it uses different methods of data collection or different sources of data in the study of certain phenomena (Mays and Pope 2000; King and Horrocks 2010). Both methodological triangulation (using various methods to

[16] Several scholars have written on the power that brokers possess given their ability to bridge structural holes in networks and connect actors or network segments that would remain disconnected in their absence in transnational activist networks (Carpenter 2011), terrorist networks (Enders and Su 2007), or state networks (Hafner-Burton et al. 2009).

answer the same research question) and data triangulation (using various data sources) are employed in this study. Data triangulation is also achieved through interviewing various actors, often with conflicting positions on the work and dynamics of the coalitions studied here.[17] By triangulating between the interviews, I made sure that I: 'check apparent contradictions and inconsistencies' (Rubin and Rubin 2005, p. 64).[18]

The volume draws on interviews with networks' members and energy stakeholder and over six months of fieldwork and participant observation. Through its choice of data collection and analysis methods (Table 1.1), the research design brings to the forefront the voices of contemporary energy policy actors and captures in this way their formal and informal policymaking and networking practices. Data sources include also official documents and other written output, specifically, European Parliament debate transcripts, official statements, organizational declarations, websites, and various newsletters of EU institutions, businesses, and NGO entities. The consultation of official documents and archives was an

Table 1.1 The mix of data collection and data analysis methods used in this research

Area of study	*Sources of data*			*Methods of data analysis*		
	Documents	*Interviews*	*Participant observation*	*Content analysis*	*Discourse analysis*	*Social network analysis*
Public-private interaction	X	X	X	X		X
Resources (including informational resources)	X	X	X	X		
Frames	X	X			X	
Social structure		X		X		X

Source: Author

[17] It is actually a common practice for researchers to: 'seek to recruit participants who represent a variety of positions in relation to the research topic, of a kind that might be expected to throw light on meaningful differences in experience' (King and Horrocks 2010, p. 29).

[18] Rubin and Rubin claim that: 'over the course of a long, in-depth interview, and better yet several, you can usually figure out where a person is exaggerating and what areas he or she is ignoring' (Rubin and Rubin 2005, p. 71).

important step in understanding the background of the case studies presented in this book and in preparing the research fieldwork. The qualitative analysis of interviews with members of advocacy coalitions is combined with the quantitative social network analysis of the connections established between these members.[19]

Social network analysis is used to generate comprehensive sociograms mapping the coalitions and to study the relations established among their members. The research innovatively combines group metrics (for instance, coalition density) and individual actors' metrics (for instance, betweenness centrality) to determine the structural factors that lead to the success of an advocacy coalition. Such a methodological approach can be replicated in other studies.

At the same time, the study provides a solid methodology for studying opposing coalitions. Very often only one advocacy coalition in a policy subsystem is studied and mapped, reflecting only one side of the policy debate (see the work of Keck and Sikkink 1998; Carpenter 2011). Such an approach cannot capture the interaction between opposing advocacy coalitions emerging from the same policy subsystem. On topics on which opposing advocacy coalitions influence each other, analysis needs to take place at the level of the policy subsystem to fully explain their success or failure. In addition to the novelty of the findings it presents, the book innovates methodologically.

Semi-structured Interviews

In my study, semi-structured interviews play a central role in the data collection process, as they allow for the collection of data in a structured and comparable way (data collection on similar issues from all interviewees), while at the same time they make possible the exploration of unanticipated topics and themes. Semi-structured interviews are suitable for studying

[19] This research follows a methodology embraced by other studies of advocacy coalitions. Well-established studies of networked structures also draw on a set of mixed methods and interviews as the main data collection method. For example, Chilvers (2008) combined interview and documentary methods with social network analysis in his study of an environmental epistemic community, while Hollis (2010) draws in his study of trans-governmental networks on a combination of interviews with network members, website analysis, and analysis of the minutes of network meetings in order to trace network connections. In their study of a religious activist network, Kenney et al. (2012) use a combination of interviews, participant observation, and analysis of documents.

less explored phenomena and social structures, such as advocacy and lobby networks operating in the field of energy at the EU level. I began my fieldwork in Brussels (1 September 2013–1 March 2014) as a visiting researcher with the Committee on Industry, Research and Energy in the European Parliament. In spring 2014 I also travelled for interviews to Bucharest, Budapest, Vienna, Paris, and Sunbury, UK. All in all, for this research 88 semi-structured in-depth interviews with policy elites working on fracking for shale gas and on the Southern Gas Corridor were conducted. Three interviewees, a US official, a consultant, and an MEP assistant worked on both cases so they were interviewed on both.

On the fracking for shale policy subsystem, I conducted 45 interviews out of the 48 interviews I intended to complete.[20] Three interviewees declined the interview invitation or postponed the interview for so long that interviewing was no longer feasible. I interviewed the key people in the organizations working on the issue studied. On the shale gas case study, I interviewed EU officials, MEP assistants, representatives of energy corporations, NGOs, individuals from energy and chemical industry associations or consultancies, and governmental officials representing EU states and states outside of the EU. All these interviewees contributed to the debate and policy on shale gas extraction in the European Union, in particular to the 'European Parliament resolution of 21 November 2012 on industrial, energy and other aspects of shale gas and oil' (European Parliament 2012a).

On the Southern Gas Corridor case study, I interviewed high-ranking EU officials, ambassadors, or high-ranking officials of EU Member States and non-EU states (from the Caspian region), individuals from energy corporations, energy consortia, and consultancies working on the Southern Gas Corridor, as well as energy experts. Those interviewed were directly involved in initiating, shaping, and making possible the development of the Southern Gas Corridor. They were in the best position to comment on the motivation and interests that several actors had in opening the Southern Gas Corridor. The interviews effectively complemented the information available on the Southern Gas Corridor in public documents. They offered insight into aspects of policymaking on which there is no written evidence.

I chose to specifically look at the dynamics of this policy subsystem in 2013, when there was fierce competition between the pipelines Nabucco

[20] Forty-two interviewees are directly quoted in this book on this case study.

West and the Trans Adriatic Pipeline around assuming a role in the opening of the Corridor. As regards governmental engagement in the development of the Southern Gas Corridor, sometimes different ministries were involved (of Foreign Affairs, Energy, Economy, etc.) and sometimes even Cabinets of Prime-ministers. I aimed to interview the highest-ranking officials from these ministries and those that were also regarded by other actors working on the Corridor as important in acting on behalf of their countries on the international stage. I interviewed 43 out of the 47 actors I identified as relevant for this research.[21] Four potential interviewees have either never responded to my interview request or have postponed the interview so many times that rescheduling the interview was impossible. In a few cases, the subjects approached declined the interview and indicated other persons they felt might have better information to offer.

In order to identify and interview all the relevant policy actors, I employed the snowball technique: 'the technique of building an exponentially increasing network of research subjects from an original subject zero' (Gusterson 2008, p. 98). The snowball technique is a good method to reach interviewees and uncover at the same time connections between them (Krahmann 2003a). By enabling the researcher to access the network sample gradually, the snowball technique also helps to define the social network (or advocacy coalition) boundaries (Goodman 1961; Wasserman and Faust 1994; Krahmann 2003a). The technique is very helpful in signalling to the researcher when interviewing should stop.[22] The snowball technique is a convenient sampling technique that usually has the limitation of creating a random sample that can generate biases. To reduce the bias and avoid being trapped in the social preference circle of a particular interviewee, I interviewed not only the policy actors that an interviewee recommended me to interview, but the actors he/she reported to have interacted with on the issue studied, including those considered policy opponents.

The starting point for my snowballing on the fracking for shale gas case was what I perceived to be a neutral interviewee, that is, the European Parliament Administrator supervising the drafting and voting process of the resolution at the Secretariat of the Committee on Industry, Research and Energy (ITRE). The starting point for the network working on the

[21] Forty-two interviewees are directly quoted in this book on this case study.

[22] The snowball technique was successfully used to map networked structures and their dynamics also in other studies (Carroll and Ratner 1996).

Southern Gas Corridor was a senior EU Commission official who was at the very centre of policy developments around the Southern Gas Corridor. In turn, these actors mentioned and recommended other interviewees. I made sure I interviewed at least one source from each of the organizations identified by my background research and my interviewees as directly involved in the two issues studied.

Towards the end of my fieldwork, I reached a 'saturation point' (Burnham et al. 2008) as no additional data was emerging through interviewing and the data gathered had led to an in-depth understanding of the dynamics that characterized the two networks.[23] In qualitative interview research, when that point is reached interviewing stops (Glaser and Strauss 1967; Rubin and Rubin 2005). All interviewees are highly educated and knowledgeable policy elites which increases my confidence in their answers. Of course, expertise does not exclude misrepresentation, but triangulation among interviews and between interviews and written sources allowed me to control for misreporting.

Interviews present the advantage that they allow for capturing the perspective of network participants on energy events, policy interactions, and developments in this particular area. They offered me access to data that only the actors that are directly involved in policymaking around the issue of shale gas or the Southern Gas Corridor are likely to have. Some information will not be available in writing given its nature (for instance, information on social interaction in the process of policymaking around a particular area), or given the secrecy with which policymakers perform some of their tasks, although they may be quite willing to talk about that issue after the policy cycle is completed:

> on truly important dossiers you never write anything down, it is the first thing. … You never expose yourself, say what you are going to do and why you are going to do it. If you do so, you just invite whoever opposes you to cause a problem. It doesn't make any sense. (interview with senior European Commission official, DG Energy 2013)

Beyond official exchanges of documents, emails, and mail, the EU policy process is characterized by a substantial amount of informality that

[23] Several network peripheral nodes were not interviewed as this process would have been very resource intensive and the probability of them generating additional information was low.

makes interviewing an essential step in the research process as interviewees are the only source that can shed light on informal interactions. Personal exchanges and personal interaction play an important role in the Brussels energy policy environment so humans remain an important source of information:

> I prefer to have meetings face-to-face as much as possible, as many as possible because it is easy to exchange information, or exchange knowledge and attitudes when you see each other. It is not always possible because of the time constraints. (interview with Polish official 2013)

Preference was given to face-to-face interviews as establishing a rapport is easier in a face-to-face context, but in a limited number of cases, interviews were conducted via Skype calls.[24] Skype was used in order to avoid data gaps in the case of respondents who were based in different locations across and outside the EU, locations that I could not travel to for logistical and financial reasons.[25] As I came to the EU energy policy field from a politics/policy background, I had to familiarize myself quickly with the economic and scientific dimension of this area to be able to 'speak the same language' as policy actors with a technical background whom I interviewed. However, the most difficult challenge encountered in this type of research is getting past the official institutional or governmental position, especially when it comes to interviewing diplomats, senior civil servants, and EU officials. A strategy I adopted in order to go beyond the formally approved answer was to indicate what I 'already know, to make it appear useless to stonewall' (Rubin and Rubin 2005, p. 195). I also left potentially sensitive questions to the second part of the interview, as advised in the methods literature (ibid. 2005, p. 32). Some interviewees approached themselves the sensitive information after a solid rapport was built during the first part of the interview.

[24] The main concern with technology-mediated interviews is that some people might not have access to it (Hewson 2007) and the sound and video quality might be poor. Otherwise, scholars express confidence in the method (Matthews and Cramer 2008; King and Horrocks 2010). Access to technology was not an issue for those interviewed for this research.

[25] Mérand et al. 2011 use a similar strategy to increase the response rate by complementing face-to-face interviews with questionnaires that the interviewees filled in themselves.

This research protects the anonymity of interviewees[26] by not disclosing the interviewees' names. The book references the interviews using only the informants' positions and, in some cases, only the organizational affiliation or the affiliation to a certain sector (when interviewees expressed a strong preference in this regard). When that position was unique and could lead to the identification of the person, special permission was requested to use that position as a reference. Making reference only to the position occupied by an informant allows the identity of the interviewee to be protected, while the social-scientific value of the research is not affected (Wengraf 2001, p. 187).

Participant Observation

Participant observation was used to reconfirm some of the general patterns in the network dynamics I became aware of through interviews. Participant observation enables the study of human behaviour in its natural setting in order to develop a scientific understanding of that behaviour or human association (Lofland and Lofland 1984). In addition to interviewing energy policymakers, I spent over six months observing EU decision-makers in their natural environment while a visiting researcher at the European Parliament, the Secretariat of the Committee on Industry, Research and Energy.[27] Physical access to the European buildings and especially the European Parliament enabled general observations on how the interaction between the MEPs, EU administration, and private energy actors takes place formally, as well as informally, in locations such as the 'Mickey Mouse' Bar in the European Parliament or the Exki cafe in Rond-Point Schuman, near the European Commission's main building.

Affiliation with the European Parliament played an important role in the successful completion of the fieldwork. First, it made it easier for me to secure interviews (for instance, with corporate representatives who may have been reluctant to disclose information on sensitive affairs such as shale gas and fracking to researchers). Second, it facilitated my participation in policy events related to my research, where I could perform

[26] The promise of anonymity also encourages sources to disclose more information than they would in its absence.

[27] Previous cases using participant observation to study this particular field include the study on the logic of access of corporate lobbying in the European Union conducted by Bouwen 2002.

participant observation or approach policy actors to ask for interviews. Affiliation as a visiting researcher with the European Parliament also helped me to network with organizations such as the Brussels Energy Club and The Energy Charter Treaty Secretariat, and so forth. Through these organizations, I gained access to energy experts I interviewed on general trends in energy policymaking. The interview process benefited from an over 90% positive response rate.[28] The high positive response rate increases the accuracy of the findings and renders more credible claims made regarding the structure and dynamics of these advocacy coalitions. Finally, affiliation to the EP provided me with a centrally situated office, which allowed for better management of my time, especially when interviewing subjects in the European quarter, and with access to the EP library, which has a broad collection of books on European Affairs.[29]

Data Analysis

Data analysis was performed on the transcribed interviews and the fieldwork observation notes. This study combines analysis of the coalition frames/narratives present in documents and interviews with social network analysis.

The literature claims that we can analyse frames by analysing certain types of discourses (Vicari 2010, p. 522). Burnham et al. 2008 define discourse as: 'the interrelated texts, conversations and practices associated

[28] I would send my interview invitations on a Tuesday (as Monday is a busier day), mentioning to the interviewee that I would like to interview them the following week and suggesting two days of that week when I could meet. The email included brief information on me, my research, and the anticipated duration of the interview, and the informed consent form in attachment. If I received no reply to my initial email, I sent a second invitation (a reminder) a week later. In the case of no reply, I sent a third and final invitation the following week and tried also to reach the person's assistant by phone and express how important the interview was for my research. Phoning is important because people I needed to interview, for instance EU officials, receive dozens of meeting/interview requests during the week via email and this showed them that I was really interested in meeting them, that I am more eager than other researchers, journalists, or lobbyists.

[29] The status of visiting researcher with the European Parliament allowed me the access I needed for participant observation. However, by associating myself with the European Parliament, I ran the risk that some interviewees might not disclose their true view on the European Union institutions in the answers they provided me with during interviews. I reduced this tendency by making it clear that I am approaching them in my capacity as an independent researcher, conducting independent research funded by an academic institution, and that my affiliation with the EP was actually intended to support my research.

with a particular object' (Burnham et al. 2008, p. 250). Discourse analysis can show how language and communication influences social action, in general, and policies, in particular, by legitimizing or marginalizing certain policy initiatives (Burnham et al. 2008). Discourse analysis will offer insight into the understandings and motivations that determine the behaviour of energy actors. In addition, a similarity between private and EU institutional discourse is indicative of the exchange of information and ideas between non-state and EU representatives.

Analysis of the frames advanced by advocacy coalitions is complemented by social network analysis (SNA) which helps to reveal the structural attributes of actors. Social network analysis involves measuring, mapping, and analysing links among a group of entities (nodes), which may be human or non-human, for instance, computer or corporate networks (John and Cole 1998). Network analysis helps to uncover: 'patterns of relationships, such as hubs, cliques, or brokers, and to link those relations with outcomes of interest' (Hafner-Burton et al. 2009, p. 561). Network analysis is: 'eminently suited for capturing, analyzing, and modelling complexity' (Maoz 2012, p. 251). International networks, including advocacy coalitions, are complex structures that social network analysis can help grasp.

Social network analysis will be used in this research for several purposes: (1) to generate network maps (sociograms) that offer a good overview of who the members of the policy subsystem and advocacy coalitions are, as well as an overview of their connections (or ties); (2) to determine how interconnected the members of a coalition are with each other; and (3) to determine the centrality of certain actors in the policy subsystem.

(1) A methodological challenge that this study encountered was to translate the concepts of policy subsystem and advocacy coalitions into the language of social network analysis. For SNA purposes, a policy subsystem will be treated in this study as the equivalent of a network out of which advocacy coalitions emerge as cliques/clusters. 'Cliques' are defined in the literature on social network analysis as: 'cohesive sub-groups into which a network can be divided' (Scott 1991, p. 103). The term 'clique' is sometimes used alongside that of 'cluster' defined as 'an area of relatively high density in a graph' (Scott 1991, p. 129). It is expected that a clique will be characterized by a high density of connections among its members, by contrast to the rest of the social network. Policy subsystems, policy networks, advocacy coalitions are concepts that assume the networked, horizontal, and non-hierarchical interaction between policy actors. The specific literature on advocacy coalitions is, however, in general limited to using

the concept 'network' as a metaphor and attempts to map in detail these networks, their membership and connections are almost non-existent. The study will map entire networks (policy subsystems) and network cliques (advocacy coalitions).

(2) This study will look at coalition level metrics such as density and geodesic distance. Density: 'is indicative of the degree of connectedness of a social structure' (Mérand et al. 2011, p. 136). Density: 'measures the number of lines in a network expressed as a proportion of the maximum possible number of lines. Density is relative unless it is 0 (no line connects actors) or 1 (all possible lines between actors are drawn)' (Mérand et al. 2011, pp. 136–137). It is of course highly unlikely that all actors will be connected with all other actors in a social network. Establishing social ties and maintaining them is resource intensive. The larger the network analysed, the lower the chances that an actor will maintain ties with all the other network actors. There is an expectation that larger networks will have lower densities (Scott 1991, p. 77). Another measure that this research will look at is the geodesic distance, defined as the distance between two network members along the shortest path established between them. A short distance indicates that the members of a network tend to form a close, tight group. Here I look at the average geodesic distance (obtained by adding all geodesic distances among all possible pairs of nodes and dividing them by the number of pairs) and at the maximum geodesic distance (the highest number of network nodes that any node needs to cross to reach any other node, along the shortest path established between them; also known as network diameter).

(3) To determine the centrality of an actor in the policy subsystem this study looks at two measures, that is, degree centrality and betweenness centrality. According to Carpenter, these are the two measures that indicate if an actor is an advocacy coalition hub (Carpenter 2011, pp. 74–75). There is usually agreement in the literature that nodes that display a high level of degree and betweenness centrality are rich in social capital (Hafner-Burton et al. 2009). Degree centrality refers to the number of connections that a member of the network has with other members, a high number implying a high degree centrality (John and Cole 1998; Carley 2006).

The problem with degree centrality is that: 'it captures in part one's belonging to a dense subgroup rather than one's reach across the whole network' (Mérand et al. 2011, p. 129). A subsystem actor might display a high degree centrality because it is connected with many other nodes in the same coalition, but this does not necessarily mean that it is equally influential in the whole policy subsystem. To tackle this problem, this research also uses the measure of betweenness centrality. Betweenness centrality refers to: 'the number of shortest paths in the network that pass through a particular node, and therefore it measures the dependence of a network on a particular node for maintaining connectedness' (Hafner-Burton et al. 2009, p. 564). Betweenness centrality indicates the extent to which an actor is an intermediary between different sections of the network that would be disconnected in its absence (John and Cole 1998; Gulati et al. 2002; Goddard 2009; Kenney et al. 2012). This research will follow Freeman (1979) and Goddard (2009) and will look at the measure of betweenness centrality in order to identify the brokers in the policy subsystem (Goddard 2009).

The analysis of policy networks can be conducted at the individual and the collective actor (organization) level (Krahmann 2003b). The decision as to whether we are studying individuals, governments, or other units is an important one that the researcher needs to make at the very beginning of the study (Hafner-Burton et al. 2009). In this research the analysis was performed at the level of organizations or units within organizations, for instance, a particular European Parliament Committee. Krahmann (2003b) argues that, when relations are analysed between collective organizations, the advantage is that the assumptions regarding their power and interests can be generalized. Interorganizational relations are more stable than relations among individuals and collective actors hold resources independently from those of their members (Krahmann 2003b). The only problem with the collective actor approach is that, at the empirical level, individuals interact among each other on behalf of organizations (ibid. 2003b). However, as long as individuals act in an organizational capacity, the analysis can still be performed at the organizational level (John and Cole 1998). In network studies, questionnaires and interviews target individuals. Even if 'the actor in a study is a collective entity, such as a corporation. … An individual person representing the collective reports on the collective's ties' (Wasserman and Faust 1994, p. 45).

Social network analysis was performed in this study on answers received to questions meant to uncover the connections between members of coalitions and of subsystems. For instance, in the case of the study on fracking the wording of one question was:

> Policymakers often interact with other persons, organizations in achieving certain policy goals (in person, via email, via phone, etc.). Did you interact

with anybody in the process leading to this resolution? Please name the relevant entities in this regard. (Please indicate the full name or official abbreviation of these entities)

The social network analysis in this study is supported by NodeXL,[30] a social network analysis software. NodeXL was used to calculate the coalition level metrics (density and geodesic distance), subsystem level metrics (density and geodesic distance), and individual subsystem actor metrics (degree centrality and betweenness centrality). NodeXL skips duplicate edges (connections) when it calculates metrics because duplicates will bias the result. This means that connections reported by two different representatives from the same organization with another entity are merged into one edge. The results tables for both coalitions' measures and individual members' measures are included and discussed for the two case studies in Chaps. 4 and 6. NodeXL also enables the connections among actors to be displayed graphically on sociograms in Chaps. 3, 4, 5, and 6. A sociogram is actually a graph (Scott 1991) that displays the connections between subsystem actors as lines between points.

Overview of the Book Chapters

The rest of the book consists of other six chapters. Chapter 2 introduces relevant developments in European energy policy and the institutional context for the case studies. It offers an overview of European integration in the field of energy and discusses what energy security entails in the EU context. It also explains how the European Commission and the European Parliament shape energy policy and what makes them the target of advocacy.

Chapters 3 and 4 discuss the findings on fracking coalitions. Chapter 3 introduces the two coalitions working on the topic, that is, the pro-fracking coalition organized by an industry association and oil and gas companies, and the anti-fracking coalition led by environmental NGOs. Chapter 4 shows that the success of the pro-fracking coalition is explained by several factors: the successful use of information and material resources, the development of a broad frame to attract allies (a frame integrating and

[30] Other social network analysis software includes UCINET and ORA (used, for instance, by Kenney et al. 2012). NodeXL was chosen because it is very user-friendly and can be used not only for data analysis but also to generate sociograms of high graphic quality.

responding to exogenous factors such as the global financial and economic crisis), and to a certain degree by the dense connections between the coalition members and the inclusion in the coalition of actors well connected in the policy subsystem.

Chapters 5 and 6 discuss developments around the Southern Gas Corridor. Chapter 5 offers a background on the Southern Gas Corridor and focuses on presenting the parameters of the race between Nabucco West and TAP, two pipelines deemed crucial for its inauguration. It also introduces the actors of the two coalitions, with their connections and position in the broader social structures. Chapter 6 discusses the TAP coalition's success and concludes that it was generated by its resources, its reach in the policy subsystem, but above all by its ability to develop an advocacy frame that was more effective in a very particular socio-economic context than the one advanced by Nabucco.

Chapter 7 further discusses the implications of the findings in Chaps. 3, 4, 5, and 6 for the literature on European energy policy, advocacy coalitions, and governance. The last chapter also recognizes the limitations of this study and discusses research avenues that future studies should embrace. I move now to providing an overview of the EU energy policy environment in which the coalitions studied in this research operate.

CHAPTER 2

The European Union and Energy Policy: Developments and Institutional Actors

This chapter aims to map the context in which the advocacy coalitions studied developed and worked. It provides an overview of developments in the EU energy field, as well as of the main institutions and actors involved in shaping EU energy policy. Although European integration began as an energy and security project, a comprehensive common energy policy (CEP) is still pending. Energy policy integration is an area that showed a lot of promise in the 1950s, but turned out to be rather slow.

As the section below will show, for a long time the EU shaped the energy policy of its Member States through its prerogatives in the EU environmental field and EU competition law. Energy seemed to follow the neofunctionalist[1] logic of 'incremental' integration, characterized by functional spillover and driven by supranational institutions. This created pol-

[1] Neofunctionalists (Haas 1958; Lindberg 1963; Hix 1999) claim that integration in a particular economic sector will trigger the integration of connected economic sectors so that the full benefits of integration can be enjoyed. They also postulate that this process will be supported by the presence of supranational institutions. National economies will consequently become increasingly integrated. Neofunctionalists argue that interest groups will also contribute to integration by seeking to interact with supranational institutions and by becoming players at the supranational level (Rosamond 2000). Transnational interest associations are likely to emerge in this context (Rosamond 2000). Politics will be increasingly defined by the competition between groups that seek to provide input to decision-making and influence policy (Alford and Friedland 1985; Rosamond 2000). Economic integration will trigger political integration as a need for a transnational regulatory system emerges.

A.-M. Bocse, *International Networks, Advocacy and EU Energy Policy-Making*, Palgrave Studies in European Union Politics,
https://doi.org/10.1007/978-3-030-49505-3_2

icy space for the work of interest groups and advocacy coalitions that tried, through their interaction with European institutions, to contribute to the development and direction of European energy policy. This book investigates the formal and informal influence on energy policy that interest groups have while operating in advocacy coalitions. But first it is necessary to give an overview of the tensions and challenges the EU has faced in the process of developing its energy policy, tensions which have created space for the 'bottom-up' influence of interest and advocacy groups.

Limited Integration Despite a Promising Start

The EU has made a lot of progress in recent years towards a common energy policy. However, tensions and disagreements remain among Member States when it comes to the development of the internal energy market, fighting climate change, and ensuring energy security. These divisions explain the slow development of EU prerogatives in the field of energy.

The current EU structures have evolved from the European Coal and Steel Community established by the EU founding states (France, Germany, Italy, Belgium, the Netherlands, and Luxembourg) through the 1951 Treaty of Paris. The Community aimed to foster peace and prosperity on the continent by promoting the integration of coal and steel resources (Glockner and Rittberger 2012, p. 16; Martin 2006, pp. 127–129 highlight the political benefits of integration). It provided a common market for coal and steel, free access of operators to these commodities, as well as minimum living standards for workers in these sectors (Marín-Quemada et al. 2012, p. 196). In 1957 the European Atomic Energy Community (Euratom) was established with the aim of creating a common nuclear power market. Energy was at the centre of the European Communities and the integration process that started with them.

Despite this very promising start, the Communities' mandate did not expand to include other sources of energy that became increasingly important. Fuels such as oil grew in significance globally in the 1950s and 1960s and European natural gas consumption increased in Europe at a yearly rate of 4.2% in the 1990s and 2% in the 2000s before the 2008 financial crisis (Honoré 2010, p. 226). By 2000, gas became more popular than oil because of its lower carbon footprint and because it was thought to reduce oil dependence on the unstable Middle East (Yafimava 2011, p. 109). Energy matters were not initially included in the European Economic Community (that developed in parallel with the Coal and Steel Community and Euratom) as a common policy area. The 1986 Single European Act set as an objective for the European Community the establishment of the single market by 31 December 1992 (European Union Member States 1986, section II). An internal energy market was added to the project by the Commission in the late 1980s to help reduce the high and variable energy prices across the Union (Helm 2012).

The 1992 Maastricht Treaty increased EU competence in the field of energy infrastructure through the Trans-European Networks, Energy (TEN-E). This initiative aimed to assist the financing and building of key transnational energy infrastructure. The Maastricht Treaty also expanded the EU mandate in the field of environmental policy that was inevitably connected to the development of the single market. Environmental pollution was considered a type of market failure that can be corrected through regulation (Burns and Carter 2012). Ambitious policy and legislative packages characterized EU work in the environmental field. These included Directive 2000/60/EC establishing a framework for the Community action in the field of water policy regulating aquatic pollution (European Parliament and the Council 2000) and Regulation No 1907/2006 of the European Parliament, and the Council of 18 December 2006 concerning the Registration, Evaluation, Authorisation and Restriction of Chemicals, REACH (European Parliament and the Council 2006a). These packages impacted the way natural resources (including fossil fuels) were exploited.

While Member States gave limited competences to the EU in the field of energy, they granted the EU powers in other policy areas, such as the internal market, competition policy, and research and environment (Behrens and Egenhofer 2008). Acquiring competences in these fields enabled EU institutions to shape policies in connected fields, including the energy policy of its EU Member States. The European Community broadened its energy legislation by linking issues related to the Single European Market and environmental protection to the energy field (Yafimava 2011, p. 106). This trend confirms neofunctionalist assumptions according to which integration in a particular economic field gives rise to integration in connected economic sectors, especially when supranational structures such as the European Commission support integration (Haas 1958; Lindberg 1963; Hix 1999).

The functioning of the internal market was based on the principle of free competition between economic operators. In order to ensure the functioning of the market, the Commission used its right of legislative initiative and developed an extensive body of EU competition law, especially directives. According to the consolidated version of the Treaty on the Functioning of the European Union (European Union Member States 2009c, chapter 2, section 1, Article 288): 'A directive shall be binding, as to the result to be achieved, upon each Member State to which it is addressed, but shall leave to the national authorities the choice of form and methods'. By making reference to principles of market-opening and anti-trust measures, in 1989 the Commission took on the task of liberalizing the electricity and gas markets, a process which continues also today. Initial rules for the EU energy market were introduced through two directives, that is, the 1996 Electricity Directive (European Parliament and the Council 1996) and the 1998 Gas Directive (European Parliament and the Council 1998). Attempts to build the internal EU energy market continued in 2003 and 2009 with directives targeting the electricity and gas sectors and the infrastructure in these sectors (Kanellakis et al. 2013). The EU took legal action against states that did not comply with EU competition law applicable to energy (Helm 2012). When a country fails to apply EU law, the Commission can take legal action by launching an infringement procedure and even refer the case to the Court of Justice of the European Union. In 2014 alone the European Commission detected twelve energy infringements, out of which five were referred to the Court (Directorate-General for Energy 2014).

This policy has been criticized that, through it, 'the Commission put the cart before the horse' (Helm 2012, p. 559). The policy focused on regulating access to existing (mainly national) networks rather than on creating a European electricity grid and pipeline system (Helm 2012). The Commission pushed for the desired legal framework, but the energy market was far from looking like a competitive, integrated market given the lack of interconnection between national infrastructures. Measures taken by the Commission contributed to increasing competition in the national markets, but did not necessarily foster competition in the EU-wide market (Helm 2012).

The EU's mandate in the field of environment and climate change policy enabled it to shape Member States' energy policy (Burns and Carter 2012). Although a common European energy policy was not formally included in the EU treaties, *de facto* such a policy began to emerge. The Commission proposed a series of directives regulating the contribution of renewable energy sources (RES) to the energy mix of Member States, as well as directives on energy efficiency in the European Union. For instance, the 2001 Directive on electricity production from RES set a target of 22.1% of RES-generated electricity in EU electricity gross consumption by 2010 (this goal did not apply to states joining after 2004). The 2003 Directive on biofuels asked Member States to set national targets increasing the ratio of biofuels in the transport fuel market (European Parliament and the Council 2003a). The EU also released and monitored the implementation of several policies and directives dealing with EU energy efficiency, including the 2006 Directive on Energy End-Use Efficiency and Energy Services (European Parliament and the Council 2006b).

The EU finally acquired formal competence on security of energy supply through the Lisbon Treaty, although it is shared with Member States. The Treaty of Lisbon amended the Treaty on the Functioning of the European Union whose current Article 194 states that: 'Union policy on energy shall aim, in a spirit of solidarity between Member States, to ensure security of energy supply in the Union' (European Union Member States 2009c, Article 194, paragraph 1, line b). The Treaty of Lisbon included a solidarity clause in the Treaty on the Functioning of the European Union that stipulates: 'the Council, on a proposal from the Commission, may decide, in a spirit of solidarity between Member States, upon the measures appropriate to the economic situation, in particular if severe difficulties arise in the supply of certain products, notably in the area of energy' (European Union Member States 2009c, Article 122, paragraph 1). Subsequent regulations defined in more detail the EU mandate in a crisis situation:

> since gas supplies from third countries are central to the security of the gas supply of the Union, the Commission should coordinate the actions with regard to third countries, working with the supplying and transiting third countries on arrangements to handle crisis situations and to ensure a stable gas flow to the Union. The Commission should be entitled to deploy a task force to monitor gas flows into the Union in crisis situations, in consultation with the third countries involved, and, where a crisis arises due to difficulties in a third country, to assume a mediation and facilitation role. (European Parliament and the Council 2010, Regulation 994/2010, paragraph 44)

However, Article 194 in the Treaty on the Functioning of the European Union states that: 'such measures shall not affect a Member State's right to determine the conditions for exploiting its energy resources, its choice between different energy sources and the general structure of its energy supply' (European Union Member States 2009c, Article 194, paragraph 2). The competence to decide on their energy mix and conclude gas supply and transit contracts remains with Member States and energy companies. The EU could, however, request changes in supply and transit contracts involving Member States if they conflicted with EU competition law. Only in 2016 the Commission secured the right to *ex-ante* check for their compatibility with EU law oil and gas intergovernmental agreements closed by Member States.

The Emergence of Energy Security Policy

The 2004–2007 EU enlargement brought to the EU several Central and East European countries. The enlargement increased the EU's overall gas import dependency and enhanced the vulnerability of the EU to gas supply disruptions, especially those generated by Russia.

Central and East European states are usually more keen for the EU to help them reduce their energy reliance on Russia through a common energy security policy, while larger Member States in Western Europe prefer to deal with Russia directly (Buchan 2010; Maltby 2013; Interview with Very Senior Hungarian Official 2014). Central and East European states tend to argue for more integration in the field of energy policy. This is motivated by their energy security concerns, especially of countries highly dependent on Russian gas.[2] There are also cases in which Member States, including from Eastern Europe, are protective of their prerogatives in areas that might impact supply security. This was the case with Poland when it came to regulating fracking in the EU.

EU energy security policy also evolved in response to several crises. Energy security became an issue at the EU level when access to energy supplies became problematic and as a result of variations in the energy price. Important events drawing attention to EU energy vulnerability

[2]There are also historical and political elements that contribute to the lack of confidence they have in Russia's foreign and energy policy (Schmidt-Felzmann 2008, p. 176; interview with Russian official based in Brussels 2013). Central and Eastern European countries became unwilling Members of the communist block led by the Soviet Union. In addition, smaller EU states have on their own modest leverage in external energy relations with Russia (Buchan 2010). Buchan argues that larger EU Members' energy relations with Russia are managed by national energy companies with the support of governments, such companies include E.ON (Germany), Gaz de France Suez (France) now Engie, and Eni (Italy). These major oil and gas companies are located in the EU larger states.

were the 2006 and especially the 2009 Russo-Ukrainian gas dispute.[3] Disagreement between Russia and Ukraine concerning the Ukrainian debts for Russian gas led to Russia cutting off the supply of gas to the Ukrainian pipeline system in January 2009 (Pirani et al. 2009). This impacted also the EU states supplied through it. Over two weeks, the EU experienced a serious interruption of energy supply (De Jong et al. 2010). At the time of the 2009 Russo-Ukrainian gas crisis, the average dependence on Russian imports was 77% in the Eastern European Members joining the EU after 2004 (European Commission 2009b, p. 2).

The crisis drew the attention of European institutions to EU energy vulnerability, increased mistrust in Russia as a gas supplier, and motivated new energy policy. The EU relies on Russia for oil, coal, uranium, and gas. Documents released by the European Parliament made reference to the fact that 'unwarranted disruption to supplies can cause severe problems, as demonstrated during the last Russia-Ukraine gas crisis at the beginning of 2009' (European Parliament 2009a, p. 2), and that: 'a number of Member States do not possess sufficient natural reserves to cope with crises' (European Parliament 2009a, p. 2). The European Commission also indicated that serious gas supply disruptions have acted as a 'wake up call' indicating EU vulnerability when it comes to energy supply (European Commission 2010).

The crisis led to scepticism on behalf of the EU regarding Russia-led energy plans. When talking to EU bureaucrats in the European Parliament and in the European Commission, the general feeling was that they regard Russia with deep mistrust (interview with European Parliament Official 3 2013; interview with European Commission official, DG Energy 2013). After the 2009 crisis, the EU enhanced its efforts to make sure the EU has access to energy supplies (Fortin 2015). Measures include diversifying energy suppliers and routes, diversifying the energy mix, energy efficiency measures, and further developing the internal energy market (Kreutler 2014).[4] Diversifying energy sources and routes is a priority for the EU according to the European Energy Security Strategy (European

[3] There is an agreement in the policy circles on this as indicated by a wide range of interviews conducted for this study: interview with Russian official based in Brussels 2013; Interview with Adviser on International Security to the President of Romania 2013; Interview with Industry Consultant 1 2013; Interview with Very Senior European Commission Official 2014.

[4] This is not to say that interest in the EU security of energy supply did not exist before 2009. For instance, in 2000 the European Commission released the Green Paper 'Towards

Commission 2014a) and the Framework Strategy for a Resilient Energy Union (European Commission 2015a).

The Russian project 'South Stream'[5] was meant to diversify existing energy routes between Russia and Europe. By developing a pipeline that would cross the Black Sea and enter the EU via Bulgaria, Russia sought to deliver gas to Europe without using the pipeline system crossing Ukraine. The EU was, however, not interested in such a project as it does not involve a diversification of gas sources and aims only to divert transit from the Ukrainian route (interview with senior European Commission official, DG Energy 2013; interview with attaché at the Permanent Representation of Greece to the European Union 2014). Unlike the Southern Gas Corridor, it does not considerably change the risk profile of the European Union:

> if you are looking at the risk profile, [the Southern Gas Corridor] is very important, to put it bluntly, it keeps the Russians on the East, and in terms of getting access to resources, Russia may have a lot of gas, off the top of my head it has 44–45 trillion cubic metres of gas in reserve, but it is one country. Whereas if you look at the Middle East, Caspian Basin resources of the Southern Gas Corridor, you have something like 78–80 trillion cubic metres of gas, one and a half times what is in Russia. Then you have 15 to 20 countries who would supply so in terms of risk profile you have a very diversified risk profile in the source countries with higher resources. In Russia you have a highly concentrated risk profile for the source country. While it is conceivable today that Russia might hate the European Union and therefore cut its gas, it is inconceivable to think that the 15 to 20 countries, if we ever made a broad-based Southern Corridor, that all 15 to 20 countries would hate the European Union all at the same time. (interview with senior European Commission official, DG Energy 2013)

The debates on European energy security have taken place after 2008 in a climate marked by the global economic crisis. The crisis has: 'reduced the appetite for radical climate change legislation amongst many member states, both East and West' (Burns and Carter 2012, p. 521). A switch

a European strategy for the security of energy supply' (European Commission 2000), but energy security efforts intensified after 2009 (Fortin 2015).

[5] Currently, the South Stream project is abandoned. The pipeline was cancelled in December 2014 owing to several factors, including opposition from the EU (on the grounds that it conflicts with EU law), and the commercial sanctions imposed by the EU on Russia after the 2014 annexation of Crimea by Russia, an event heavily criticized by the EU.

from a focus on climate to a focus on competitiveness took place in the European energy debate since 2008 as a result of the global financial crisis (interview with representative of the US Chamber of Commerce 2014). The EU rate of economic growth was quite slow at the time when the policy debates presented in the rest of this book took place and was challenged by resource shortages in the public and private sector, the fragmentation of the financial system, and by unemployment (European Commission 2013). In this context, taking measures that contribute to economic growth was a priority for EU leaders and improving access to reliable and sensibly priced energy was considered a measure contributing to economic growth.

Supply and economic crises contributed to placing energy higher on the EU agenda. There has been growing interest in energy security policy in Brussels over the last decade. The European institutions, especially the European Commission and the European Parliament, have set EU energy security high on their agenda. In one of its core documents on energy policy, *Energy 2020,* the European Commission claims that: 'energy is the life blood of our society. The well-being of our people, industry and economy depends on safe, secure, sustainable and affordable energy' (European Commission 2010, p. 2). In the Commission discourse, the security referent objects are individuals, businesses, and collective actors such as the society itself. In *Energy Roadmap 2050* the European Commission states that: 'the overall functioning of society is dependent on safe, secure, sustainable and affordable energy' (European Commission 2011, p. 2). The lack of energy constitutes a major threat that would negatively impact the very core of European well-being. The European Parliament discourse is quite similar to that of the European Commission in the emphasis it places on energy security threats and in the way it considers independence from Russian gas an EU energy security priority. The Parliament sees energy security as an important part of overall EU security: 'whereas energy security constitutes an essential component of the overall security, stability and prosperity of the European Union and a key element for the pursuit of economic and social development in Europe' (European Parliament 2009a, pp. 1–2).

The 2014–2019 European Commission set ambitious targets for itself in the energy field. Developing the Energy Union was one of the ten[6]

[6] Other priorities included creating jobs; growth and investment; the digital single market; a balanced EU-US Free Trade Agreement; migration; and the EU becoming a stronger global actor.

priorities of the Commission (European Commission 2015b). The Energy Union was introduced in 2014 as an institutional and policy framework aiming to support additional EU integration in the energy field by generating enhanced coordination among five policy areas: supply security; an integrated energy market; energy efficiency; climate action; and research and innovation. The Energy Union Framework Strategy was launched on 25 February 2015. As a proof of the fact that energy is a priority for the Commission, the Energy Union was led by one of the six vice-presidents of the European Commission. Supply security is an important objective of the Energy Union as its aim is to diversify EU sources and suppliers of energy and make better use of the energy produced in the European Union (European Commission 2015a). The Energy Union Package mentions that: 'producing oil and gas from unconventional sources in Europe such as shale gas is an option, provided that issues of public acceptance and environmental impact are adequately addressed' (European Commission 2015a, p. 5). The Energy Union project is based on previous EU work and commitments, for instance the Energy Security Strategy of May 2014. The strategy identifies long-term measures that would contribute to EU energy security, among which are 'increasing energy production in the European Union', and: 'diversifying external suppliers and related infrastructure' (European Commission 2014a, p. 3). Particular attention is given to the Southern Gas Corridor:

> The Union must reduce its external dependency on particular suppliers by diversifying its energy sources, suppliers and routes. Notably, a reinforced partnership with Norway, the acceleration of the Southern Gas Corridor and the promotion of a new gas hub in Southern Europe should all be pursued. (European Commission 2014a, p. 20)

The strategy mentions negotiating with existing energy partners such as Russia, Norway, Saudi Arabia, and new partners, for instance, countries in the Caspian region (European Commission 2014a, p. 16). The same strategy also recommends: 'speaking with one voice in external energy policy' (European Commission 2014a, p. 3).

The Energy Union can greatly contribute to the development of the EU Common Energy Policy and particularly to a policy on energy security. One of the benefits of a CEP would be that it would allow the EU:

'to speak out consistently with a single voice in international matters, so that Europe would be able to exert influence and wield bargaining power when dealing with third countries in the context of an effective foreign policy' (Marín-Quemada et al. 2012, p. 208). The next section seeks to clarify what energy security entails in the EU context. Such a conceptual clarification is needed given that 'energy security' is used by different actors, in different environments, and with different meanings.

The Energy Security of the EU: What Does It Entail?

After the end of the Cold War, what falls within the scope of 'security' was redefined to include economic, political, ecological, social, and cultural elements (Buzan et al. 1998; Kirchner 2006, 2007). Energy security is tackled by EU states at the national level, but also through supranational structures such as the EU, the North Atlantic Treaty Organization (NATO), or specialized agencies such as the International Energy Agency (IEA).[7] Governments consider energy to be a strategic commodity vital to national security (De Graaff 2011; Eberlein and Newman 2009). Energy security has been, particularly since 2006, a hotly debated topic in the EU (Keukeleire and MacNaughtan 2008). Security of supply gained an increasing role in EU energy policy from the mid-2000s (Youngs 2009). The shifting concern towards the security of supply took place in a particular context: the energy dependency on Russia of new members entering the EU in 2004–2007; the 2006 and 2009 Russian gas crises; and to a certain degree the loss of faith in nuclear energy as an alternative, internal energy source following the 2011 accident at the Fukushima nuclear plant in Japan. Traditionally an internal policy topic, energy was 'securitized' and, in this way, entered the 'high politics' agenda of EU foreign and security policy (Youngs 2009; Young 2010).

> The Report on the Implementation of the European Security Strategy approved by the European Council in December 2008 highlights the growing reliance on imported energy as a significant additional risk for the Union's security of energy supply and stresses energy security as one of the

[7] Energy security was also placed on the NATO agenda in the mid-2000s, although its role has remained limited in subsequent years (interview with Deputy Assistant Secretary General of NATO 2014; Interview with Energy Section Official, NATO 2015).

> new challenges for security policy. (European Parliament and the Council 2010, Regulation 994/2010, paragraph 11)

We can talk about the energy security of a state, region, or continent, or about global energy security. What energy security entails for each entity depends on whether that state or political unit is an importer, exporter of energy, or a transit entity (Proedrou 2012). This research will discuss energy security mainly in relation to the European Union, a net importer of both gas and oil. From an energy importer's perspective, energy security is usually considered to be achieved when there are adequate energy supplies from reliable sources, at competitive prices, and that cause limited harm to the environment (Proedrou 2012 building on the definitions of: Eng 2003; Qingyi 2006; Bolton et al. 2007).[8] Also, 'the degree of insecurity a country feels revolves around its dependence on a given type of energy and the number of its sources for that energy' (Buchan 2009, p. 87). Access to energy supply is important for economic development and growth, but is also a matter of justice (Sovacool and Dworkin 2014). According to Sovacool and Dworkin 2014, energy justice 'involves the right of all to access energy services, regardless of whether they are citizens of more or less greatly developed economies' (p. 5).

Recommendations and policy papers offer considerable insight into the way European institutions, in particular the European Commission, think about energy security. In 2000 the European Commission made it clear that:

> the European Union's long-term strategy for energy supply security must be geared to ensuring, for the well-being of its citizens and the proper functioning of the economy, the uninterrupted physical availability of energy products on the market, at a price which is affordable for all consumers (private and industrial), while respecting environmental concerns and looking towards sustainable development. (European Commission 2000, p. 2)

[8] This definition coexists with other definitions. For instance, for an energy exporting country 'energy security' refers to the security of demand at competitive prices that will generate profit without major costs to the environment (Proedrou 2012). The interests of exporters include avoiding recession in importing states that might trigger a reduction in energy demand and preventing importers from switching to alternative sources or diversifying supply (Proedrou 2012). Other energy security definitions attempt to reconcile the points of view of the importers and exporters and define energy security as the balance between energy supply and demand, facilitating sustainable economic and social development (Daojiong 2006).

In the EU context 'energy security' tends to be considered the equivalent of 'security of energy supply' (Escribano and Gracía-Verdugo 2012, p. 26). Access to energy can be secured through the exploitation of existing domestic energy resources or by importing energy at reasonable prices from abroad. In order to enhance its energy security, the EU followed a policy of diversification of energy supplies and energy routes.[9] Diversification is, therefore, a policy that enables a polity to reduce its energy insecurity:

> the diversification of gas routes and of sources of supply for the Union is essential for improving the security of supply of the Union as a whole and its Member States individually (European Parliament and the Council 2010, Regulation 994/2010, paragraph 7);

> well, energy security, the more diversified your supplies are, the more energy security you have, diversified both in terms of sources, the need really to work on the diversification of the sources, but also on the diversification of the routes. And maybe I should have changed the order, so the diversification of the routes, but also of the suppliers as factors which are key to the EU's energy security. (Interview with Very Senior European Commission Official 2014)

Several official documents released by the European Commission in the last decade establish a strong connection between EU energy security, security of energy supply, and the diversification of energy sources and energy routes. The 2006 Green Paper introduced the foundations of EU energy policy: sustainability; competitiveness and energy efficiency; and security of supply (Marín-Quemada et al. 2012, p. 199). The Paper's provisions related to supply security cite objectives such as: 'diversifying the EU's energy mix with greater use of competitive indigenous and renewable energy, and diversifying sources and routes of supply of imported energy' (European Commission 2006, p. 18); 'creating the framework which will stimulate adequate investments to meet growing energy demand' (European Commission 2006, p. 18); and 'improving the conditions for European companies seeking access to global resources'

[9] There are studies that look at EU-Russia relations not in terms of EU dependence on Russia, but in terms of interdependence between the EU and Russia in the energy field as the EU is the main market for Russian energy (Finon and Locatelli 2006, p. 8; Esakova 2012, p. 17). However, this is not the dominant understanding of energy security that informs EU action and policy in the energy field.

(European Commission 2006, p. 18). The Green Paper also calls for a: 'common external energy policy' (European Commission 2006, p. 19). According to the European Council Presidency conclusions released in the aftermath of the first Russo-Ukrainian gas crisis, energy security was to be achieved through: 'effective diversification of energy sources and transport routes, which will also contribute to a more competitive internal energy market' (European Council 2007, p. 18). The *EU energy security and solidarity action plan: 2nd strategic energy review* released by the Commission in 2008 insisted on the diversification of energy supplies, developing external energy relations, and the best use of indigenous energy resources coming from renewable and nuclear sources (European Commission 2008).

But how many suppliers or routes does the EU need to be energy secure? While some scholars considered EU worry for its energy security to be legitimate (Duffield and Birchfield 2011; Proedrou 2012), others felt that European concerns with energy shortages, especially gas shortages, are not justified (Stern 2006, p. 33). Stern argues that the percentage of energy supply that a country receives from another country tells us little about the importing country's vulnerability to supply disruption. Any assessment concerning its energy security performed by an entity is at least to a certain degree subjective. The energy security of a polity is dependent on factors such as a system of energy supply corridors that the country can access, the geopolitical situation affecting the exporting and transit countries, and the overall international situation (Escribano and García-Verdugo 2012). However, very important is 'the country's perception of energy security' (ibid. 2012, p. 29) that filters realities and events. Perceptions and understandings of energy security entertained by governmental and intergovernmental actors are fluid and built in interaction with other policy actors, including non-state actors. This study will demonstrate that understandings of EU energy security and what contributes to it are shaped by the subjective interpretation of objective factors advanced by the different actors (supranational, governmental, corporate, etc.) involved in energy policymaking at a particular time.

This book will discuss EU energy security in relation to the gas sector. This is motivated by the EU's dependence on imported gas, as well as by specifics of the gas sector that make it more vulnerable to international political developments. Political analysis is a good tool for explaining developments in this field.

Gas constituted 23% of overall EU energy consumption in 2010 (Directorate-General for Energy, DG Energy 2013, p. 35).[10] This share remained stable over the next decade with gas accounting for 23.8% of the EU-28 gross inland consumption in 2019 (DG Energy 2019, p. 22). The EU is highly dependent on imported gas. EU-28 energy import dependency in the field of natural gas was 65.3% in 2013 (DG Energy 2015, p. 24). The EU-28 gas import dependency has increased from 48.9% in 2000 to 74.3% in 2017 (DG Energy 2019, p. 24). In addition, some predict that gas will play an increasingly important role in the EU energy mix in the future. Gas demand might increase slowly as Europe will rely less on nuclear power given that nuclear facilities are ageing and countries such as Germany intend to phase out such facilities for safety reasons by 2020 (Interview with Senior International Energy Agency Official 2015). The discovery and exploitation of shale gas reserves in North America and in the Eastern Mediterranean might extend the gas lifetime (Gény 2010). Gas also has a reduced carbon footprint compared with coal.

Gas imports go through fixed pipelines and create dependence on long-term suppliers that are usually located in the physical proximity of the EU, while other forms of energy are domestic (renewable) or easier to import and less dependent on fixed infrastructure (coal, oil, and nuclear fuel). Pipeline gas is traded at the regional level, given the fixed infrastructure and transportation systems (Yafimava 2011, p. 25). This places Russia in a privileged position as an exporter of gas to the EU and it is highly unlikely that the EU will ever be able to fully exclude Russian gas from its energy mix. In 2013, 39% of EU gas imports came from Russia (DG Energy 2015, p. 26), in 2017, 38.7% (DG Energy 2019, p. 26). Gas is also more difficult to store than oil which makes developing strategic gas reserves more difficult[11] and reduces the means of coping with unexpected gas shortages. As gas cannot be stored at its place of consumption, flexibility needs to be incorporated in the supply system in order to meet fluctuations in demand, especially those between winter and summer demand (Honoré 2010).

These factors imply that: 'gas-based relationships are more vulnerable to political influences than oil based relationships' (Esakova 2012, p. 27).

[10] EU gas consumption in 2013 was 471 billion cubic metres (bcm) (IEA 2015, p. 196).

[11] Gas can be stored in caverns, as well as depleted gas fields and aquifers. The commercial storage capacity is mainly concentrated in Europe in Germany, Italy, and France (Honoré 2010, p. 205). These are countries that are less prone to supply disruptions.

States play an important role in gas transit given the sovereignty they exercise over their territory so any transit disputes in the field of natural gas are commercial, as well as political (Yafimava 2011, p. 139). Increases in the price of gas (the oil-linked gas prices in long-term contracts tripled in 1999) also contributed to an increasing association between EU energy security and gas (Yafimava 2011, p. 109).

The responsibility for EU energy security is divided between the European institutions, the Member States, energy companies, and in certain cases even energy consumers:

> security of gas supply is a shared responsibility of natural gas undertakings, Member States, notably through their Competent Authorities, and the Commission within their respective areas of activities and competence. Where appropriate, the national regulatory authorities, where they are not the Competent Authorities, should also contribute to security of gas supply within their areas of activities and competence in accordance with Directive 2009/73/EC. Moreover, customers using gas for electricity generation or industrial purposes may also have an important role to play in security of gas supply through their ability to respond to a crisis with demand-side measures, for instance interruptible contracts and fuel switching, as this directly impacts on the supply/demand balance. (European Parliament and the Council 2010, Regulation 994/2010, paragraph 23)

Corporations are significant partners for governments in generating energy security in the EU context (Proedrou 2012). Companies 'operate in the energy field, sign supply contracts, form joint ventures, invest money in exploration and transportation schemes and provide energy to industries and households' (ibid. 2012, p. 50). The role of energy corporations in European energy security policy was formalized in 2010:

> in the event of a supply crisis, market players should be given sufficient opportunity to respond to the situation with market-based measures. Where the reactions of market players are not sufficient, Member States and their Competent Authorities should take measures to remove or mitigate the effects of the supply crisis. Only where these measures are insufficient should measures be taken at regional or Union level to remove or mitigate the effects of the supply crisis. Regional solutions should be sought as far as possible. (European Parliament and the Council 2010, Regulation 994/2010, paragraph 24)

Even in the case of a gas crisis, governmental intervention should take place only when the energy market fails to deliver the necessary gas supplies (paragraph 43). If we recall the definition of energy security advanced by the European Commission (European Commission 2000), energy security not only has an energy access component but also has a price and an environmental dimension (Escribano and García-Verdugo 2012, p. 27). As subsequent chapters will show in more detail, at various times, in the EU policy environment access to energy or pricing can be the element that dominates the EU energy security debate. Certain Directorate-Generals (DGs) in the EU Commission, such as DG Energy, will pursue energy security as a primary target, while others, such as DG Environment, will stress the environmental component.

Various EU policy areas have an impact on EU energy security and this makes designing policy tackling energy insecurity extremely difficult. Some scholars refer to energy security as a specific part of EU energy policy (Buchan 2010; Helm 2012). Helm identifies and writes on distinct areas of EU energy policy, that is, the completion of the internal energy market, EU climate change policy, and the security of supply (Helm 2012, pp. 556–569). In practice, energy security is closely related to the development of the EU internal energy market and an energy transport infrastructure that would increase the speed and direction of energy flows towards the EU Members that are more likely to face supply disruptions. At the same time, energy efficiency measures triggered by climate change considerations reduce the EU energy demand. EU energy security policy cannot be separated from EU economic integration and EU environmental and climate policy. There is also a strong connection between EU energy security and the overall Common Foreign and Security Policy (Buchan 2010). This is particularly the case when energy supplies come from outside the EU borders, as is the case with the gas that will enter the EU through the Southern Gas Corridor.

The External Dimension of EU Energy Policy

The integration of the EU Foreign and Security policy is limited as Member States are unwilling to transfer prerogatives to the EU in the field of Foreign Policy and often remain divided on many international developments. Division also persists in the field of EU external energy relations. It is beyond the scope of this chapter to present a comprehensive picture of all the instruments and engagements of the EU in external energy relations. Eleftheria Neframi (2012) offers a useful overview of this.[12] This section will present aspects of the EU external engagement that help frame and understand the case studies presented in this book. The EU's ability to speak with a single voice when interacting with energy suppliers such as Azerbaijan positively impacts its diversification of energy sources and routes and the development of projects such as the Southern Gas Corridor.

In the field of international energy affairs, the European Commission shares its mandate with the Member States and energy companies. Energy companies purchase gas for the EU consumers. In addition, the Commission relies on companies to actually build the pipelines that bring gas to Europe. The Commission can, however, liaise with governments in exporting countries in order to make a case for this gas to be sold to Europe. As an EU official indicated: 'when we are talking about countries outside of the EU, it can be very helpful to have a political willingness paving the way for the companies to come in afterwards' (Interview with Very Senior European Commission Official 2014). For instance, the energy diplomacy conducted by the Commission persuaded several countries to commit gas to the Southeastern 'energy corridor' promoted by the Commission, that is, Egypt (2 bcm/year), Iraq (5 bcm/year), and Turkmenistan (10 bcm/year) (Buchan 2009, p. 81).

One of the most common instruments used by the EU in its external relations is diplomatic dialogue with energy suppliers. Energy is on the agenda of the EU talks with Russia, the Persian Gulf countries, the Central Asian states, and bodies such as the Organization of the Petroleum Exporting Countries (OPEC). Building stronger diplomatic relations with key gas suppliers, including the US and Russia, is stipulated in the EU Energy Diplomacy Action Plan (Council of the European Union, Foreign Affairs 2015) and European Union Global Strategy (European External Action Service, EEAS 2016). The dialogue with the US on energy takes place in the framework of the EU-US Energy Council and in recent years the EU-US interaction was impacted by the shale gas revolution in the US that led to regulatory exchanges between the EU and the US as will be discussed in greater detail in Chaps. 3 and 4 of this book. US shale gas

[12] Aspects of EU external energy relations concerning the help provided to developing countries to improve access to energy are not included in this study. For instance, as part of the Cotonou Agreement, the EU supplied the African, Caribbean, and Pacific countries (ACP countries) with energy services that are environmentally friendly (Neframi 2012, p. 165).

exports are regarded by experts as a solution for the EU gas source diversification away from Russian gas (Leal-Arcas 2018). However, an important condition for this to happen is the EU to invest in and diversify its network of LNG terminals (Leal-Arcas 2018).

The EU's need to speak with a single voice in external energy relations is recognized by various energy policymakers and experts based in EU institutions or international organizations. The 2006 *Green Paper: A European Strategy for Sustainable, Competitive and Secure Energy*, released by the European Commission in the aftermath of the 2006 Russia-Ukraine crisis, recommended the creation of an EU external energy policy (European Commission 2006). The document *An energy policy for Europe: Commission steps up to the energy challenges of the twenty-first century* of 2007 included provisions on a common external energy policy and highlighted the need to establish a connection between energy affairs and general EU external relations (European Commission 2007; Marín-Quemada et al. 2012).[13] The IEA's 2008 Energy Policies Review on the European Union stated that: 'it may be valuable to consider proposing the creation of a more central role for the European Commission in the external energy relations of the EU, beyond its existing legal competences, by providing in particular for stronger co-ordination of Member States, namely supplier and transit countries, and outline which increased powers and responsibilities may be necessary to achieve this' (IEA 2008, p. 85).

The European Union acquired a formal, explicit mandate in the field of external energy relations through the Lisbon Treaty, but this competence is shared with the EU Member States (European Union Member States 2009c, Article 194). The fact that each Member State is responsible for its energy mix can be a source of weakness for the EU's ability to defend its interests at the international level. The EU often fails to speak with a single voice on the international stage in energy and many other policy areas: 'we are the biggest buyer so we have a lot of market power, but we don't act as the bigger buyer in the world, we act as twenty seven Member States pursuing their own personal interests, with different preferences so it's very difficult' (interview with European Parliament official 3 2013). There is a certain resistance on the part of EU Member States when it comes to transferring their power in external energy relations to the European

[13] The issue was also tackled by the paper released by Javier Solana 'An External Policy to Serve Europe's Energy Interests' (European Commission and the Secretary General of the Council of the European Union 2006, p. 3).

Union. As one governmental official admitted in an interview, this makes the mission of the European Commission more difficult: 'we do not want the Commission to have too many powers, it is not so easy for the European Union to really find the way, so to say' (Interview with Austrian Official 2014).

A step forward to enhancing the work of the EU in energy diplomacy is constituted by the 2015 EU Energy Diplomacy Action Plan aiming 'to support the external aspects of the Energy Union' (Council of the European Union, Foreign Affairs 2015, p. 5). The Council indicated that the Southern Corridor remains a priority for the EU energy diplomacy (Council of the European Union, Foreign Affairs 2015, p. 3). The EU Energy Diplomacy Action Plan stressed the need for the EU to formulate a common message in energy diplomacy: 'Systematic efforts should be made for the EU to speak with one voice on major energy issues both in bilateral relations and in multilateral frameworks' (Council of the European Union, Foreign Affairs 2015, p. 7). Of course, coordination among entities in charge of energy diplomacy remains a challenge, with the implementation of the Action Plan itself divided between the High Representative of the Union for Foreign Affairs and Security Policy, the Commission, and the Member States.

The EU has often failed to act as a single actor in its interaction with Russia over energy. The lack of common energy policy concerning the EU energy mix (remaining in the competence of the EU Member States) prevented the EU from effectively using its market power to secure a better deal with Russia (Raszewski 2018). Russia approaches Member States bilaterally and applies a divide-and-rule strategy. The EU Member States have been incapable of coordinating their position regarding Russia-sponsored pipelines such as Nord Stream and South Stream (Yafimava 2011, p. 104). These projects entailed a diversification from the unstable gas transit route across Ukraine, but not diversification away from Russian sources. Nord Stream led to tensions between Germany, which supported the project, and the Baltic states, Sweden, and Poland, that opposed it. These states opposed the offshore route that the project took (Poland given the loss of transit revenues) and opposition intensified after the 2006 Russo-Ukrainian gas crisis (Yafimava 2011, p. 95; confirmed also by interviews conducted for the book: interview with energy executive 2013, etc.). Italy and France also denounced the project (Belyi 2008). In Southern Europe the competition between Nabucco and the Russia-supported South Stream led to an additional divide among the EU

Member States in the late 2010s. Nabucco was supported by its transit states, Turkey, Bulgaria, Romania, Hungary, and Austria, while South Stream was supported by Italy, Bulgaria, Hungary, and Greece; Hungary and Bulgaria being also partners in Nabucco (Simonet 2012, p. 236). As this study will show, the competition between Nabucco West and TAP in the framework of the Southern Gas Corridor further contributed to the divide amongst EU Member States regarding energy infrastructure projects.

The European Council conclusions of February 2011 required the High Representative of the European Union for Foreign Affairs and Security Policy to integrate energy security in her work. Consequently, the European External Action Service (EEAS) attempted to enhance its energy diplomacy resources. An EEAS Energy Diplomacy Network was established as part of the Multilateral Relations and Global Issues Directorate of the EEAS and a coordinator was appointed. The network comprises desk officers in the EEAS working on countries and regions key to EU energy security, as well as officials in the EU delegations to the US and Russia. The network is supposed to cover aspects of energy diplomacy defined in the words of one of its key officials as an: 'act of diplomacy aiming to ensure energy security' (Interview with Official in the European External Action Service, EEAS, Network on Energy Diplomacy 2013). The staff and analysis capacity of the Energy Diplomacy Network are limited; although it received a new boost through the EU Energy Diplomacy Action Plan in 2015, its ability to deliver remains dependent on cooperation with other structures, for instance the Strategic Group on International Energy Relations.

The Commission-based DG Energy plays a leading role in opening energy corridors. The EEAS can support the Commission in this work through several instruments. In the case of the Southern Gas Corridor, such instruments included: 'contacts at the foreign policy level, ministerial dialogues, EU delegations gathering and assessing information' (Interview with Official in the European External Action Service, EEAS, Network on Energy Diplomacy 2013). The network also exchanges information and consults in the formulation of policies with large energy companies.

The EU external energy policy reflects the regulatory nature of the EU, its identity as a regulatory state (Goldthau and Sitter 2015, p. 75). According to Goldthau and Sitter, the EU and in particular the European Commission have the tendency to use a 'regulatory policy toolbox' (Goldthau and Sitter 2015, p. 6) to respond to global developments in the energy field and enhance the EU energy security, which they define as 'uninterrupted energy supplies which are both affordable and sustainable' (Goldthau and Sitter 2015, p. 7). When it comes to gas markets 'the EU has sought to build rule-based markets internationally and regionally, and to project its own rules and principles well beyond its own borders' (Goldthau and Sitter 2015, p. 79). The EU was successful in its regulatory state approach in relation to Russia when it comes to implementing some of its anti-trust principles (for instance, the abolition of destination clauses in contracts closed with Gazprom), but these achievements were supported by broader changes in the IPE of energy, including the shale gas revolution in the US and lower EU gas demand as a result of the 2008 financial and economic crisis (Goldthau and Sitter 2015). Goldthau and Sitter conclude that the EU can be referred to as 'Regulatory Power Europe' defined as 'an actor in its own right with a liberal outlook, a focus on market-making and operation, and a long reach beyond its own borders' (Goldthau and Sitter 2015, p. 129).

The EU attempted in recent decades to export energy policy and rules in its neighbourhood through several intergovernmental structures (such as the Energy Charter Treaty or the Energy Community) or by simply demanding that EU law be applied to pipeline projects connecting the EU with non-member countries. The Trans-European Energy Networks (TAN-E) constitute an area in which the EU has competence and can be used to shape external energy relations (interview with former officer at the German Marshall Fund, Brussels office 2013). The EU transfers its rules and standards to non-EU countries through the relations that it establishes with these countries in developing energy corridors (Escribano 2012, p. 278). For instance, the Nabucco gas pipeline was intended to be built under EU public procurement rules:

> when we were looking at how to secure the Southern Gas Corridor, not only were we looking for a pipeline through Turkey, but we were looking for a pipeline through Turkey which had significant legal guarantees as to its operations. This is why we put lots of time into the Nabucco gas pipeline legal framework. (interview with senior European Commission official, DG Energy 2013)

This makes the investment climate more predictable for energy companies interested in investing in countries in the EU neighbourhood.

The Energy Charter Treaty signed in 1994 after the collapse of the Soviet Union aimed to establish a legal framework that would encourage investment in the energy sector of the former Soviet states. The Treaty focused on four main areas: the protection of foreign investments, including against non-commercial risks; provisions securing the energy flow through different types of energy transport infrastructure (including pipelines and grids); a mechanism for conflict resolution between signatory states and between host states and investors; and measures aimed at reducing the environmental footprint of energy generation and use (The Energy Charter Treaty Signatory States 1994). As Russia did not ratify the Treaty, it is not currently applicable to a key energy player and its impact is limited.

The EU played a key role in establishing the Energy Community in 2005. The organization brings together the countries of the European Union, as well as those of South-Eastern Europe and the Black Sea. The Community aims to extend the EU energy market and its rules to the Western Balkans, Moldova, and Ukraine in order to promote investment in the energy grid of the former Yugoslavia. The organization also aims to contribute to the political and economic stability of South-Eastern Europe (Neframi 2012, p. 163). Members from Western Balkans participate in the organization in preparation for EU membership. The full participation of Turkey would be important to the construction of new pipelines aiming at EU supply diversification, but Turkey is currently just an observer in the Community. INOGATE (Interstate Oil and Gas Transport to Europe Programme) constituted a softer attempt to promote EU policy and norms that facilitate cooperation on energy policy with the countries of the Black and Caspian seas. The initiative was re-branded in 2004 as the Baku Initiative, but its effectiveness has been limited.

The Commission does not have the authority to negotiate (on behalf of companies) or sign gas purchase contracts. The Commission can, however, ask for changes to be made to gas contracts closed between companies in case they violate EU competition law. Another prerogative that the European Commission can exercise according to the Third Energy Package (Directive 2009/73/EC) is granting exemptions from EU law to infrastructure that enables the import of gas from outside the EU (European Parliament and the Council 2009). Article 36 of the Directive 2009/73/EC concerning common rules for the internal market in natural gas stipulates that: 'Major new gas infrastructure, i.e. interconnectors, LNG and storage facilities, may, upon request, be exempted for a defined period of time, from the provisions of Articles 9, 32, 33 and 34 and Article

41(6), (8) and (10)' (European Parliament and the Council 2009, Article 36 of the Directive, paragraph 2). Unbundling and third party access rules applicable to transmission and distribution systems, storage facilities, and upstream pipeline networks are rendered exempt.[14] Unbundling prohibits an entity to own energy generation, transmission, and sale facilities simultaneously, while third party access rules grant access to networks to those who do not own the actual physical network infrastructure in order to encourage competition and the functioning of the energy market.

However, these rules might reduce the incentive to make investments in energy infrastructure. When it comes to unbundling, massive investment in gas extraction facilities might not be made if there is uncertainty regarding the possibility to transport that gas through a reliable system to a market. Third party access impacts the right of an investor to hold exclusive control over the energy transport infrastructure developed and in its absence the investment might not make financial sense. Therefore, exemptions from these rules are meant to encourage projects that would contribute to EU energy security and which would not be developed in the absence of the exemption (Article 36). Once an exemption is approved at the national level, the Commission is notified and within two months it will confirm the exemption or ask for amending or withdrawing the exemption request (Article 36, paragraph 9). Exemptions can also be given to investments that aim at a: 'significant increase of capacity in existing infrastructure and to modifications of such infrastructure which enable the development of new sources of gas supply' (European Parliament and the Council 2009, Article 36 of the Directive, paragraph 2).

These provisions show an awareness of the fact that fully implementing the principles of free market and competition sometimes goes against EU energy security interests. In order to encourage investment in these capital-intensive infrastructure mega-projects, rules such as unbundling and third party access are suspended. Some would claim that this suspension is sometimes arbitrary. Article 36 does not define what a 'major' gas infrastructure entails and it is silent on what should be the capacity or the cost of a 'major' investment. This gives the European Commission a certain level of discretion over exemption decisions. The European Commission granted additional exemptions to the Nabucco West project, as well as to

[14] These exemptions are also confirmed by Regulation (EC) No 715/2009 of 13 July 2009 on conditions for access to the natural gas transmission networks and repealing Regulation (EC) No 1775/2005 (Ministerial Council 2009).

TAP in May 2013 (Azernews 2013), but required the Russia-supported South Stream to comply with the provisions of the EU law.[15] This led to accusations that the process of granting an exemption is politicized and lacks objectivity and transparency (Yafimava 2011, p. 128). As we shall see, the European Commission's capacity to offer exemptions to pipelines has influenced developments around the Southern Gas Corridor.

In addition to an accommodating legislative framework, the European Commission can also facilitate access to funding for certain energy infrastructure projects. The TEN-E programme aims to support additional internal energy interconnections and in the natural gas field to increase the supply and route diversification through pipelines, LNG terminals, and gas storage facilities (Kanellakis et al. 2013).

Through the European Energy Programme for Recovery (EEPR) established in 2009, 4 billion euro was dedicated to co-financing energy projects that can help also with economic recovery. Electricity and gas infrastructure was funded by 2.4 billion euro. The EEPR provides grants to energy projects to: 'boost the economic recovery, increase the security of energy supply and contribute to the reduction of greenhouse gas emissions' (European Commission 2016). The EEPR funded the first Polish LNG import terminal with 80 million euro. The EEPR also supported projects that are part of the Southern Gas Corridor.

The EU also supported the Europe 2020 Project Bond Initiative implemented by the European Investment Bank and that began its operation in 2012 (European Parliament and the Council 2012). The initiative aims to stimulate investment in key energy infrastructure by increasing the creditworthiness quality of the bonds that private companies involved in the project generated. This funding is meant to complement the funding available through public grants and loans made by banks. The projects that are eligible for this funding are those that are considered commercially viable and already eligible for funding under TEN-E.

This section shows that the Commission has a number of policy instruments at its disposal (diplomatic support, exemptions from EU law, and financial assistance) and that it can use these instruments to support the energy projects that help the Commission generate EU energy security,

[15] The Commission found that the intergovernmental agreements on which South Stream was based did not comply with principles such as ownership unbundling and third party access to the pipeline and the European Commission also stated that exemptions might be granted only in the distant future (Euractiv 2013).

according to its own understanding of what EU energy security entails. The European Commission has a developing record of using such instruments to enhance EU energy security. The next section will discuss the growing role of the European Parliament in EU energy policy.

The European Parliament and EU Energy Policy

As we have seen, the European Commission can pave the way diplomatically for international energy projects, can provide exemptions from EU law for energy infrastructure, and financially support key energy transport projects. The previous sections also showed that the Commission can influence energy policy through the use of legal instruments related to the internal market and environmental policy. All these factors make the Commission a very attractive target for the advocacy and lobbying of various interest groups. The Lisbon Treaty turned energy security policy from a national into a competence shared between the EU and the Member States and in this way strengthened the role of the Commission (Proedrou 2012). This section will argue that it also strengthened the role of the European Parliament.

Energy security emerged in the discourse and agenda of the European Parliament especially after the accession of new EU members in 2004–2007. Around the same time, the Parliament began to call for more extensive EU involvement in providing for the energy security of its Member States. In 2003 the European Parliament adopted a report by the German MEP Peter Mombaur which counteracted a proposal of the European Commission to increase the amount of European oil stocks (Mombaur 2003). Such a proposal was seen to conflict with the powers of EU Member States. However, in 2007 the Parliament approved a report by Jacek Saryusz-Wolski, the Polish chairman of the Committee on Foreign Affairs. The report called for a stronger 'common European foreign policy on energy, covering security of supply, transit and investment related to energy security' (Saryusz-Wolski 2007, p. 6), which was to be coordinated by a 'High Official for Foreign Energy Policy' (Saryusz-Wolski 2007, p. 7). This shows that, from 2003 to 2007, the European Parliament's position on EU energy security prerogatives changed. The European Parliament became an advocate of integration in the field of energy (Dinan 2014). To provide an argument for integration in this field, and in the fields of defence and the digital single market, the European Parliament Research Service engaged in the ambitious project of 'Mapping the Cost of Non-Europe, 2014–19', the cost of the lack of EU action in certain areas. According to the EP Secretary-General, Klaus Welle, through this exercise the Parliament 'has thus put itself in a position to be able to shape the agenda for the coming five years' (Welle 2014, p. 3). In this way, the European Parliament was looking to take the initiative on EU law making more or less formally (Dinan 2014).

The Treaty of Lisbon enhanced the EP's role in the development of EU law, including laws that might have implications for EU energy policy. Under the Treaty of Lisbon, the number of areas in which the EP is involved in legislative work through co-decision increased. Co-decision was extended from 44 areas (Sampol 2009) to 83 under Lisbon and was renamed as the 'ordinary legislative procedure' (European Commission 2012b). New areas to which the procedure applies since the Treaty of Lisbon include services of general economic interest; personal data protection; immigration; border checks; European intellectual property rights; public health; and energy (provisions related to the internal market and energy were under co-decision already). The Treaty has enhanced the EP's ability to shape energy policy developments:

> the Treaty has changed a lot of things obviously, starting for example, with the role played by the Parliament, now in the specific case of energy it has changed also in the sense that it's giving much more power to the Parliament, the Parliament is definitely now on an equal footing with the Council, except on the nuclear matters. (interview with policy adviser to the European People's Party, EPP, in the European Parliament 2013)

The introduction of Article 218 in the Treaty on the Functioning of the European Union (European Union Member States 2009c, Article 218, paragraph 6, line a), an article dealing with the conclusion of international agreements, enhanced the Parliament's role in energy matters (Braun 2011). This article stipulates that agreements covering fields to which ordinary legislative procedure applies require the consent of the European Parliament. Agreements concerning energy projects of European interest, such as the gas interconnector Nabucco, now require the consent of the Parliament. Article 218(6a) also provides for the Parliament's consent when it comes to agreements related to energy or which establish cooperation with other organizations (such as the IEA, the Energy Charter Treaty, and the Energy Community).

In areas in which the Parliament has more legislative power, we would expect intense lobbying (Mazey and Richardson 2006, p. 261). The expansion of EP legislative power since 1986 has attracted the attention of interest groups (Kohler-Koch 1997; Mazey and Richardson 2006). As Mazey and Richardson argue:

> the gradual increase in the EP's powers has, of course, further increased the complexity of the Brussels lobbying game. Few interests now dare risk leaving the parliamentary arena to their opponents and, hence, parliamentary hearings attract the full melange of stakeholders. (Mazey and Richardson 2006, p. 261)

'Intergroups' emerge at the EP level through informal meetings at which MEPs discuss various policy issues, for instance the Pharmaceutical Intergroup (ibid. 2006, p. 260). As the following chapters will show, such a group also emerged in the European Parliament around the issue of fracking for shale gas.

Existing literature explains interest groups' access to the European Parliament as they are holders of 'access goods' such as information (Bouwen 2004a). Bouwen argues that the information that groups supply to the European Parliament is not technical and expert, as is the case with information supplied to the European Commission, but rather information on European interests and national preferences (Bouwen 2004b). On the other hand, Christiansen and Dobbels 2013 claim that: 'the EP is traditionally disadvantaged vis-à-vis the other two institutions [the Commission and the Council] when it comes to both technical expertise and time' (Christiansen and Dobbels 2013, p. 1167).[16] This should increase the EP interest in technical information. Bouwen (2004a) notwithstanding, this book will show that, on highly technical and controversial issues such as fracking, the European Parliament is very interested in technical information.

The European Parliament claims to speak on behalf of the European people, as shown by resolutions it has released, including the 'European Parliament resolution of 20 February 2008 on the Treaty of Lisbon' (European Parliament 2008). This gives the European Parliament

[16] Christiansen and Dobbels (2013) claim that, whilst EP powers in the field of delegated acts, for instance, have formally increased, the EP is not able to fully use its powers as it lacks resources, including personnel and expertise.

legitimacy and constrains the freedom of action that other institutions (especially the European Commission and the European Council) might have in relation to the preferences of the European Parliament. The Parliament influenced the election of Jean-Claude Junker as the head of the European Commission in 2014 (Dinan 2014; Fabbrini 2015). According to Dinan, the President of the European Parliament and the EP Secretary-General: 'exploited the minor modifications in the Lisbon Treaty to build a case for an entirely new approach to selecting and electing the Commission President' (Dinan 2014, p. 115). This way the European Parliament managed to make the most of unclear treaty provisions. The Parliament is an increasingly vocal actor, also making the most of its right to release non-binding initiative reports:

> the Parliament has become more vocal and more intent upon influencing the Commission's legislative agenda. At a meeting of the directors in a DG in the Commission, one of the main elements they mentioned was that they need to pay attention to the legislative initiatives demanded by MEPs through parliamentary questions, because in general people do not pay attention to parliamentary questions. But the fact that the Parliament became much more vocal will change things, I believe. Also, in the long term it will change the dynamics and in general the interests that corporations have regarding what non-binding legislation entails. (interview with European Affairs consultant 2014)

This point of view is also highlighted by European Commission officials:

> the people upstairs here in the Commission will react to what the Parliament says, although they might not react to what I say. However, if the European Parliament says it, they will take it seriously just because it is the European Parliament, although the content might be 100% the same. (interview with senior European Commission official, DG Energy 2013)

Some scholars argue that the European Parliament mainly plays a discursive role in energy policy (Proedrou 2012). The study on fracking presented in this book will show that even this discursive role is not to be neglected and that groups are interested in influencing policy discourses from an early stage, that is, at the parliamentary level when the EP takes the initiative on an issue. Groups recognize: 'that the EU policy process demands a multi-track lobbying strategy' (Mazey and Richardson 2006, p. 260).

Conclusion

This chapter captured the context in which the work of the advocacy coalitions studied by this research takes place. Energy policy rose on the EU agenda and at the same time the EU and its institutions have gained and are seeking a broader mandate in EU energy policy, especially in EU energy security policy.

Both in the field of energy policy, in general, and external energy policy, in particular, the European Commission seems to have been very proactive in acquiring a greater role and taking over several functions previously performed by Member States. As Maltby notes: 'From the mid-2000s, the Commission contributed to a shift in political norms, successfully framing import dependency as a problem requiring an EU-level solution, based on the institution's pre-existing preferences for a diversified energy supply and internal energy market. Whilst Member States retain significant sovereignty, the Commission has achieved since 2006 creeping competencies in the internal, and to a lesser extent external, dimensions of EU energy policy' (Maltby 2013, p. 435). The Commission appears to have been a 'demandeur' (Buchan 2010, p. 368) in the field of energy security, looking to play a role not formally granted by the Member States, especially when it comes to negotiations with external suppliers (Buchan 2010). Recent crises have created momentum and made the European Commission demands appear more legitimate:

> there have been some examples, actually some rather unfortunate examples, like the gas crisis of 2009, which have acted as an alarm bell and indicated that actually Member States on their own are not really in a position to face some challenges which energy may pose. That has led Member States to agree to the need to Europeanize the energy policy of the EU because, indeed, if we speak with one single voice in this field, the EU can be much stronger than by having 28 different voices. (Interview with Very Senior European Commission Official 2014)

The European Commission is at the very centre of EU action in the field of energy. However, in recent years the European Parliament, alongside non-state actors, has also come to play an increasing role in EU energy policy. The EU has traditionally shaped the energy policy of Member States through EU environmental and competition rules, somewhat predictably given that the main function of the EU is regulation, employing law as an instrument to achieve policy results (Peters and Pierre 2010,

p. 99). The fact that it can provide exemptions from these rules, funding, political and diplomatic support constitutes an additional incentive for groups promoting various energy technologies and projects to persuade EU institutions of the validity of their energy exploitation or energy infrastructure projects.

Without doubt, energy companies play an important role in EU energy security policy given their prerogatives in energy extraction and transport. The EU and its Members have formally recognized the companies' central role in responding to and preventing the gas crises that the EU might face. Companies are dependent on what the EU and its states do as they design the legislative framework in which corporate actors operate. In addition, as energy trade takes place in the realm of international politics and is influenced by geopolitics, companies seek EU and governmental support in order to gain access to energy contracts in third countries (Proedrou 2012). Non-governmental organizations are drawn to energy policymaking processes by the environmental and climate implications that fuel choices inevitably have, with this book discussing particularly the implications of natural gas. There is little insight so far into the way in which the interaction between EU institutions, states, corporations, NGOs, and so forth is structured in energy and particularly energy security policymaking processes. This study seeks to change this. The next chapter introduces this interaction and the structures that shaped it in the issue-area of fracking for shale gas.

CHAPTER 3

Fracking in the European Union: Coalitions in Collision

This section will explore the interaction between public and private actors in European energy policy by analysing two coalitions that clashed over shale gas exploitation through fracking in Europe. In the early and mid-2010s fracking constituted a much debated issue in Brussels. This study does not aim to take a stance on whether shale gas exploitation is beneficial or not to the European Union, but to look at the interaction between the actors involved in this issue and to shed light on their role in shaping European institutional positions on fracking for shale gas in the EU.

This chapter will present the context and background of the fracking debate and the two coalitions clashing over the merits of fracking. The study on the coalitions will concentrate mainly on the work of the two advocacy coalitions at a particular point in the policymaking process, that is, the drafting of and voting on the 'European Parliament resolution of 21 November 2012 on industrial, energy and other aspects of shale gas and oil', P7_TA(2012)0444 (European Parliament 2012a) initiated by the Committee on Industry, Research and Energy (ITRE). This is due to the fact that this was a completed stage in the policy cycle when this research was conducted and to the relevance of the resolution for EU energy policy. The resolution was considered an important milestone in the policymaking process that would decide on the regulatory framework in which fracking will take place in Europe. The resolution benefited from

A.-M. Bocse, *International Networks, Advocacy and EU Energy Policy-Making*, Palgrave Studies in European Union Politics,
https://doi.org/10.1007/978-3-030-49505-3_3

a lot of attention from both industry and NGOs as it was perceived to be essential in framing any kind of future debate on shale gas at the European level:

> it set the tone and the kind of parameters of the debate that we are still having now. It is the first real and political discussion of shale gas in Europe which is why it was so important for us to try and make sure that people involved in the debate had facts listed as much as possible, as much as they were interested in having facts and data or examples. (interview with representative of industry association 2014)

The European Union and Fracking: Background and Developments

Since 2010, fracking for shale gas has been of great interest to the Brussels-based policy community. The successful exploitation of shale gas in the US through fracking gave hopes that a similar development could be replicated in the EU (interview with policy adviser to a Polish Member of the European Parliament, MEP 2013; interview with policy adviser to the European Conservatives and Reformists, ECR in the European Parliament 2013). The shale gas revolution in the US had an important impact on the domestic and international gas markets and impacted the political economy of oil and gas, while stimulating new debate regarding energy and environmental sustainability (Raszewski 2018). Interest in shale gas extraction in Europe intensified in 2011 and remained very high for a few years: 'there is a large interest in the society, in the policy society, there was a moment when we had lots of invitations to conferences, speeches as if the whole world was going crazy' (interview with policy adviser to a Polish Conservative Member of the European Parliament, MEP 2014).

Shale gas is natural gas found in natural underground rock fissures and rocks need to be broken open ('fractured' or 'fracked'). This procedure involves pumping water, sand, and chemicals into the rocks under high pressure to break the rock and facilitate gas extraction. In Europe hydraulic fracturing has been used to a limited degree in conventional and shale gas reservoirs, usually in vertical wells (European Commission 2014c). Exploiting shale gas resources through fracking was and remains a very contentious issue in Europe. On the one hand, supporters of fracking argued that the development of shale gas in Europe needs to be encouraged and that additional EU regulation on fracking is unnecessary and would prevent the development of this area by placing an unnecessary regulatory burden on it (interview with policy adviser to a Polish Conservative MEP 2014). Pro-fracking groups also claimed that exploiting shale gas contributes to the EU energy security by tapping into a domestic supply source and that shale gas exploitation through fracking can be done in a safe way:

> their job is to try and explain to an MEP why shale gas in this instance is important for Europe's energy security and to try and convince an MEP that it can be done safely. Those are the main two things they are trying to sell. (interview with policy adviser to an ITRE MEP 2013)

On the other hand, NGOs and Green politicians opposed fracking on environmental (groundwater pollution and climate considerations) and health grounds and argued that developing renewable energy in the EU is the preferable way to enhance the EU energy security.

The EU Member States were and remain divided on the issue. By 2012 France and Bulgaria had banned shale gas exploration and exploitation through fracking under pressure from environmental groups and public opinion (interview with policy officer at Friends of the Earth France 2015). However, in 2012 Poland remained very interested in fracking and was providing exploration permits to several companies. Shale gas extraction through fracking was still banned in France, Bulgaria, and Cantabria region in Northern Spain when this empirical study was undertaken in 2013–2014. The exploration of shale gas reserves was taking place in Poland, the UK, and Romania.

Given the interest that the issue generated with European citizens and states, it was not long before European institutions formally began to work on fracking. In September 2010, a group of MEPs from Central and Eastern Europe, members of the European People's Party in the European Parliament, released a written declaration on the possibility of using gas from alternative sources in Europe (Grzyb et al. 2010). The declaration asked the European Commission to conduct: 'an initial analysis of the possibility to extract gas from alternative sources within Europe and to prepare a technical and economic feasibility study of extraction' (Grzyb et al. 2010, p. 2).

In 2011 the Committee on Industry, Research and Energy in the European Parliament started drafting a 'Report on industrial, energy and other aspects of shale gas and oil' (European Parliament 2012b). The report was voted on by the plenary of the European Parliament on 21

November 2012 (492 votes in favour, 129 against and 43 abstentions) and in this way became a European Parliament resolution reflecting the opinion of the entire European Parliament, not only of ITRE. The ITRE resolution did not recommend a ban on fracking and stated that the existing EU legislative framework: 'adequately covers all aspects of shale gas licensing, early exploration and production' (European Parliament 2012a, paragraph 29). The resolution noted that, in the future, 'large-scale extraction of shale gas may require the comprehensive adaptation of all EU's relevant existing legislation' (European Parliament 2012a, paragraph 29), but did not call for new, and specific, legislation in 2012.

Voices in the energy industry praised the report on which the ITRE resolution was based: 'I have to say I think the Rapporteur[1] did a good job on that [report] on shale, the quality of what went in was pretty damn high, you looked at it with an industry background and you thought this is sensible stuff' (interview with source in the gas industry 2014). The industry welcomed the content of the ITRE resolution, claiming that it was important to address some of the misunderstandings about shale gas and hydraulic fracturing and it was also relevant to create momentum in the discussion on Europe's energy resources (interview with representative of an Italian energy company 2014). The Green movement in Brussels did not praise the resolution. Sources from the pro-fracking sector, anti-fracking sector, and EU institutions agreed that the ITRE resolution met mainly the policy interests of the pro-fracking sector (interview with representative of an Italian energy company 2014; interview with policy adviser to the Greens/European Free Alliance, EFA, in the European Parliament 2013; interview with European Commission official, DG Energy 2013).

The European Parliament: A Target of Advocacy

The European Parliament debates were merely the first stage in the policymaking process. The outcome of the European Parliament debates was considered important as they would shape the position on fracking taken

[1] 'Rapporteur' is the French term designating an MEP entrusted by peers to report on an issue and to write a report on it. Reports are first subjected to the vote of one European Parliament Committee. They contain proposals for amendments or resolutions which, if also voted by the European Parliament plenary, become European Parliament resolutions. This was the case with the report of the Committee on Industry, Research and Energy discussed in this study.

at a later stage in the policymaking process by other institutions, such as the Commission and the Council of the European Union, in case the Commission decided to propose binding EU law on the conditions of the exploitation of shale gas through fracking.

Members of the anti-fracking coalition demanded a ban or at least a moratorium on fracking (interview with policy officer at Food and Water Europe 2013; interview with policy officer at Friends of the Earth Europe 2013; interview with European Commission official, DG Environment 2014). However, the EU cannot legally impose such a ban as EU law recognizes the right of a Member State: 'to determine the conditions for exploiting its energy resources, its choice between different energy sources' (European Union Member States 2009c, Article 194, paragraph 2). De facto, the prerogative of the EU Members to decide on their energy mix can be restricted by the EU: 'as you see, the Treaty says that is up to each Member State to decide on its energy mix, but the reality is very different, we keep impacting, affecting through our policies, through our positions the energy mix in Member States, the reality is very different than what the treaty says about it' (interview with policy adviser to the European People's Party in the European Parliament 2013). The EU impacts the exploitation of natural resources, especially when this has implications for the environment and public health.

From the European Parliament, the policy debate moved to the European Commission. The Parliament played an important role in placing fracking for shale gas on the agenda of the Commission:

> from the decision-making point of view, the Commission is the only body that has the right of legislative initiative. What happened is that on shale gas, on this subject especially, the Parliament pushed the Commission to adopt a point of view immediately. I do not know if you could call this an indirect right of initiative, but the reality is that this is what happened. (interview with European Affairs consultant 2014)

Existing literature indicates that engaging and convincing policymakers early in the policy debate on an issue enables groups and organizations to influence policy (Chilvers 2008, p. 2998). Mazey and Richardson claim that: 'Lobbying resources allocated to this early stage of EU agenda-setting are likely to produce bigger policy pay-offs than resources allocate to lobbying later in the policy process' (Mazey and Richardson 2006, p. 249). This is especially true with the social structures that rely upon their capacity to transmit knowledge to policymakers when influencing policy (Zito 2001). This explains why the shale gas debates in the Parliament attracted the attention of various groups, despite the fact that legally EP resolutions do not have the same weight as a potential European Commission directive (a legal act that Member States need to transpose in national law), or a regulation (a legal act that becomes enforceable in all Member States as soon as it is released).

The shale gas debate was central to the work of the European Parliament in 2011–2012. It created a lot of tension at the European Parliament level (interview with policy adviser to a Polish Conservative MEP 2014) and emotions (interview with representative of industry association 2014), especially during the plenary vote in November 2012:

> I think this was one of the most emotional debates that there ever was in the Parliament, that is what MEPs said in the plenary as well. One of them said that this was the first real debate he participated in at the Parliament. (interview with representative of an American energy company 2013)

After lengthy debates, the European Commission decided not to propose any new binding legislation and released a Communication and a Recommendation on 22 January 2014. The Commission limited itself to a Recommendation, despite the fact that its own Communication indicated that:

> since the EU environmental legislation was developed at a time when high volume hydraulic fracturing was not used in Europe, certain environmental aspects associated with the exploration and production of fossil fuels involving this practice are not comprehensively addressed in current EU legislation. This in particular concerns issues such as strategic environmental assessment and planning, underground risk assessment, well integrity, integrated and consistent requirements in terms of baseline and operational monitoring, capture of methane emissions and disclosure of fracturing fluid composition on a well by well basis. (European Commission 2014c, p. 8)

Recommendations do not have legal force and are not binding for EU states. The Commission argued that: 'this Recommendation laying down minimum principles to be applied as a common basis for the exploration or production of hydrocarbons with high-volume hydraulic fracturing is necessary at this point of time' (European Commission 2014b, introductory clause 11, p. 3). The Recommendation:

> should help all Member States wishing to use this practice address health and environmental risks and improve transparency for citizens. It also lays the ground for a level playing field for industry and establishes a clearer framework for investors. (European Commission 2014d)

The Commission took the position of the Parliament into consideration when formulating its arguments. Both the Communication and the Recommendation released in January 2014 quote the ITRE resolution in justifying the position of the Commission. The ITRE resolution provided the frame for understanding the: 'significant potential benefits of producing shale gas and oil' (European Commission 2014b, p. 1). Sources from the Commission confirmed that the ITRE resolution offered them a mandate not to propose additional and fracking specific legislation. The ITRE resolution and signals coming from Member States (particularly the UK) that they will not support new EU binding legislation determined the Commission not to propose a new directive at that point (interview with European Commission official, DG Clima 2014; interview with European Commission official, DG Environment 2014).

The Commission's decision to make only recommendations was very well received by shale gas supporters (interview with European Affairs consultant 2014; interview with representative of a French energy company 2014; interview with policy adviser to a Polish MEP 2013). These outcomes seem to indicate that supporters of fracking managed to project their arguments better at the European level than the Green movement did during the first stage of EU policymaking on fracking (2011–2014).

The rest of this case study concentrates on the first stage of the policymaking cycle, the debates in the European Parliament. That was the only stage that had been completed at the time when my fieldwork took place and on which reasonably broad access to data could be secured. The debates in the European Parliament attracted an impressive amount of advocacy and the organizations involved in advocacy were divided into two main coalitions, presented in the next section.

Introducing the Clashing Coalitions

Fracking for shale gas attracted the interest of a wide variety of actors from both the national and supranational levels. Energy companies, industry associations, NGOs, European institutions, governments, European politicians, and consultancies made up the policy subsystem working on fracking in Europe. The sociogram below (Fig. 3.1)[2] gives an overview of the policy subsystem involved in the debate around the ITRE resolution of 21 November 2012. The sociogram aims to capture the interactions taking place in 2012.[3]

The reporting in this chapter is performed at the level of policy subsystem inclusive of coalitions that emerge as clusters in the subsystem. This enabled me to generate a sociogram that presents the two coalitions (their

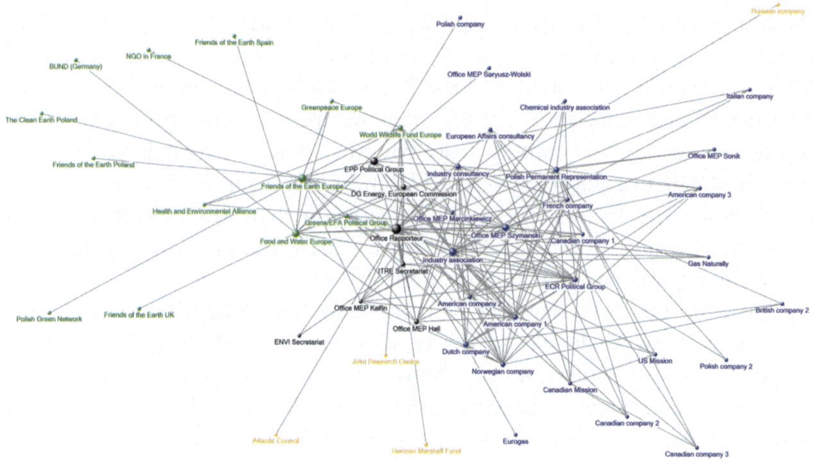

Fig. 3.1 Sociogram of the fracking for shale gas policy subsystem (generated with NodeXL). Anti-fracking coalition: Green; Pro-fracking coalition: Blue; Targets of advocacy: Black; Other actors: Orange. (Source: Author)

[2] The sociogram is based on the analysis of the connections that actors in the policy subsystem declared they have established with other actors working on the same issue.

[3] This research did not aim to collect systematically data on the subsystem nodes and edges before and after 2012 so that very accurate maps of the subsystem can be generated for different moments in time, nor did it aim to discuss in detail the coalition-formation process. That said, the membership of the two coalitions remained relatively constant from 2012 until 2014 when the European Commission released its Recommendation (European Commission 2014a). The claim that network membership remained quite constant is based on interviews with policymakers (interview with European Affairs consultant 2014) and on the fieldwork observations. This finding fits with the assumptions in the advocacy coalition framework literature that advocacy coalitions tend to be stable. Structures, especially in the context of major controversies when policy core beliefs are contradictory (Jenkins-Smith and Sabatier 1994, p. 180). Jenkins-Smith and Sabatier argue that coalition membership can remain almost the same for decades.

members and connections that bring them together), as well as the connections between each coalition and the policymakers that it aims to influence. At the same time, it captures the connections between the actors in opposing coalitions, if such connections exist. Social network analysis run on a single coalition does not allow for this. As will be shown below, although limited, contacts between the pro-fracking and the anti-fracking coalitions took place. In order to recreate and analyse the subsystem structure, I consider both network members and the connections between them, enabling mainly information exchanges and displayed on the sociogram using lines. The interviews with subsystem participants enabled the recreation of a social structure that included 51 members connected through 141 edges.[4]

Out of the subsystem, two advocacy coalitions emerged and targeted their advocacy towards the European Parliament (more exactly to the ITRE Rapporteur, policy advisers, officials, MEPs). The targets of advocacy are represented in black on the diagram. Advocacy groups targeted in particular the office of the Rapporteur in the process of developing the ITRE resolution. The office of the Rapporteur and the policy adviser to the Rapporteur (appointed by the Rapporteur) had great influence on the wording of the ITRE resolution, especially the initial draft, later subjected to amendments. Academic literature usually fails to acknowledge the role that the assistants and advisers of the Members of the European Parliament play in the policy process. Interest groups were very keen to be involved in a dialogue with this policy adviser because: 'he held the pen at the beginning' (interview with source in the gas industry 2014). He was extremely influential in the resolution writing process (interview with European Parliament official 1 2013). His role brought him in direct contact with various stakeholders. He ended up intermediating the interaction of his MEP with the industry, NGOs, and other stakeholders. In his own words:

> companies, NGOs, anyone who has any kind of stake, we had a lot of meeting requests, yes, and also there were during that time a lot of think-tanks organizing events on shale gas and, because neither I nor my boss have a geological background, it was interesting for us to attend these meetings at think-tanks. There were lots of experts there from the environmental side and from the industrial side so we thought it was quite important, that, in

[4] The term used in SNA to designate the connecting lines between actors on the sociogram.

order to get a good grasp of the issue, to expand our geological knowledge. (interview with policy adviser to an ITRE MEP 2013)

The centrality of this policy adviser in the resolution writing process is indicated by the fact that almost everybody I interviewed in Brussels on this issue mentioned him. As one interviewee pointed out: 'he was really great in getting in touch and keeping in touch' (interview with official at the Mission of Canada to the European Union 2013). His position in the network at the crossroads of information flows made him the target of immense amounts of information that he had eventually to filter, present to the Rapporteur, and help get incorporated into the wording of the resolution. He brokered the flow of information in the policy subsystem.

The Rapporteur and her office was the target of advocacy during the report-writing process, but also before the vote on the report in the plenary of the EP on 21 November 2012. The Rapporteur for the file was Niki Tzavela, Greek MEP and a member of the Europe of Freedom and Democracy (EFD) political group in the EP. In the report-writing process, the Rapporteur and her adviser were very aware that the report needs to reflect the views of the whole Parliament, not only of her relatively small political group, for the report to secure enough votes in the plenary (interview with policy adviser to an ITRE MEP 2013). Before voting takes place, the Rapporteur usually negotiates and accepts amendments from different political groups in the EP in order to ensure that the report will be voted on by the plenary. In order to have this report voted on, the ITRE Rapporteur integrated many amendments coming from the Progressive Alliance of Socialists and Democrats (S&D) in the European Parliament, the second group in the EP in terms of its number of seats in 2009–2014. The Rapporteur needed to dilute her approach and adopt some of the suggestions made by the Greens in the EP in order to satisfy the Socialists (interview with European Parliament official 1 2013).

The office of the Rapporteur benefited in the report-writing process from substantial input from an administrator in the Secretariat of the Committee on Industry, Research and Energy[5] (interview with European Parliament official 1 2013). The ITRE Secretariat and this particular

[5] Each committee in the European Parliament has a secretariat that offers administrative and secretarial support. Very often, the senior officials in the Secretariat also shape policy by providing input for reports and other committee work.

policy officer were also the target of advocacy, but not to the same degree as the office of the Rapporteur and her adviser.

Political groups and MEPs in the European Parliament were also subject to intensive advocacy, especially before voting on the report. The European People's Party in the European Parliament was the target of substantial advocacy given its large size (the largest group including a third of the EP seats in the 2009–2014 Parliament) and given that it had no pre-determined position on the issue. In the end, the EPP rejected a potential ban on fracking for shale gas in the EU and did not see the need for additional EU fracking regulation. The EPP advisers found it premature to recommend specific EU legislation on fracking for shale gas given that shale gas extraction was not yet taking place on a large scale in Europe (interview with policy adviser to the European People's Party in the European Parliament 2013).

The clash of opinion on fracking between the energy and chemical industries, on the one side, and environmental groups, on the other side, led to polarization and the emergence of two opposing advocacy coalitions in the fracking policy subsystem. The two groups began to advocate for and, respectively, against the extraction of shale gas through fracking. Both coalitions attempted to expand their ranks in 2011–2012 and to find allies in the Brussels policymaking circles. The next section will discuss the membership of the two coalitions starting with the anti-fracking coalition, as revealed also by Fig. 3.2.

In the anti-fracking coalition, interviews revealed that a central role was played by two NGOs, that is, Food and Water Europe and Friends of the Earth Europe (interview with policy adviser to an ITRE MEP 2013). The Brussels offices of these NGOs led the anti-fracking campaign at the EU level. Cooperation between the policy officers working on the shale gas file in these two organizations was very strong, as one of them put it: 'we are Siamese twins on this, it's a priority for both our organizations to coordinate this work across Europe' (interview with policy officer at Food and Water Europe 2013). They played the role of coordinators of the anti-fracking coalition and were joined in the campaign by the World Wildlife Fund, WWF, Europe, and Greenpeace European Unit (interview with policy officer at Greenpeace European Unit 2013). NGOs were driven by the belief that shale gas extraction through fracking poses considerable threats to the environment and to public health, and that only renewable energy can increase EU energy security in a sustainable way. Food and Water Europe and Friends of the Earth Europe also claimed that, by

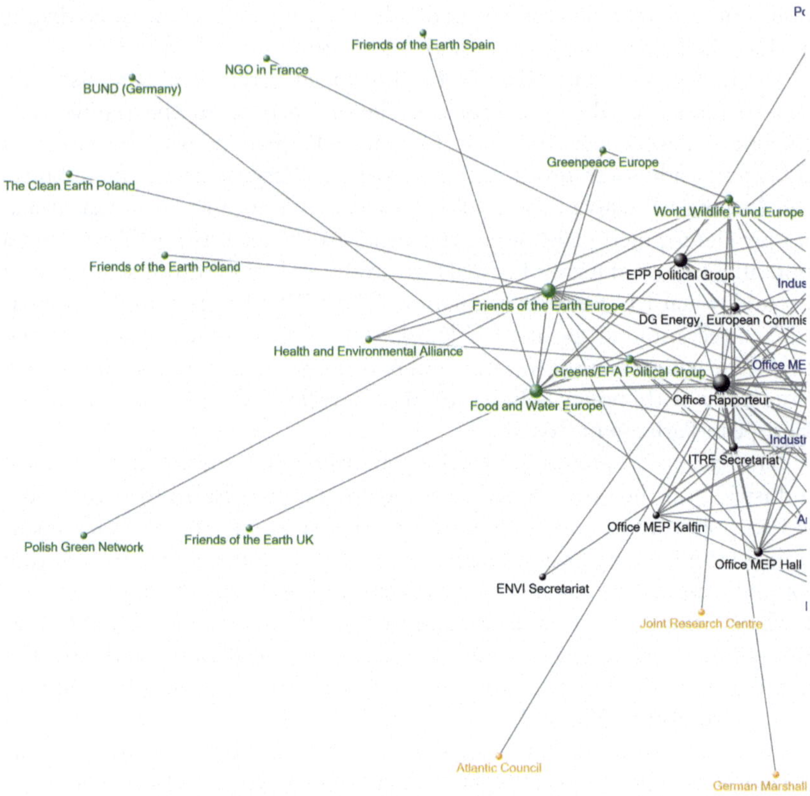

Fig. 3.2 Sociogram of the anti-fracking coalition (in Green). Anti-fracking coalition: Green; Pro-fracking coalition: Blue; Targets of advocacy: Black; Other actors: Orange. (Source: Author)

diverting investment from renewable energy, shale gas will sabotage the EU in its attempt to develop a climate-friendly energy system.

NGOs were joined in the coalition by the group of the Greens/ European Free Alliance in the European Parliament, who took a position against fossil fuels such as shale gas, stating that it will have a negative impact on the EU commitments to renewable energy sources (interview with policy adviser to the Greens/EFA in the European Parliament 2013). French Green MEPs were especially hostile to fracking. The Greens were quite radical and demanded an EU level ban on fracking for shale gas, although, according to current EU treaties, this is not possible (European

Union Member States 2009c, Article 2, paragraph 6). The Greens also rejected green or waterless fracking, the rationale behind this being that: 'in terms of the actual processes, when you dig that deep into the ground, you uncover lots of naturally occurring radiations and chemicals so, even if you are not injecting chemicals into the ground, you are still uncovering them in the ground' (interview with policy adviser to the Greens/EFA in the European Parliament 2013).

By the time the ITRE resolution was voted in the European Parliament in November 2012, the anti-fracking campaign had won over a substantial part of the Progressive Alliance of Socialists and Democrats in the European Parliament, the Greens, and the Confederal Group of the European United Left-Nordic Green Left (interview with European Parliament official 1 2013; interview with policy adviser to the European People's Party in the European Parliament 2013).

There has been a lot of speculation in the media and Brussels-based policy circles that Russia and Gazprom[6] might be funding some opposition to shale gas at the EU level or in the Member States (see for instance the articles of Higgins 2014; Harvey 2014), but this study did not find any evidence of this for the EU level anti-fracking campaign. None of the people interviewed for this research seemed to have any direct, first-hand evidence on the involvement of Gazprom in supporting anti-fracking groups in Brussels. Several interviewees from both coalitions stated that, as far as they knew, Gazprom is not part of the debate and interaction in Brussels around this issue. Environmental organizations that spearheaded the anti-fracking lobby in Brussels denied any financial connection with Gazprom, pointing to the fact that they campaign against fossil fuels in general and are against the increase of gas in the energy mix whether from unconventional or conventional sources, as it is the case with gas sold by Gazprom (interview with policy officer at Friends of the Earth Europe 2013). Furthermore, sources close to Gazprom in Brussels denied any kind of connection between Gazprom or Gazprom funding and European anti-fracking advocacy (interview with public affairs consultant working for Gazprom 2013). The anti-fracking coalition aiming to prevent fracking for shale gas in Europe developed in opposition to a pro-fracking coalition and its membership is revealed by Fig. 3.3.

[6] Gazprom is a Russian state-controlled company and all strategic decisions are approved by the state so the Russian government strongly influences Gazprom's decisions (interview with Russian academic and energy law expert 2013).

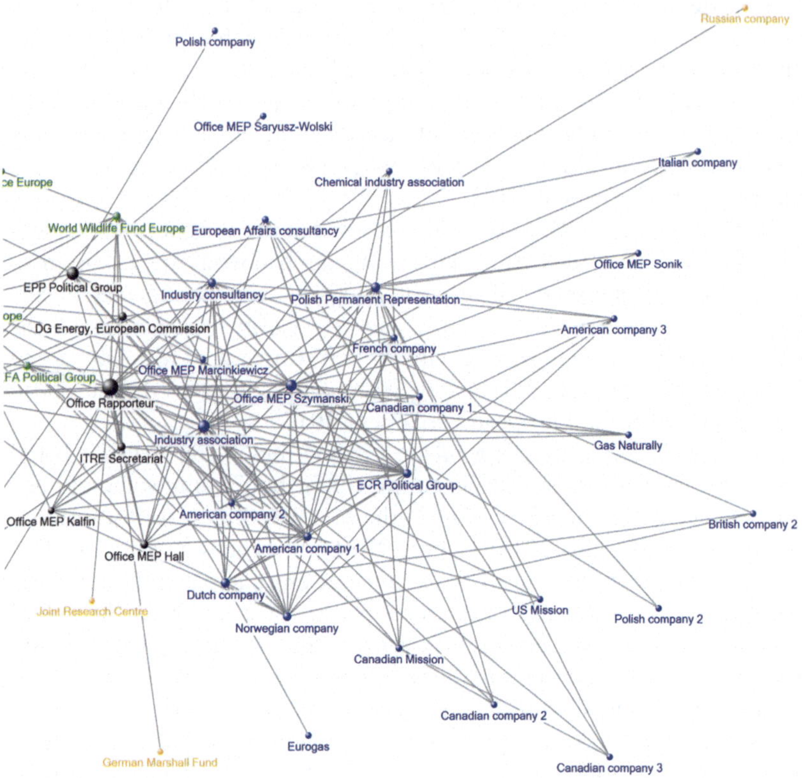

Fig. 3.3 Sociogram of the pro-fracking coalition (in Blue). Anti-fracking coalition: Green; Pro-fracking coalition: Blue; Targets of advocacy: Black; Other actors: Orange. (Source: Author)

The pro-fracking coalition included large American oil and gas companies such as ExxonMobil and Chevron interested in exploiting shale gas in the European Union and in the revenues that this might generate. They were joined in their campaigns efforts by large European energy companies and middle-level Canadian companies involved in exploring for shale gas in Poland. The coalition also included an industry association, the Organization of Oil and Gas Producers (OGP), and public affairs and consultancy firms based in Brussels. Consultancies were hired by energy companies to manage the relation with the EU sector and, to a certain degree, with the public opinion. They were remunerated for their consultancy services. The oil and gas industry did not welcome the idea of new legislation on fracking which they claimed would be an excessive measure and insisted on proper implementation of the existing EU legislation that they argued covered well this industrial activity (interview with representative of an American energy company 2013).

In addition to the oil and gas industry, the chemical industry was involved marginally in the pro-fracking campaign, working in cooperation with the oil and gas industry. The main rationale for the chemical industry to support shale gas is the hope that it will provide this industry with non-expensive gas that will decrease its production costs and will close the competition gap between the EU and the US in the chemical field (interview with representative of chemical industry association 2014).

The pro-fracking coalition was joined by Polish, British, and Czech Conservative MEPs. The Polish MEPs were great believers in and promoters of the shale gas as a solution to energy insecurity in Poland and the EU (interview with policy adviser to a Polish Conservative Member of the European Parliament 2014; interview with policy adviser to the European Conservatives and Reformists in the European Parliament 2013; interview with European Affairs consultant 2014). The position adopted by many Polish MEPs is that the EU should not further regulate shale gas extraction at the EU level, nor should it operate changes to existing EU legislation such as the Water Framework Directive (Directive 2000/60/EC) (European Parliament and the Council 2000) or the Directive on the Registration, Evaluation, Authorisation and Restriction of Chemicals (European Parliament and the Council 2006a) in light of potential shale gas exploitation through fracking in Europe (interview with policy adviser to a Polish MEP 2013). The argument is that it would be unfair towards investors who are already operating in Poland to change the rules and that additional regulation will increase investments costs and discourage the development of shale gas extraction facilities.

Poland was the most involved Member State in the shale gas debate at the European Parliament level and also the main state supporter of shale gas exploitation through the Polish Permanent Representation. The shale gas debate occupied an important place on the agenda of the Representation: 'for the Permanent Representation it seems to be quite an important part of the policy and, definitely, one of the main priorities in energy and environmental policy' (interview with Polish official 2013). The Polish government feared that the EU might impose excessive regulation and increase the administrative burden on Member States that want to go ahead with shale gas exploitation. Poland was and remains very interested in developing its shale gas potential given its energy security concerns:

> when you see the reserves that some countries like Poland have, it is obvious that they see it [shale gas] as, firstly, an energy security issue. It's basically replacing the gas coming from Russia and it's giving them a choice. They are not, let's say, hostage to one single provider so for them it's obviously the first reading that is done, that of energy security. (interview with policy adviser to the European People's Party in the European Parliament 2013)

Poland had a background of mistrust and tensioned relations with Russia, its main gas supplier, and was very interested in becoming more independent from Russian gas. Being energy independent should be seen in the context of its deep energy and political dependence during the communist era (interview with policy adviser to the European Conservatives and Reformists in the European Parliament 2013), dependence that Poland strives to leave behind.

Polish governmental representatives also claimed that shale gas will increase the competitiveness of the Polish economy (by providing access to cheaper gas) and that it can generate revenue for local communities (interview with Polish official 2013). In Poland shale gas development was supported by both government and opposition parties, as well as by public opinion at national level. Opposition developed in the areas in which shale gas projects are expected to be implemented.

The UK began to play an increasing role in the EU shale gas debate in 2013 as the debate moved from the European Parliament to the European Commission, but was not very active at the moment of debating and voting the ITRE resolution. The UK supported shale gas as a source of energy security, low energy prices, and an aid in the fight against climate change. The government led by David Cameron showed a lot of support for fracking in the UK and rejected the possibility of a ban on fracking in its public interventions (Carrington 2015).

The US Mission to the EU, as well as the Mission of Canada to the EU, was also involved in the shale gas debates. Both missions monitored developments in the EU legislation applicable to shale gas exploration and extraction and facilitated exchanges between the North American regulators and their European counterparts (interview with official at the United States Mission to the European Union 2013; interview with official at the Mission of Canada to the European Union 2013). According to the official at the US Mission: 'European regulators meet with our regulators some at the federal, but most at the state level so they can exchange experiences and learn best practices, ask questions'.

The Canadian Mission was more open to expressing its support for shale gas developments in the EU than the US Mission. In the words of the Canadian official liaising with the EU on this issue: 'our position is supportive, we believe it can be done safely if done properly and you do it properly through proper regulation, impact assessments, that sort of thing' (interview with official at the Mission of Canada to the EU 2013). Canada attempted to prevent any kind of negative impact that the EU shale gas debate might have on the Canadian industry operating in and outside Europe:

> you know, Canada does care. We don't just want to share information, we do care about what happens in shale gas because it can have potentially negative impacts on Canadian industry that's active and, you know, there's this effort going on to make anything unconventional seem bad and dangerous. (interview with official at the Mission of Canada to the EU 2013)

The US Mission seemed more reluctant to directly advocate for shale gas, taking the position that: 'we are willing to offer help to the ones who want to do it, but we are not gonna push people to do it, if they don't want to' (interview with official at the United States Mission to the EU 2013). American companies have contacted the Mission to try to find out what steps the EU Commission will take on shale gas, but did not rely on the US government's support in advocating with the EU and conducted their own advocacy campaigns as part of the pro-fracking coalition (interview with official at the United States Mission to the EU 2013).

By November 2012, certain groups in the European Parliament also joined the pro-fracking coalition. The European Conservatives and Reformists (ECR) and the Europe of Freedom and Democracy (EFD) Group were most in favour of fracking for shale gas. The Conservatives seemed to share the industry fear that over-regulating shale gas extraction will simply kill any endeavour in this field:

> there is the risk of too much legislation, we may just lose competitiveness in the field because the sector will be over-regulated even before it has started so from an investment point of view it is not the wise thing to do. (interview with policy adviser to a Polish Conservative MEP 2014)

The first chapter introduced the idea that actors in an advocacy coalition: '(a) share a set of normative and causal beliefs and (b) engage in a non-trivial degree of co-ordinated activity over time' (Sabatier 1998, p. 103). While members of the anti-fracking coalition are mainly driven by environmental considerations and the belief that shale gas does not constitute a sustainable source of energy, the energy and chemical industries are driven by economic and profit considerations, as well as the belief that shale gas is the best solution for tackling the EU energy security concerns. As explained in the first chapter, this study will adopt a broad definition of what a belief constitutes, allowing for corporate actors operating in the field of energy (who seek material benefits, to maintain a certain level of profit or to increase it) to be seen as actors in advocacy coalitions.

As revealed by the sociogram on the policy subsystem working on shale gas, members of the same coalition are connected by a dense web of links indicating resource exchanges and coordination. Interaction and exchange among the members of the same coalitions was driven by the need to generate a cohesive message for the outside world: 'everybody knows and everybody works on the principle that you have to send the same message or that at least it needs to be coherent' (interview with European Affairs consultant 2014). In both coalitions certain organizations coordinated the advocacy of the coalition. The pro-fracking coalition relied to a great degree on the industry association, while the anti-fracking coalition relied on the NGOs Food and Water Europe and Friends of the Earth Europe to coordinate its work.

Studies, briefs, and position papers were circulated among members of the same coalition and they jointly signed papers to be sent to the European Parliament (interview with policy adviser to the European People's Party in the European Parliament 2013). Exchanges of opinion took place in the coalition on the text of the resolution, as well as on amendments proposed to initial versions. In the pro-fracking coalition exchanges between governmental actors and corporate actors took the following shape: 'we exchange the information, we share our hesitations, we express our expectations and then it is up to the companies and up to us which way we choose' (interview with Polish official 2013). Companies wish to know where allied governmental actors stand on an issue, how firm is their support. The corporate members of the coalition, who have technical knowledge and information on shale gas exploration and exploitation given their direct involvement in these processes, provide it to other members of the coalition (interview with industry consultant 1 2013).

In 2010–2014 there were events on shale gas and fracking almost every day in Brussels. Interaction between policy actors took place around the ITRE resolution during meetings and events organized by the European Parliament Secretariat, by Members of the European Parliament, by European Parliament political groups (interview with European Parliament official 2 2013). In addition to the formal events organized in the institutional setting (hearings, consultations), there were also a wide variety of events (workshops, seminars, conferences, round table discussions) organized by industry associations, environmental NGOs, and organizations such as the German Marshall Fund (GMF) Brussels. The GMF did not take a firm position for or against fracking for shale gas, but was heavily involved in mediating the interaction between policymakers in the EU, policymakers in the US, and experts on shale gas (interview with former officer at the German Marshall Fund, Brussels office 2013; interview with former researcher at the German Marshall Fund, Brussels office 2013).

Platforms such as that constituted by the GMF provide a good environment in which members of opposing advocacy coalitions can meet and interact. As Sabatier (1998) argues in his work on advocacy coalitions, 'professional fora' are critical for promoting learning across coalitions (Sabatier 1998, p. 118), given that this is much more problematic than learning processes among members of the same coalition (Sabatier 1998, p. 105; Radaelli 1999, p. 665; Rozbicka 2013, p. 842). Members of the same coalition are more willing to engage in information and knowledge exchange with each other, consequently learning is more likely to happen in the same coalition.

However, on the issue of fracking, competition and mistrust led to little interaction between the two coalitions as they emerge as almost two independent segments on the sociogram. Advocacy coalitions tend to see opposing coalitions as being more malignant and powerful than they probably are (Sabatier 1998, p. 110). This was visible in the case of the coalitions working on fracking. For instance, members of the pro-fracking coalition pointed in interviews to the advantages that environmental NGOs derive from hiring experts with good networking skills when it comes to approaching policymakers, especially young EU advisers and officials who actually draft policy proposals (interview with source in the gas industry 2014). Fieldwork in Brussels allowed me to observe that this perception is not accurate and that industry advocates can also be quite good at networking with policymakers. On their side, the anti-fracking coalition claimed that industry has 'giant pockets' (interview with policy officer at Greenpeace European Unit 2013). Although industry has more material resources than NGOs, their governmental affairs and advocacy funding are not unlimited and usually are the first area to suffer cuts when the companies are doing less well. Both coalitions tended to misperceive and overestimate the tools that the opposing coalition uses.

Both the data collected through interviews describing the networking patterns in the policy subsystem working on fracking and the social network analysis performed on the subsystem indicate limited exchanges between the pro-fracking and anti-fracking coalitions. An interviewee showed that:

> the industry kind of self-isolates itself in the sense that they listen to one another, each shares what he/she hears from the other, but nobody goes to the source, you know, or only a few are the ones that go to the source. This is one of the weaknesses of the corporate lobbying in Brussels, at least from my perspective. (interview with European Affairs consultant 2014)

Despite some attempts to interact, there is recognition that it is difficult for dialogue between the two coalitions to take place on fracking:

> so we have some good relationships with them but, once we say that we are in favour and once they say they are opposed, the dialogue on this issue cannot go very far. … When we have some true divergence, I do not think a long dialogue is useful. On some other issues we can discuss, in some reduction of CO_2 emissions we may have the dialogue because we may converge with the objective and discuss the means to achieve it. But issues like shale gas are more difficult, I think. (interview with representative of a French energy company 2014)

That being said, certain organizations played a bridging role between the two coalitions. This was the case with the World Wildlife Fund (WWF) Europe. WWF's priority was fighting climate change, so it placed more emphasis on phasing out coal, which has a higher carbon footprint than gas: 'essentially keeping the pressure on coal, but not worrying too much about gas is a Europe-wide position of the WWF' (interview with former policy officer at WWF Europe 2013). The WWF considered that gas can be a potential bridge fuel to an economy based on renewable energy (interview with former policy officer at WWF Europe 2013). From this point of view, the WWF position was closer to that of the gas industry than was the case with NGOs such as Food and Water Europe and Friends of the Earth Europe that rejected the role of gas as a transition fuel. As the WWF representative confessed in an interview, he had a reputation in Brussels and with the industry: 'of being a kind of moderate or sensible NGO person' (interview with former policy officer at WWF Europe 2013). This created more opportunity for the WWF and its representatives to establish links not only with the anti-fracking coalition (of which it was part), but also with the pro-fracking coalition. Given its connections, the WWF concentrated a lot of relational power.

Empirical data confirms that the main policy officer working on fracking on behalf of the WWF had more opportunities to communicate his ideas and points of view to the industry than other members of the anti-fracking coalition, maybe even to socialize them with these views up to a point:

> because I have that kind of reputation [of being moderate and sensible NGO person] often industry players will stop and talk to me, saying: 'hey, what do you think of this?' and it's just a way of them chatting, you know, looking in the mirror, really, finding what's going on by listening to different perspectives. (interview with former policy officer at WWF Europe 2013)

Such an NGO representative offers the industry access to information and perspectives that its representatives might not be able to access by moving only in the industry circles.

The European Parliament's intention to write a report on the industrial and energy aspects of shale gas extraction in Europe triggered exchanges and interactions beyond the borders of the EU giving the two coalitions a strong international character. Although aiming to influence EU policy, the membership of the two advocacy coalitions working on fracking in Europe surpassed the borders of the European continent, as revealed by the sociogram. The policymaking on fracking in Europe benefited from the contributions of international NGOs (such as Friends of the Earth and Greenpeace), of international oil and gas corporations (ExxonMobil, Chevron), and of the US and Canada. In this way, the European debates were influenced by shale gas debates taking place in the US, while foreign regulators provided extra-European regulatory expertise to EU legislators. Ideas and concerns travel well across the Atlantic.

This chapter also showed that the European Parliament can affect the decision-making process on an issue area through its own initiative reports. Even if they are not legally binding as such, they can greatly influence and frame the European policy debate, especially when it comes to highly controversial issues such as shale gas exploitation in the EU. After being voted on in the European Parliament on 21 November 2012, the ITRE resolution went on to influence the European Commission's position on fracking for shale gas and its decision not to propose additional regulation on shale gas extraction in Europe. This is indicative of the increasing power of the European Parliament in the EU institutional game.

The next chapter will look at the factors that helped the pro-fracking coalition in shaping to a greater degree than the anti-fracking coalition the EP position and particularly the 'Resolution on industrial, energy and other aspects of shale gas and oil'. It will, at the same time, provide additional insight into the resources, information flows, and structure that characterize this policy subsystem and the coalitions that are part of it.

CHAPTER 4

Fracking in the European Union: The Power of Resources, Words, and Structure

This chapter will discuss the factors increasing the chances of an advocacy coalition to reach its goals by looking at the empirical data on coalitions that advocated for or against fracking for shale gas in Europe. The introductory chapter hypothesized that a coalition is more likely to be successful ***if it possesses and makes good use of resources; if it develops a broad, timely, and dynamic frame; and if it is well interconnected and includes members who are central to the policy subsystem working on a particular issue.*** This chapter will discuss the degree to which the actions of coalitions working on fracking confirm or contradict these hypotheses. The ITRE report adopted by the European Parliament plenary states that it:

> recognises, therefore, the important role of worldwide shale gas production in ensuring energy security and diversity of energy sources and suppliers in the medium to long term; is aware that domestic production of shale gas could offer an opportunity for some Member States to further diversify their natural gas supply sources, bearing in mind Member States' dependence on natural gas imports from third countries. (European Parliament 2012a, paragraph 10)

And:

A.-M. Bocse, *International Networks, Advocacy and EU Energy Policy-Making*, Palgrave Studies in European Union Politics,
https://doi.org/10.1007/978-3-030-49505-3_4

> points out that shale gas will help to strengthen the position of customers vis-à-vis gas suppliers and should therefore lead to lower prices. (European Parliament 2012a, paragraph 6)

The same resolution expresses a concern regarding the competitiveness of the European industry in the context of the shale gas revolution in the US:

> observes that US spot prices have fallen to a historic low, thus widening the price gap between the US and a Europe bound by long-term contracts, and having an impact on the competitiveness of Europe's economies and industry. (European Parliament 2012a, paragraph 3)

and argues that shale gas can assist the EU to meet its climate change commitments as shale gas can contribute to the:

> transformation of the energy system, as stated in the Energy Roadmap 2050, since it represents a quick, temporary and cost-efficient way of reducing reliance on other, dirtier fossil fuels before moving to fully sustainable low-carbon power generation, thereby lowering greenhouse gas emissions, particularly in those Member States that currently use large amounts of coal in power generation. (European Parliament 2012a, paragraph 14)

Such Member States also include Poland, a strong advocate for shale gas at the EU level. As will be shown below in more detail, the resemblance between the arguments of the pro-fracking coalition and the clauses of the ITRE resolution is striking and solid evidence of the influence that the pro-fracking coalition had on the document. This chapter will explain why the pro-fracking coalition was more successful than the anti-fracking coalition in its advocacy campaign with the European Parliament.

The first section of the chapter will discuss the role of resources and particularly of informational resources in shaping policy outcomes. Information: 'is the most important resource to study in order to understand the exchange between business interests and the EU institutions' (Bouwen 2002, p. 369). Information provides advocacy coalitions with access to policymakers. Access can easily translate into influence. As the next section will show, technical information on fracking can be traded for information that helps improve the advocacy strategy. Once a trust relationship is established, interest groups might even propose amendments to be integrated word-by-word in official documents.

The Power of Resources

This section will argue that the pro-fracking coalition was better at reaching and persuading the European Parliament than the anti-fracking coalition, given its rich informational and material resources. The exchange of information is crucial in the creation and work of advocacy coalitions (Rozbicka 2013). Scholars claim that information is central to lobbying in the EU context (Bouwen and McCown 2007; Eising 2009; Chalmers 2012). Information, knowledge, and expertise constitute important 'access goods' (Immergut 1992; Bouwen 2002) that provide members of coalitions with access to policymakers. Non-state actors influence European institutions because they are credited with possessing information that can be of great help to policymakers based in the institutions. Network-like forms of organization (including advocacy coalitions) are thought to be structures very suitable for information transfer and learning (Powell 1990; Podolny and Page 1998; Watts 2003; Kenney et al. 2012).

Possessing Information of Technical Nature

Members of the European Parliament and European civil servants are dependent on corporations and NGOs acting as information providers. That corporations and NGOs perform such information services is currently accepted in Brussels and is part of the normal political processes taking place here. This has become obvious through the participant observation I engaged in during my fieldwork and is consonant with testimony given by policy actors in interviews:

> it's the way we work, internally. Even in our group we are not saying, well, NGOs are the bad guys or corporations are the bad guys, as I mentioned to you, they are doing their job, it is part of the game, it has always been like that and honestly it's very useful in terms of providing information because we cannot be expert on everything. Here, for example, working for the EPP, we are working in ITRE. ITRE is covering issues like space policy, like telecommunication, research, energy in all the dimensions. The guy that is telling you that he is expert in all those areas is simply lying. So in that context, such information is very useful to us. (interview with policy adviser to the European People's Party in the European Parliament 2013)

The informational input of non-state actors is welcomed by MEPs, EU civil servants, and policy advisers that cover a wide range of issues, lack time to conduct their own research, and sometimes do not have a strong technical background. Communities of experts engage broadly with policymakers and influence policy especially in highly technical areas or areas characterized by a high degree of uncertainty (Haas 1992a). The information provided to policymakers during the fracking campaign falls into what Bouwen named 'expert knowledge' and defined as an access good that 'concerns the expertise and technical know-how required from the private sector' (Bouwen 2002, p. 369). Fracking was perceived in the EP from the moment the subject entered its agenda as a technical process whose understanding requires specific knowledge many MEPs and in-house advisers did not have. Both the members of the pro-fracking coalition and of the anti-fracking coalition did not argue with this perception as this provided them with access to MEPs and advisers, although the type of technical information offered by energy companies and NGOs was different, as indicated later in this section.

Under conditions of uncertainty, policymakers turn to experts for advice. Reducing uncertainty is an important goal for both policymakers and legislators. According to Zito, there are several sources of uncertainty:

> issue uncertainty results from problem complexity. This occurs when the problem has an impact across a wide range of territory involving a broad range of actors, and the issue is linked to a number of other policy issues in a way that problem definitions and solutions cannot separate neatly. Uncertainty also involves situations where the definition of what the problem is, the measuring and gathering of evidence, and the question of solutions are disputed by significant actors. Newness of the issue area, prevalent in both the EU and environmental policies, also creates uncertainty. (Zito 2001, p. 588)

Shale gas extraction through fracking is characterized by uncertainty. We have only estimates on the shale gas reserves available in the EU. We do not know how many of those resources are easily exploitable, it is unclear if fracking generates problematic methane emissions (scientific research has not reached a conclusion on this), and we do not know how a shale gas boom in Europe will impact EU climate change commitments or EU energy insecurity. There is a major disagreement between policy actors on all these issues, as well as between scientists. As one NGO representative mentioned, the debate around fracking is also: 'a battle between scientists. … You have scientists on either side doing research and producing very different results. ... There is nothing like scientific certainty, there is always, you know, new ideas or new methods' (interview with policy officer at Food and Water Europe 2013). Exploiting shale gas had just entered the EU agenda during the period discussed in this study so it was a rather new topic on which policymakers had little information. In such a context, we would expect the information transmission services of energy companies, consultancies, and environmental NGOs that translate the work of scientists into the language of policymakers to be in great demand.

This study found that, when it comes to taking a decision on shale gas, the European Parliament has relied on corporations, the consultancies they employ, and NGOs for data on technical aspects related to fracking for shale and the economic and environmental aspects of shale gas extraction and use. As a key policy adviser in the ITRE resolution writing process highlights:

> expertise is the most important thing you can gain from them, in having an understanding of what the process entails. Not all MEPs are geologists so we are talking mainly technical expertise, as well as having a good understanding of what kind of regulations are necessary, as well as having a picture of what would be too excessive, in terms of having commercially viable projects and then competitiveness issues in terms of energy pricing, but that is mainly important because of the global context of energy prices. (interview with policy adviser to an ITRE MEP 2013)

And:

> we are talking mainly about information transfer in the sense that we have best practice guidelines that we intend to implement including, in Europe, if no additional binding legislation is released meanwhile, or we are talking about being open in offering them several analyses more or less of business, more or less economic related, for instance on how much it costs to dig for a shale gas project. (interview with European Affairs consultant 2014)

In addition to approaching decision-makers with information, interest groups were open to answering specific questions on a wide variety of issues when approached by decision-makers: environmental aspects; the type of technology that will be used for shale gas extraction; energy market aspects (for instance the effects of the shale gas boom on the US energy market); and energy security implications, especially for Eastern European EU Member States (interview with European Parliament official 1 2013).

What Cross argued in relation to epistemic communities also applies to advocacy coalitions. It is less important if the information they provide is proven or not, what is important is that the information be 'socially recognised' (Cross 2013, p. 158). The recognition that companies and NGOs receive from policymakers as valuable sources of information made them influential, as they use this authority to persuade policymakers, to alter their opinions and policy aims.

Developing and voting a report on industrial, energy, and other aspects of shale gas and oil implied that the MEPs have a basic understanding of hydraulic fracturing and particularly the energy industry took the opportunity to present itself to them as the ultimate expert on the actual fracking and drilling operations. Companies directly involved in energy exploration in Europe and exploitation beyond Europe argued that they are in an especially good position to provide information to policymakers on the drilling for shale gas process:

> I can imagine MEPs or people in the Commission, they are not petroleum engineers or drilling engineers, they need someone to sit down and explain to them how things really happen so they can make informed decisions about policy. This is our role, so we have the best people to inform about this because we do this every day. (interview with representative of a Dutch energy company 2013)

And:

> we are supporting the idea of shale gas. We do that because we have been involved with shale gas in the United States now for four years, we have ownership and operations in the United States, in North Dakota, so based on that experience we definitely think that this is feasible in Europe. (interview with representative of a Norwegian energy company 2014)

Also governments, such as the Canadian government that supported the pro-fracking campaign in the European Union, claimed that their regulators' extensive experience in fracking recommends their opinion as a reliable and trustworthy one to European regulators:

> the Alberta regulator gave a very good example. He was saying that in Alberta we've drilled extensively since we started drilling 100 years ago. In

> the EU they drilled 27 wells so obviously there are some lessons that can be learnt and the EU should learn from, not just Canada's mistakes, but those of the US as well. (interview with official at the Mission of Canada to the EU 2013)

The Canadian and American missions to the EU, part of the pro-fracking coalition, provided information mainly on the regulatory practice associated with shale gas in Canada and in the US. For instance, the information that the Canadian Mission offered mainly concerned how the regulatory framework is set up in Canada, extractive industry best practice in Canada, and the good environmental record of shale gas extraction in Canada (interview with official at the Mission of Canada to the EU 2013). The interaction between the Canadian Mission and the European Parliament entailed providing information on shale gas exploitation in Canada to the Secretariat, to the MEPs, and especially to the Rapporteur of the Committee on Industry, Research, and Energy through her policy adviser (interview with official at the Mission of Canada to the EU 2013). In this way, the Canadian Mission contributed to the preparation of the ITRE report on shale gas. Also, in the meetings with Polish MEPs, the Canadian Mission offered its view on shale gas extraction and to follow up on the issue if MEPs need further information (interview with official at the Mission of Canada to the EU 2013). The mission let MEPs know that fracking can be done safely and can constitute a feasible solution for a country seeking to enhance its energy security by increasing its domestic gas production through fracking.

NGOs were also engaged in communication processes targeting the European Parliament, but for a long time such communication was restricted to highlighting the negative effects that shale gas might have on the environment:

> we prepared some position papers that we circulated to make some recommendations, and to also raise awareness of the number of impacts, because it was the first time that the European Parliament was discussing these issues so there was obviously a huge lack of knowledge of the number of these impacts and it was important for us to highlight what these impacts were. (interview with policy officer at Friends of the Earth Europe 2013)

In addition, my empirical research shows that advocates also help policymakers process large amounts of information. Technological advances that facilitate contacts between policymakers and interest groups have led to an increase in the amount of information that policymakers need to digest these days, unlike in the early 2000s: 'nowadays everything is much faster than it was, much more easy also, easy in the sense of facilitating contacts, speaking of this kind of stuff, but it's more complicated because you have much more content to digest, many more things to deliver' (interview with policy adviser to the European People's Party in the European Parliament 2013). Therefore, policymakers welcome the guidance that experts, whatever their policy agenda, might offer in navigating this informational labyrinth.

Possessing Financial Resources

Financial resources enabled the industry to organize events or pay consultancy firms to organize meetings with MEPs and EU officials where the pro-fracking coalition engaged in acts of advocacy:

> of course, it is a question of how many resources you have and how much you can dominate the public debate so I can't tell you how many oil and gas industry events I've been invited to and they just have the money to do that and frame the debate and control the debate. ... No question that they are giants and that they have giant pockets for this sort of thing and it's cost effective for them to invest their money in this if they prevent some little piece of environmental legislation going through and if this cuts their costs in the long run. (interview with policy officer at Greenpeace European Unit 2013)

Several sources deeply involved in EU energy policymaking on fracking for shale gas reported that energy companies invested more material resources, more money in organizing events, workshops, and meetings with decision-makers than the NGOs (interview with journalist at an influential Brussels-based media outlet 2013; interview with policy officer at Food and Water Europe 2013; interview with European Commission official, DG Clima 2014; interview with European Affairs consultant 2014). Working dinners or breakfast meetings were also often organized by pro-fracking campaigners to discuss shale gas and its potential implications for Europe (participatory observation during fieldwork; interview with representative of a French energy company 2014, recalling having attended such a breakfast; interview with representative of industry association 2014, recalling having organized a working dinner on shale gas during a European Parliament plenary session in Strasbourg). Polish MEPs supporting fracking organized the regular round table on shale gas in the European Parliament, working lunches and circulated pro-shale gas newsletters to other European Parliament Members (interview with policy adviser to a Polish MEP 2013).

Being able to host such events matters, especially as personal rather than technology-mediated interaction is central to Brussels-based energy policymaking. I found that policy actors use email, phone, and social media in their policy interaction, but that face-to-face communication remains crucial. On the issue of shale gas, interaction in person was the preferred means of communication for Brussels-based policy actors be they European civil servants, policy advisers to MEPs, industry, or NGOs. It is easier to persuade people in a face-to-face meeting than over the phone, especially when defending a point of view that is strongly contested by opposing coalitions. This is the case with most statements concerning shale gas (given its environmental, economic, and social implications). Brussels is a policy environment where oral communication is important, especially when it comes to interacting with the European institutions:

> we prefer face-to-face meetings because you can have an exchange, by email we send some documents, the result of a study or an invitation, but not have a conversation [...] the way we communicate here with the Commission and the Parliament is more on the personal level, face-to-face meetings or events, more human interaction. (interview with representative of a Dutch energy company 2013)

The preference for communication in person is also shared by NGOs, using technology-mediated communication to establish a contact and a trust relationship with officials, in preparation for meetings:

> you first send emails and then once you create kind of a trust relationship, you can phone them directly and then you can arrange a number of face-to-face meetings, because we believe it's probably the most effective way to pass our messages and recommendations. And, of course, use the opportunity of public events to sometimes speak to officials that we usually cannot have access to, like the highest officials, for example. (interview with policy officer at Friends of the Earth Europe 2013)

It is usually at these events that informal contacts are established, officials communicate on publicly unavailable information and interest groups, be they industry or NGOs, make informal policy suggestions. As one interviewee with several years of experience working in Brussels on energy policy mentioned, this is the level of:

> the informal Brussels village. There are things that are drafted, bits of legislation that come completely from outside because people have just been talking with each other. That process of informal engagement is something which is also part of the story. (interview with source in the gas industry 2014)[1]

The access that advocacy coalitions gain using their informational and financial resources is also used to gather information that can make them more effective advocates. Rarely is any meeting in Brussels only a unilateral information flow. Exchanges between EU institutions and coalitions are reciprocal. As indicated by Bouwen 'the key to understanding the lobbying activities of business interests in the European institutions is to conceive of the relation between these private and public actors as an exchange relation between two groups of interdependent organizations' (Bouwen 2004b, p. 339). Lobbyists and advocates (corporations and NGOs alike) are provided with information by politicians, policy advisers, and other decision-makers and this information helps them to organize and implement their campaigns. As Mazey and Richardson claim: 'knowing what is going on may be just as important to an adaptive interest organisation as trying to influence what is going on' (Mazey and Richardson 2006, p. 249). The type of information that advocates receive is of a different nature than the information they offer. They are interested in receiving information providing insight into political moods and policy preferences:

> the discussion is always a two way process. We bring some information and we get, I would say, some political feeling about the way they see the issue from a political standpoint and sometimes we can draw some conclusions for

[1] Whilst face-to-face meetings remain the preferred means of communication, time constraints might not always make them possible. Email and phone are used when policy actors have a very busy agenda and when the problem can be solved in a faster and more effective way in a technology-mediated manner. Technology is also very important when staying in touch with established policy contacts (according to participant observation and several sources: interview with policy adviser to an ITRE MEP 2013; interview with industry consultant 1 2013; interview with representative of a Norwegian energy company 2014).

our advocacy depending on their reactions. (interview with representative of a French energy company 2014)

And:

you can receive information in the sense that a coalition between EPP and ALDE might happen or maybe they did not reach a compromise so far, internal things that you normally do not have access to because they are not public. Information related to bilateral negotiations or negotiations behind closed doors is the kind of information you can generally get from the people who are on your side. (interview with European Affairs consultant 2014)

In addition, interest groups received information on the parliamentary procedure, but also on the position and preferences of certain MEPs. This helps outsiders understand better how the Parliament and EU institutions work: 'access to information to understand how the parliamentary process works because that can be really difficult to feel from outside of the Parliament, just to understand what will happen exactly, how it will happen' (interview with policy adviser to a Liberal Member of the European Parliament 2013). From the ITRE Secretariat, they received information about the compromise amendments that the Rapporteur will integrate in the resolution (interview with policy adviser to a Polish Conservative MEP 2014).

In particular, members of the pro-fracking coalition received information on the positions and preferences of MEPs that helped them map the opinion spectrum in the European Parliament (interview with representative of industry association 2014) and design their strategies:

it's most of the times very specific, concrete examples, for example which Rapporteur or which MEP is proactive, it's involved in the discussion, whether an MEP has a very objective approach to things or is open for arguments or some MEPs block everything which comes from industry, this kind of information. Sometimes, they advise, yes, you could speak with this one about these things, etc. (interview with industry consultant 1 2013)

Usually, for this information flow to take place policymakers in the EP have to identify themselves with the position and preferences of a certain coalition, to share similar beliefs.

> if, for example, an MEP believes shale gas is a good thing, I do not think they would hesitate to say you should talk to that person because he might help you with something else, he might help you with German constituencies, for example, or you should talk to this Polish Member because she is having problems in her constituency and it would be interesting to get feedback on what residents there were saying about effects on water, etc. (interview with policy adviser to an ITRE MEP 2013)

If they found out what worries the voters in their constituencies, advocates had a better chance of addressing those issues when approaching the MEPs and of getting them on their side. Advocates also wrote amendments and sent them to MEPs who embraced them. As one MEP policy adviser indicated during an interview: 'they will send me their ideas for, say, amendments and of course we will take them on board. … For them, it is pure policy influence' (interview with policy adviser to a Liberal MEP 2013). Both industry (interview with representative of industry association 2014) and NGOs sent such amendments on fracking. When it comes to NGOs, in particular Food and Water Europe and Friends of the Earth Europe pushed for these amendments to be adopted by the European Parliament (interview with policy officer at Greenpeace European Unit 2013).[2]

This section showed that there was a dense exchange of information taking place between the two coalitions and the MEPs whom they tried to influence, often in an indirect way, through their policy advisers and political group advisers. Fracking is a process surrounded by a lot of uncertainty and this makes the knowledge and expertise of energy companies directly

[2] This study has provided data mainly on information exchanges. This is not to say that it excludes the possibility of exchanges involving financial resources and staff. It is, however, very difficult to check if exchanges of financial resources take place between interest groups and policymakers, especially as this would be an illegal activity. Some interviewees mentioned that a particular MEP benefited from financial favours from the industry or a certain MEP has shares in a particular shale gas company (interview with policy adviser to the Greens/ EFA in the European Parliament 2013; interview with senior policy adviser to the Greens/ EFA in the European Parliament 2013). In most such cases the information came from a policy actor who had opposing political views, especially advisers to the Greens in the European Parliament and could not be checked with that particular MEP or his political group so it has to be considered with caution. There is also an exchange of personnel in the field of energy in Brussels between EU institutions and the private sector, corporations, or NGOs. Usually the flow of personnel takes place from institutions to energy corporations or NGOs and less often the other way around. However, the exchange of personnel did not emerge as a prominent phenomenon in the cases studied in this research.

involved in the fracking process particularly valuable to policymakers. Their reputation as rich information sources and material resources provided the pro-fracking coalition with more opportunities to interact with policymakers and pass on its information, positions, and understandings of the benefits of fracking. After access is secured, advocates attempt to persuade policymakers to embrace their policy preferences. They do this by altering facts and prioritizing certain lines of argument that fit their policy goals.

The Power of Words

The main resource for advocates is information. This might be technical information, economic information, or simply data on the preferences of certain groups that play a key role in policy implementation. Policymaking is finally based on this information. However, as this section will show, the information that advocates provide tends to be filtered to fit their interests and this filtering is what makes it a valuable political weapon. The information that interest groups provide is framed in a particular way, tailored to an audience and to a particular goal that the coalition seeks to reach. For the purpose of this study: 'to frame is to select some aspects of a perceived reality and make them more salient in a communicating text, in such a way as to promote a particular problem definition, causal interpretation, moral evaluation, and/or treatment recommendation' (Entman 1993, p. 52).

Most policymakers are aware that the information that corporations and NGOs deliver might be biased. Policy actors who admit to engaging in dialogue with interest groups stress that they are aware of the biases that might be inherent in the information they are provided with, but they still use this information in order to cope with information shortage:

> we deal with so many issues at some times, we need expertise, obviously we know that there is no such thing as independent expertise. It's always biased in some direction so it is not that we trust in everything that we are told, but we need people to get some background because otherwise we are simply unable to cope with everything on our own. (interview with policy adviser to the European Conservatives and Reformists, ECR in the European Parliament 2013)

Even knowledge that is presented to the decision-makers as 'science' is framed in a particular way. For instance economic estimates on the number of jobs that will be created in Europe as a consequence of shale gas exploitation or data on greenhouse gas emissions generated by shale gas extraction. Usually the studies on best shale gas extraction practice in North America are quoted by the industry and studies on average practice are quoted by the NGOs because they tend to indicate higher greenhouse gas levels, especially when it comes to methane emissions resulting from shale gas extraction (interview with policy officer at Food and Water Europe 2013).[3] Research can and is manipulated to fit certain policy positions: 'you can find research, as you know, there is research on any point, you have an argument, you find research for it, that's how it works with research' (interview with policy adviser to a Liberal MEP 2013).

Framing was an important tool through which the two coalitions studied in this chapter sought to get policymakers on their side. Framing took place through the position papers that organizations wrote and sent to policymakers, through presentations and arguments adopted in meetings, and through the selection of experts that coalitions chose to introduce to policymakers. The NGOs arranged meetings where they brought scientists, experts sharing their point of view (interview with policy officer at Food and Water Europe 2013) and so did the industry or the consultancies hired by it: 'we also coordinated a lot of very technical experts either in water or waste or drilling to come to the Parliament and talk to the MEPs as well, and we gave some ideas, for example when there were hearings, we proposed academics or experts in a particular topic' (interview with representative of industry association 2014).

The introduction to the book advanced a few theoretically grounded hypotheses regarding the effectiveness of framing that will be tested against the coalitions working on fracking. Based on the existing literature, we would expect frames to make an impact if they are: ***(1) broad and resonate with many actors; (2) respond to exogenous unfolding events, and (3) respond effectively to opposing frames***. In this section I show that the pro-fracking coalition advanced a broad frame, enabling it to attract institutional support; integrated better than the anti-fracking coalition the financial and economic crisis in its frame; and engaged in a fruitful way with the frame advanced by the anti-fracking campaigners in order to dismiss their arguments. This contributed to the success in persuading the EP of its point of view.

[3] Sometimes NGOs 'request research to be carried out for lobbying purposes' (interview with policy officer at Greenpeace European Unit 2013).

The pro-fracking coalition advanced a frame that was meant to appeal to a wide range of policy actors during the shale gas debates taking place in the European Parliament. The actions and the interpretation of the world that the pro-fracking coalition advanced tried to align with the interests, values, and beliefs of key actors. The fracking supporters engaged in frame extension defined as the process through which: 'an SMO may have to extend the boundaries of its primary framework so as to encompass interests or points of view that are incidental to its primary objectives but of considerable salience to potential adherents' (Snow et al. 1986, p. 472).

Broad Frame and Resonating With Many Actors

The pro-fracking frame was broader than the anti-fracking frame, which focused only on the environmental and potential health impact of fracking for shale gas, especially in the 2011–2012 debates that informed the ITRE resolution. Arguments for fracking for shale gas multiplied in order to respond to the interests of a varied audience and to attract its support. The frame was extended to include the public goods that fracking might generate: energy security (meaning access to both energy supply and affordable energy); boosting EU competitiveness (especially in the context of the global financial and economic crisis); and helping the EU transition to a carbon-free economy. Shale gas exploitation through fracking was presented as meeting a triple interest:

> this [shale gas] is important for Europe, this is important for security of energy supply, this is important for the competitiveness of Europe, this is important also for the climate and the environment. ***This is important for security of energy supply.*** Conventional natural gas is declining. Currently our import dependency is 60%, that will rise to 80%. ***Second, there are issues of competitiveness.*** You have energy intensive industries who are vocal right now because of the shale gas revolution in the US and there I am not saying that we are going to have the same shale gas revolution as in the US, but still it could help competitiveness. ***Third, you see that in the US there is a decrease of greenhouse gas emissions because of the shift from coal firepower generation to gas firepower generation*** so if you would do the same in Europe you can have a decrease of greenhouse gas emissions. (interview with representative of an American energy company 2013)

The shale gas debate benefited from a lot of attention at the EU level owing to the potential contribution that shale could make to EU energy security. This was the case in the US. The energy security argument became quite popular in the Brussels-based policy community:

> the whole idea of talking shale gas in the first place is the security and the security of supply and the new source of energy and so forth, but then whether you choose to develop that or not depends on what price tag it has, but first and foremost is an energy source so of course you start with the energy argument. (interview with European Parliament official 4 2013)

And:

> energy security is definitely a very important argument, one of the main arguments in favour of developing these resources. (interview with policy adviser to the European Conservatives and Reformists, ECR in the European Parliament 2013)

My research found that the pro-fracking coalition played an important role in associating shale gas with EU energy security in the policy subsystem working on the ITRE resolution. In relation to shale gas, the energy security argument was used by big companies, those with good reputations, not only in extraction but also in the dialogue with communities and stakeholders (interview with policy adviser to an ITRE MEP 2013). This point of view is confirmed by other key players in the shale gas debates: 'I think this argument is mainly used by the energy companies and through us. I mean energy companies, consultancies, and public affairs firms, and think-tanks, yes, make that link' (interview with industry consultant 1 2013).

The pro-fracking coalition argued that the contribution of shale gas to the EU energy mix is even more welcome given declining internal gas production at the level of the European Union in recent years. As one industry representative pointed out:

> production is declining in the conventional gas fields so the EU dependence on imported gas is increasing and so from our perspective it makes sense that at least we explore any potential new reserves of gas in Europe and see if they are commercially viable, maybe produced in a sustainable, environmentally protective way. So from our point of view it is important that Europe at least analyses what it has and then makes a decision politically. We

> think it makes sense to also exploit domestic resources, especially for Central and Eastern European Countries. (interview with representative of industry association 2014)

The industry pointed to the fact that increasing the amount of domestically produced gas can help the EU reduce its dependence upon external suppliers and gain more flexibility when negotiating gas contracts with external suppliers, particularly Russia:

> in Europe shale gas is home-grown resources, so it's indigenous resources and from this point of view it helps when you have something produced at home, it helps when you go out and negotiate supply contracts from outside Europe, it helps in your negotiation with other suppliers because you have an alternative which is indigenous gas production, it helps balance the power between supply and demand. (interview with representative of a Dutch energy company 2013)

The industry admits that generating energy security, which can be considered a public good, is not necessarily very high on their agenda, but they resorted to this argument when interacting with politicians. The pro-fracking coalition was aware that their message needs to be adapted to the audience they are approaching:

> for us it is a question of, when we go to an MEP, understanding where they are from, tailoring our argument. You might meet one MEP from Lithuania and talk about security of supply. You might meet an MEP from Germany and focus on competitiveness so each argument is equally valid. It is a question of which resonated most with the person that you are talking to. (interview with representative of industry association 2014)

And:

> if you have a firm that is interested in Poland, of course the argument around security of supply will work with every MEP or with every Polish decision-maker, beyond debate. But sometimes, in certain phases you have to adapt your messages to the agenda of the person you are meeting. ... Then of course you rely on security of supply in a general way, because it is an argument that is obvious, but you also rely on all that triggers local employment or investment at the local level. (interview with European Affairs consultant 2014)

The energy security argument was more likely to convince Members of the European Parliament from states in Central and Eastern Europe.[4] Eastern European states are very interested in reducing their dependence on Russian gas and placing themselves in a better position to negotiate gas prices with Russia. Central and Eastern European understanding of energy security is strongly related to the idea of access to supply:

> all of what we used to call East Europe from Estonia down to Greece and Bulgaria because they still have a huge amount of over-reliance on Russian supply, or electricity in the case of the Baltics, on Russian gas in almost all of Eastern Europe, some places also on coal and also on oil, but they are focused on energy security in terms of supply. (interview with official at the United States Mission to the EU 2013)

By contrast, the anti-fracking frame was mainly grounded in environmental, climatic, and public health arguments and narrower than the pro-fracking frame. Environmental NGOs warned that shale gas extraction might have a negative impact on the environment at different levels. NGOs pointed to the negative consequences of shale gas exploitation on groundwater and on air quality (interview with policy officer at Food and Water Europe 2013; interview with policy officer at Greenpeace European Unit 2013). The questions that they raise are related to the 'flowback water', a by-product of the fracking process, its treatment, and its reintegration in the natural water circuit. NGOs also argued that shale gas exploitation poses threats to public health (interview with policy officer at Friends of the Earth Europe 2013).

The anti-fracking coalition as a whole argued that shale gas extraction can generate gases that will contribute to climate change and will prevent the EU from meeting its climate change commitments[5]:

[4] As revealed by various interviews: interview with policy adviser to the Greens/EFA in the European Parliament 2013; interview with representative of an American energy company 2013; interview with policy officer at Food and Water Europe 2013; interview with policy officer at Greenpeace European Unit 2013; interview with European Commission official, DG Energy 2013.

[5] Within the anti-fracking coalition, there were variations of position regarding the relation between gas and climate change. WWF's individual position was that phasing out coal, which has a higher carbon footprint than gas, is their top priority. They also agreed that gas can be a potential bridge fuel in the transition to renewable energy (interview with former policy officer at WWF Europe 2013). However, in the campaign targeting the European Parliament and as part of the anti-fracking coalition, they supported a more critical position of gas, position preferred by the coalition partners.

> for climate reasons as well because we believe that there is a whole range of fugitive methane that are inherent to that process and that goes directly into the atmosphere and seriously contributes to climate change and in that sense we do not believe that shale gas is any kind of transition fuel because it's still a very dirty fossil fuel and the only type of energy that could allow us to go towards a decarbonised economy is renewable energy and energy efficiency policies. We've also seen a whole range of examples that show that the shale gas industry requires massive investments to be developed, and if it directly competes with the renewable sources in that sense, we do not see how it really complements renewable energy development. (interview with policy officer at Friends of the Earth Europe 2013)

Shale gas suddenly made possible the option of cheap shale gas versus expensive renewable energy and in times of economic crisis such an option became very attractive (interview with policy officer at Food and Water Europe 2013; interview with policy officer at Greenpeace European Unit 2013).

Members of the anti-fracking coalition indicated that the technology to extract shale gas is not developed enough and that the industry cannot offer guarantees against all the potential environmental impacts. They also advise that: 'until certain requirements can be met, there needs to be much more research into the environmental and health impacts of shale gas' (interview with policy officer at Greenpeace European Unit 2013). Under these conditions, they argued that the best solution is to avoid exploiting shale gas:

> we see that there are some technological obstacles that the industry cannot fix, that generate a whole range of long-term environmental impacts that then generate massive health and climate impacts, that we think shouldn't be ignored and as a consequence we think that we should leave that shale gas in the ground. (interview with policy officer at Friends of the Earth Europe 2013)

The potential negative impact that fracking has on the environment and the action against climate change raised issues of energy injustice. One dimension of energy justice is related to intergenerational equity entailing an obligation to prevent energy-related negative externalities from harming future generations (Sovacool and Dworkin 2014, p. 17). Engaging in practices that harm the environment places an additional burden on future generations that will need to deal with the negative effects of fracking that are not visible today, but might become evident in the future. Conventional gas extraction practices and in particular fracking generate huge amounts of produced water and the environmental and health costs of oil and gas extraction are not always internalized to the fuel price (Sovacool and Dworkin 2014, p. 132). Similarly, greenhouse gas emissions generated in the process of exploiting and using gas resources might generate economic benefits for current generations, but bites into the overall carbon budget and leaves future generations with a reduce amount of clean air and with the task of dealing with the consequences of climate change.

Anti-fracking groups rejected the perspective of a shale gas revolution taking place in Europe on the same scale that it has taken place in the US and that in this way shale gas can contribute to EU energy security. What sets the US aside from the EU is: 'an entirely different starting point with decades of geological knowledge that has built up, huge service industry, lax environmental regulation, where the US energy market is highly integrated with all these hubs that are connected' (interview with policy officer at Food and Water Europe 2013). The anti-fracking coalition excluded shale gas as a solution for EU energy insecurity and advised energy efficiency and the development of renewable energy:

> for us, energy security is renewables because they are renewable and sustainable. We are not going to run out of them in the way that you will run out of fossil fuels because it's true security in that we secure health and the climate, so I think, we have our own definition of energy security. (interview with policy adviser to the Greens/EFA in the European Parliament 2013)

Overall, the framework that the anti-fracking coalition advanced was narrower than the framework of the pro-fracking coalition. Table 4.1 presents in a comparative way the elements included in the frames of both coalitions:

As the next section will show, one of the factors that enabled the anti-fracking coalition to expand its frame was the fact that it integrated into its arguments a response to developing exogenous events.

Table 4.1 Elements of the pro-fracking and anti-fracking frames presented in a comparative way

Coalition	*Frame elements*						
	Energy security			*Environmental concerns*		*Economic competitiveness*	*Public health*
The pro-fracking coalition	Shale gas will help increase EU domestic energy production	Shale gas will help decrease gas-dependence on Russia	Shale gas will help keep gas prices low or reduce gas prices	Shale gas will help the EU keep its climate change commitments	Fracking will not harm the environment if the best industry practice is adopted	Shale gas will enhance EU economic competitiveness	
The anti-fracking coalition	Renewable energy is the best source of energy security			Shale gas will not help the EU meet its climate commitments; renewable energy will	Fracking will harm the environment		Fracking will negatively impact public health

Source: Author

Responding to Exogenous Unfolding Events

The pro-fracking coalition integrated exogenous events in their policy argumentation very effectively. Coalition members need to be entrepreneurial in order to induce policy change by taking advantage of changes in the policy context (Jenkins-Smith and Sabatier 1994). These changes might entail: 'significant perturbations external to the subsystem (e.g. changes in socio-economic conditions, system-wide governing coalitions, or policy outputs from other subsystems)' (Jenkins-Smith and Sabatier 1994, p. 179). The global financial and economic crisis was an event that was used by the pro-fracking coalition to build a case for large-scale fracking in Europe. Zito argues that a crisis will make policymakers more open to radical solutions in order to advance new policy (Zito 2001). The crisis provided the context in which policymakers were more willing to take additional risks in order to secure energy at lower prices.

The pro-fracking coalition used the security of supply argument in conjunction with the EU economic competitiveness argument to advocate for shale gas development in Europe in times of financial and economic crisis. The pro-fracking coalition played an important role in bringing the economic argument to the debate and in linking energy security with cheap energy prices triggered by large-scale fracking in Europe, prices that can lead to economic competitiveness. This is a discourse that can be very successful in an era of recession. Energy security is redefined in this context as access to cheap gas that can contribute to economic development and job creation.

The economic competitiveness argument extended the frame of the pro-fracking coalition to respond to the interests of Western European EU Members, as well as those of the chemical industry. The access to energy argument responds very well to the interests of East European Member States and MEPs from there, but was of less interest to MEPs from Western Europe. Members of the EU in Western Europe are not as interested in access to energy as they are in low gas prices and MEPs from these countries were persuaded especially by arguments related to gas pricing:

> you see much more push in Romania because their driver is security of energy supply, which is much more an issue than in this part of Europe [Western Europe] because here we never had this issue. When you plug in, you always get electricity. For this part of the world, energy prices, competitiveness is becoming more important, more of an issue than security of

> energy supply. (interview with representative of an American energy company 2013)

Interest in accessing affordable gas and supporting the European economy grew in the context of the global financial and economic crisis. The global context made advocacy more difficult for the anti-fracking coalition:

> they are lobbying at a harder time for them given the economic crisis, given the fact that the US is making substantial progress economically due to the cheaper shale gas and so it's more difficult for them to influence the debate than it would have been maybe in 2007–2008. (interview with journalist at a trade specialised publication 2014)

Several interviewees reported a discursive shift towards competitiveness as the debates on fracking and shale gas in Europe were progressing (interview with representative of industry association 2014; interview with representative of the US Chamber of Commerce 2014). As a policy officer in the European Parliament indicated, at the moment of the debates on fracking in the EP, energy prices became an important policy consideration:

> at that point we were already starting discussions about energy costs, energy prices associated with that, mainly costs. Many, many complaints from some industry, some producers, that the energy costs represent a growing part of the price of the product and therefore they are losing some competitiveness, for example when compared with the States. (interview with policy adviser to the European People's Party in the European Parliament 2013)

In addition to contributing to the economy by keeping energy prices low, fracking was also seen as contributing to the European economy by employing new people in the extractive and adjacent industries (interview with representative of a French energy company 2014; interview with representative of a Norwegian energy company 2014). The pro-fracking coalition expanded its frame and advocacy base by responding to exogenous events, as well as by responding to the frame articulated by its adversaries in a slightly more efficient way than the anti-fracking coalition.

Responding Effectively to Opposing Frames

Neither coalition develops its discourse in isolation. Both coalitions engaged in a process of counterframing, which: 'includes refutations of the logic or efficacy of solutions advocated by opponents as well as a rationale for its own remedies' (Benford and Snow 2000, p. 617). The pro-fracking coalition included in its frame elements regarding the protection of the environment and argued that fracking will help the EU meet its climate change commitments by enabling the EU to reduce its CO_2 emissions. The US example was very often used by advocates to illustrate their points. US sources corroborated their claims:

> what shale has allowed is basically to dramatically reduce our use of coal in electricity production which had significant impact on our ability to transition away in terms of climate policy. I think a year and a half ago, for the first time gas was producing more electricity than coal at a lower cost, which has allowed us, even though we were coming out of the recession, to make this transition so it's made a real fundamental contribution to climate policy. (interview with official at the United States Mission to the EU 2013)

Fracking advocates claimed that shale gas can substitute fossil fuels that are more carbon-intensive, such as coal, and can help build a 'greener future' for Europe (Shale Gas Europe 2015). This was a response to the frame advanced by the anti-fracking coalition that centred around environmental and climate arguments at the very beginning.

By claiming to protect common interests, environmental groups claim the high moral ground. The energy security argument advanced by the pro-fracking coalition also brought an important public interest and emotional dimension to the pro-fracking discourse. Several interviewees representing organizations and structures involved in the pro-fracking coalition claimed that NGOs use emotions to make their case (interview with representative of a Dutch energy company 2013; interview with official at the Mission of Canada to the EU 2013). The energy security argument matched the emotional dimension of the environmental, climatic, and public health arguments against shale gas brought by NGOs:

> it adds an emotional dimension. The industry often criticizes the citizen movement and the NGOs for being too emotional and, you know, for not sticking to the facts. These are the kind of accusations. I think talking about it in terms of energy security is a very emotional kind of argument because

> you make it sound as if everyone is going to be insecure. I think there is an emotional kind of connotation with the word ['security'], because security is really fundamental. (interview with policy adviser to the Greens/EFA in the European Parliament 2013)

According to fracking advocates, shale gas is a generator of energy security, the source of a public good, and its exploitation has become important for society. The industry involved in the pro-fracking campaign managed to convey the message that it is not arguing only for its own economic interests, but for a public good which can be as important as environmental protection and public health.

In turn, the anti-fracking coalition changed its frame by integrating economic arguments in order to respond better to a frame developed by the pro-fracking coalition that had an important economic component. According to Sabatier: on the basis of perceptions of the adequacy of governmental decisions and/or the resultant impacts, as well as new information arising from search processes and external dynamics, each advocacy coalition may revise its beliefs (primarily in the secondary aspects) and/or its strategies (Sabatier 1998, p. 104). When they felt they were losing ground by focusing on environmental arguments, as the debate moved under the influence of the global financial crisis towards the field of economics, environmental NGOs decided to engage with the economic aspect of the debate:

> it seemed like all the economic arguments were winning over the environmental ones so that's why we have been working quite extensively on these economic arguments, to analyse why the US example was showing this image of shale gas as cheap and abundant gas, cheap and abundant energy. We released two facts sheets on the issue. We invited an American energy analyst to a conference that we organized with a Socialist MEP in order to speak and to analyse these economic aspects of the shale gas industry. (interview with policy officer at Friends of the Earth Europe 2013)

Organizations such as Food and Water Europe and Friends of the Earth Europe attempted to deconstruct the argument that shale gas will contribute to lower energy prices in Europe and will enhance the competitiveness of the European industry (interview with policy officer at Food and Water Europe 2013).

The two coalitions seemed to be involved in a genuine 'framing contest', a concept developed by Ryan (1991, pp. 75–94) that can be used to describe the competition for the best frame between the pro-fracking and the anti-fracking coalitions. Unfortunately for environmental NGOs, their arguments resonated less with and were less able to convince the European institutions. The economic arguments were integrated late in the anti-fracking coalition's frame. MEPs and DGs in the European Commission (such as DG Clima, DG Energy, and DG Enterprise and Industry) believed in late 2013-early 2014 that gas can facilitate the transition to a carbon-free economy by replacing coal in the EU energy mix (interview with European Commission official, DG Clima 2014; participant observation at events at which European officials made statements) and that cheap shale gas from Europe or the US can help increase EU competitiveness (interview with European Commission official, DG Enterprise and Industry 2014).

This section showed that coalitions will try to adapt their discourse to the audience they seek to co-opt or to persuade to adopt a specific position or action, in this case, European Parliament officials, advisers, and parliamentarians. The pro-fracking coalition resorted to frame extension to produce a broad enough frame that would attract the support of the European Parliament (MEPs coming from Central, Eastern Europe, and Western Europe) and of several sectors of the European industry. Analysis of the discourse developed by different policy actors enabled me to show that members of the pro-fracking coalition embraced and promoted the energy security discourse in relation to shale gas. These actors were very resourceful. Industry, which in general is perceived to possess more extensive material resources than NGOs, was an important promoter of this discourse.

The previous sections show that resources, as well as a well-articulated frame, contributed to the success of the pro-fracking coalition. The next section will show that certain structural characteristics of the coalition and its Members also accounted for its success. Some actors occupied a central position in the subsystem working towards the ITRE resolution of 21 November 2012 and this position enabled them to share information and to shape the understanding of the European Parliament on the benefits and drawbacks of fracking in Europe, especially for European energy security.

The Power of Structure

This section will examine the subsystem structure and the relative positions that key actors occupy in the subsystem in order to determine if social structural factors advantaged the pro-fracking coalition in its advocacy work. Whereas the previous sections focus on the actors that make up the policy subsystem, this section will concentrate on the ties that connect them in the policy subsystem. The analysis of these ties through social network analysis enabled me to recreate the structure of the coalitions and the subsystem. As discussed in the introduction to the book, social network analysis also enables the computation of different coalition level metrics and individual actor metrics that will be presented in this chapter.

Interconnected Coalition

Using the group metrics function in NodeXL, I calculated the density and geodesic distance for both coalitions, as well as for the whole subsystem. The results are included in Table 4.2:

In addition to consisting of more nodes, the pro-fracking cluster in the network also seems to have been denser (density of 0.225) than the anti-fracking cluster (density of 0.218). The difference in density is not very large, but its significance increases if we take into consideration that the pro-fracking coalition size is twice the size of the anti-fracking coalition (Fig. 4.1) and that achieving a high density in larger structures is more difficult.

Table 4.2 Including the coalition level metrics and the subsystem level metrics for the shale gas study

Graph metrics	*Anti-fracking coalition*	*Pro-fracking coalition*	*Whole subsystem*
Nodes/members	13	27	51
Number of ties/connections between members (excluding duplicate ties)	11	62	141
Density	0.218	0.225	0.141
Maximum geodesic distance (diameter)	3	4	4
Average geodesic distance	1.764	1.805	2.229

Source: Author

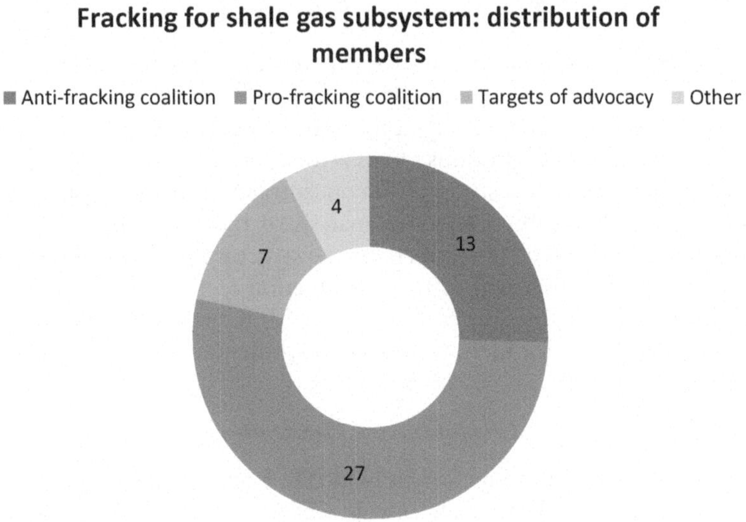

Fig. 4.1 Fracking for shale gas subsystem's distribution of members. (Source: Author)

This indicates that the pro-fracking coalition was connected by a denser web of ties which facilitated the exchange of information, the pooling of resources, and the development of a coherent frame used in the advocacy campaign. As indicated by previous studies, densely interconnected networks are thought to support more efficiently flows of resources, policy ideas, and preferences in the network (Krackhardt 1990; Faul 2013).

In an ideal coalition in which everybody is in direct contact, the distance between coalition members would be 1, all members being able to communicate with the other members directly. In reality, this is rarely the case. The values for average geodesic distance (in Table 4.2) show that, on average, in order to reach another member, a member of the pro-fracking coalition would go through 1.805 nodes, while the member of the anti-fracking coalition would go through 1.764. Given that these figures are very close, it is hard to claim that they had an impact on the success of one coalition or another. The diameter of the coalition is influenced by the size of the coalition, a smaller coalition being more likely to have a smaller diameter. It is therefore less relevant to compare the diameters of the two coalitions in this case study.

Once a frame is built at the coalition level, it needs to spread in the policy subsystem in order to influence policy. Given that the aim of the two coalitions was to influence the position of the European Parliament, this chapter will be looking especially at actors that emerged as brokers at the subsystem level.

Including Nodes Central to the Subsystem

Social network analysis can help determine the position of an actor in a social structure (Scott 1988; Wasserman and Faust 1994) and the power that derives from this position. Certain actors played a greater role in mediating the exchange of information and understandings of fracking in Europe owing to their central position in the policy subsystem working on this issue (these brokers are revealed by Fig. 4.2). They played an important role in mediating the interaction between the coalition they were part of and the object of their advocacy, the European Parliament (represented by the office of the ITRE Rapporteur working on the issue, the ITRE Secretariat that also provided some input to the ITRE Rapporteur, and MEPs that were likely to make a difference in the resolution voting process). The key position that these actors occupied in the policy subsystem

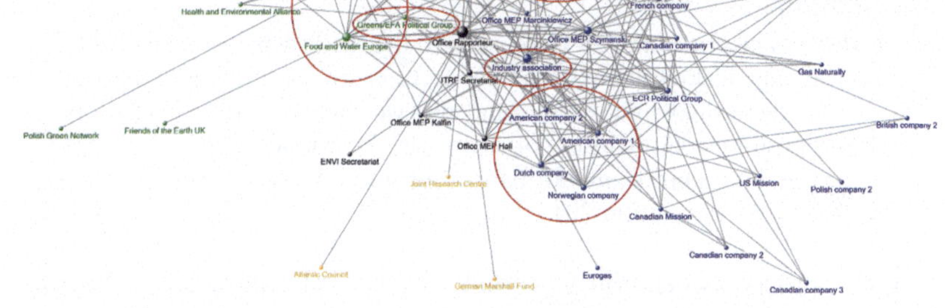

Fig. 4.2 Brokers in the fracking for shale gas subsystem. Anti-fracking coalition: Green; Pro-fracking coalition: Blue; Targets of advocacy: Black; Other actors: Orange. (Source: Author)

was revealed by the description of their role in the coalition and subsystem during interviews, as well as by social network analysis (SNA).

The interviews with subsystem participants revealed that the pro-fracking coalition was advantaged in the process of engaging in information and frame exchanges with the European Parliament. The pro-fracking coalition reached the EP through three main types of actors central to the policy subsystem, that is, through the industry association, through the governmental affairs offices of energy companies that had such offices in Brussels, and through consultancies. By contrast, the anti-fracking coalition had more reduced access. The role of brokers in relation to the EP was played in its case by two NGOs and by the Greens/EFA in the EP.

In the pro-fracking coalition, the energy industry association played a leading role. The industry association was prominent in the information transfer that took place in the policy subsystem, not only because most of the industry chose to act through it but also because it was favoured as an interaction partner by the European Parliament. As one consultant explains: 'in general the institutions prefer to talk directly with a representative of the industry, with the trade association, mainly this is the preference in general because of course it is more time efficient' (interview with European Affairs consultant 2014). The industry association also benefited by increased legitimacy and credibility, given its broader membership: 'if you only talk as one company then you are far less credible, it's just your own interest, but if you can widen it to your own sector then it gains an importance, becomes more credible, because it's not only you arguing for it' (interview with industry consultant 1 2013). The industry association communicated on different aspects of shale gas extraction on behalf of the industry. According to an industry representative, it acted as an information office:

> the idea was just to comprehensively talk to the MEPs who were involved, if they had any technical questions about how we do drilling, how does hydraulic fracturing work, where companies were already drilling in Europe, industry positions on disclosure of chemicals, those kind of things. We basically just became a bit of an information bureau. (interview with representative of industry association 2014)

The industry association was joined by several companies in its pro-fracking advocacy with the European Parliament. Four large oil and gas companies registered in the US, Norway, and the Netherlands were very involved in the campaign. These companies maintain governmental/EU Affairs offices in Brussels and were in direct contact with the European Parliament in the decision-making process on fracking for shale gas in Europe. They sent their in-house European Affairs experts to convey the position of their particular company, although they were also members of the industry association and also advocated through it (interview with representative of a Norwegian energy company 2014).

Companies also hired consultancies to mediate some of the communication with European institutions by organizing meetings and events that brought together energy company officials and EU decision-makers (interview with representative of an American energy company 2013; interview with representative of a Norwegian energy company 2014). In this way the companies externalized some of the tasks that their rather small European Affairs offices could not handle at the pick of the debate on fracking in Europe. Consultancies are used by energy companies for several reasons, as a representative of an industry association indicated:

> most of our members work with consultancies. It is basically a matter of resources to them because a lot of the offices are very small, maybe one or two people, or they are not even here in Brussels so they need people to monitor the debate, monitor the policy developments, keep an eye out if there are any parliamentary questions that relate specifically to their operation. Most of our members use consultancies for kind of monitoring, intelligence gathering, some of them use them to set up meetings with MEPs and officials if they are not physically here in Brussels, some of them use consultancies to help them condense materials or to change materials from North America for a European audience, it depends. I don't want to say all our members, but I would say a good 90% of our members use consultancies for one or another task. (interview with representative of industry association 2014)

Consultancies were also employed by smaller companies that did not have a permanent in-house European Affairs officer and were involved in shale gas exploration in Europe (interview with European Affairs consultant 2014). Mediating the communication with the European Parliament was one of the most important functions that such consultancies performed.

Food and Water Europe and Friends of the Earth Europe brokered the communication between the anti-fracking coalition and the European Parliament. Organizations such as Greenpeace European Unit or the

World Wildlife Fund entrusted them with this role, while they remained involved in the campaign by signing statements that Food and Water and Friends of the Earth distributed to European Parliament Members, by allowing their logos to be used on campaign documents, or contributing advice for the amendments to the ITRE resolution proposed by Food and Water Europe and Friends of the Earth Europe (interview with policy officer at Greenpeace European Unit 2013). This kind of task distribution enables NGOs to remain efficient despite their reduced resources:

> for purposes of being more efficient with the resources that they have, very often, when NGOs lead on a particular issue, they basically do most of the work, to be honest, and they may seek the support of other NGO allies and we do the same with other NGOs on other issues. (interview with policy officer at Greenpeace European Unit 2013)

This statement confirms some of the claims in the literature according to which one of the reasons why interest groups form coalitions is that they enable resource sharing and the more effective use of resources (Mahoney 2008, pp. 168–169). The Greens in the European Parliament acted as a bridge between the anti-fracking coalition and other Members of the European Parliament. They were at the same time members of the coalition and members of the target of the coalition's advocacy, the EP.

The role of intermediators played by all these actors in the subsystem was also indicated by the SNA performed on the connections that members of the coalitions reported they had with other members of the policy subsystem (members of the same coalition, targets of advocacy, members of the opposing coalition, or other actors). SNA complements the insight into the network dynamics offered by analysis of the qualitative descriptive interview data.

In order to determine the network's hubs through SNA, according to Carpenter (2011), we look at measures such as degree and betweenness centrality. Degree centrality refers to the number of connections a member (node) of the network has with other nodes, a high number implying a high degree centrality (John and Cole 1998). The two coalitions differ in size. With 27 members, the pro-fracking coalition includes twice the number of members of the anti-fracking coalition which has 13 members. A larger coalition size increases the likelihood of members in the pro-fracking coalition having more ties with other actors in their coalition and implicitly in the policy subsystem. To avoid such bias, the SNA for this case study will not discuss degree centrality and will centre on betweenness centrality.

High betweenness centrality is generated by the position of an actor as a connector between different sections of the network (John and Cole 1998; Gulati et al. 2002). Nodes with high betweenness centrality are brokers or gatekeepers between network subgroups (Goddard 2009; Kenney et al. 2012). Brokers are a type of network hubs. In the case of this study, they intermediate between the pro-fracking coalition or the anti-fracking coalition and the target of their advocacy, the European Parliament.

Betweenness centrality was calculated for all the network nodes (51) and the top 20 nodes are included in Table 4.3. Table 4.3 also includes information on which of these subsystem nodes were in the pro-fracking coalition and which were part of the anti-fracking coalition.

Table 4.3 Betweenness centrality scores of actors in the fracking for shale gas subsystem (top 20 scores)

Policy actor	*Betweenness centrality*	*Coalition that it belongs to*
Office rapporteur	331.721	–
Friends of the Earth Europe	183.722	Anti-fracking
EPP political group	179.830	–
Food and water Europe	163.966	Anti-fracking
Industry association	149.274	Pro-fracking
Office MEP Szymanski (polish)	117.206	Pro-fracking
Polish permanent representation	63.410	Pro-fracking
Dutch company	60.334	Pro-fracking
ECR political group	42.431	Pro-fracking
DG energy, European Commission	41.404	Pro-fracking
Industry consultancy	41.318	Pro-fracking
Norwegian company	40.001	Pro-fracking
Office MEP hall	39.732	–
World Wildlife Fund Europe	35.183	Anti-fracking
ITRE secretariat	34.069	–
American company 1	31.615	Pro-fracking
Greens/EFA	26.129	Anti-fracking
Canadian Mission	8.678	Pro-fracking
American company 2	7.756	Pro-fracking
European affairs consultancy	6.762	Pro-fracking

Source: Author

The data (Table 4.3) provides quantitative evidence of the fact that the industry association, large oil and gas companies, and specialized consultancies played an important role in the transfer of information and understanding of the benefits of fracking in the policy subsystem. The two leaders of the anti-fracking campaign (Food and Water Europe and Friends of the Earth Europe) display high scores when it comes to betweenness centrality. Friends of the Earth have the second highest betweenness centrality and Food and Water Europe the fourth betweenness centrality in the policy subsystem. NGOs have a good reputation for being able to network and establish connections, especially among themselves, to work in a net, and to back each other in different campaigns (interview with policy adviser to the European People's Party in the European Parliament 2013; interview with source in the gas industry 2014).

The quantitative data included in Table 4.3 shows that 12 of the 20 most central members of this policy subsystem, based on their betweenness centrality, were part of the pro-fracking coalition. On the contrary, only 4 members of the anti-fracking coalition displayed a top 20 betweenness centrality. Twice the size of the anti-fracking coalition, the pro-fracking coalition included more well-connected nodes than the anti-fracking coalition and this helps explain why its frame dominated the policy subsystem.

Brokers possess relational power. The relational power of an entity is determined by: 'its position in the network, defined by its persistent relationships with other nodes. Power is no longer derived solely or even primarily from individual attributes, such as material capabilities' (Hafner-Burton et al. 2009, p. 570). Brokers in the pro-fracking coalition seem to concentrate overall more relational power than the ones in the anti-fracking coalition. This power allows them to reach different segments of the subsystem and facilitate information sharing and learning (Kenney et al. 2012, p. 740). Both actors inside and outside the network perceive the policy positions of hubs as proxies for the network (in this case, coalition) position (Carpenter 2011, p. 74). In this way, the likelihood that their claims will be taken seriously by external audiences, including policymakers, increases. The pro-fracking brokers facilitated the exchange of information, beliefs, and understanding of fracking in the EU and influenced the overall understanding of fracking in the policy subsystem.

The examples offered above indicate that in the subsystem working on the ITRE resolution on shale gas, certain actors were in a better position to intermediate the information flow between the anti-fracking coalition and the European Parliament (the case of Food and Water Europe and Friends of the Earth Europe, the Greens/EFA in the European Parliament), others to intermediate communication between the pro-fracking coalition and the European Parliament (as was the case with the industry association, certain companies, and consultancies). The organizations mentioned above can be considered subsystem brokers. The presence of brokers points to differences in the way the two coalitions organized their work and were structured, with the pro-fracking coalition benefiting from more access paths to the European Parliament. This section seems to validate the hypothesis according to which coalitions that are denser are more likely to shape policy and shows that coalitions that include more brokers of the policy subsystem have an advantage over other coalitions. In addition to the power they have as a result of possessing large material and informational resources, the members of the pro-fracking coalition are endowed with substantial relational power in the informal subsystem structure of which they are part. The policy subsystem analysis and map included in this book capture attributional power that is already converted into relational power as reflected by the connections (edges) on the sociogram.

This study does not deny that attributional power can be converted into relational power. Although it cannot be denied that material resources can be mobilized to establish new ties and to increase the connectivity of an actor in the policy subsystem, there is no perfect correlation between the amount of material resources (attributional power) and relational power. Organizations such as Friends of the Earth Europe and Food and Water Europe are as well connected as large oil and gas companies in the policy subsystem working on fracking for shale gas. This shows that the development of connections is not dependent only on the possession of financial resources. Networking skills can compensate for the lack of material resources. In addition, social connections cannot simply be 'bought' overnight; they are established in time and are based on relations of mutual trust.

Conclusion

The analysis performed in this chapter seems to indicate that the success of the pro-fracking advocacy coalition is not due to a single set of factors, but rather to the interplay between resources, frames, and structure, with a special focus in this case placed on informational resources and framing (Fig. 4.3).

This chapter showed that the pro-fracking coalition possessed valuable material and, especially, informational resources and articulated a credible frame. Information and knowledge resources enhanced its ability to make an impact. The study showed that exchanging information remains an important part of the EU policymaking process and is a way of coping with uncertainty. The literature on policy narratives argues that scientific uncertainty is translated into political certainty by the use of dominant narratives in the policy process (Garvin and Eyles 1997; Radaelli 1999). Advocates working on fracking helped decision-makers navigate the unknown. They helped them translate scientific uncertainty into political

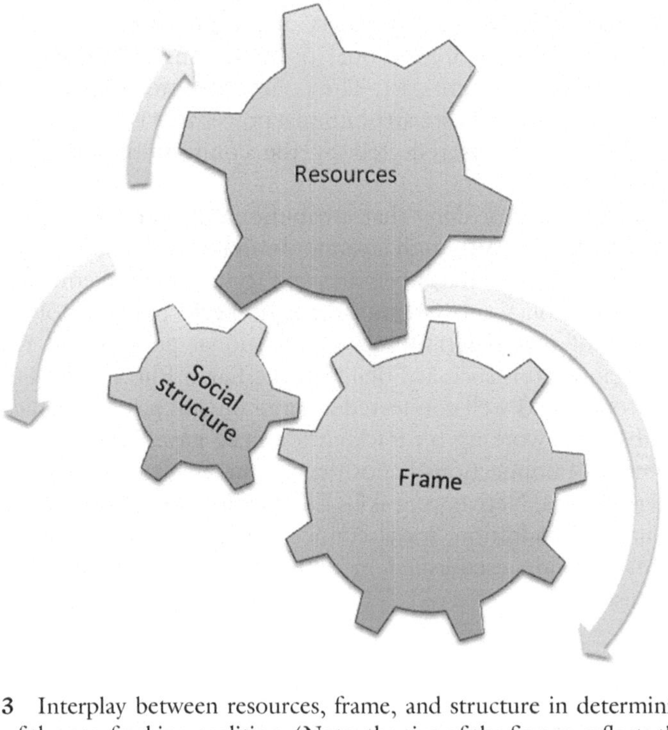

Fig. 4.3 Interplay between resources, frame, and structure in determining the success of the pro-fracking coalition. (Note: the size of the figures reflects the relative contribution of these factors to the pro-fracking coalition success. Source: Author)

certainty by articulating certain frames. The energy security argument combined with the economic competitiveness discourse determined an important number of EU MEPs to support shale gas despite the objections brought up by the anti-fracking coalition.

Decision-makers are usually aware that none of the information they receive from interest groups is objective beyond debate, that everybody has an interest when communicating. Despite recognizing the bias, decision-makers often admit to being influenced by that information. As one official in the European Parliament noted, 'inevitably, when discussing an issue, to a degree your approach will be framed by what you were told, you will pick stuff up' (interview with European Parliament official 1, 2013). Analysing the association between shale gas and energy security is important because it: 'had an important role to play in the way pro-shale gas arguments were framed' (interview with European Parliament official 1, 2013). Studying actors interacting as part of a networked policy subsystem helps to explain how conceptions of shale gas as an energy security solution are shaped and reinforced at the EU level. As one policy actor central to this network points out, the final understanding of what fracking entails for Europe was the result of a collective framing process: 'we all managed to put this discussion into frames of competitiveness, security of supply, environment and climate issues and industry issues' (interview with Polish official 2013).

Companies are driven by the opportunity to make profit (interview with former officer at the German Marshall Fund, Brussels office 2013; interview with representative of a Norwegian energy company 2014), but energy policy is a field in which they can also generate public goods. They can provide European citizens with an uninterrupted flow of energy that will keep their homes warm and their appliances working. Linking energy security with economic competitiveness meant that shale gas could help Europe cope with economic stagnation and unemployment challenges. In this way, shale gas could create additional public goods. This discourse is consonant with, and helps perpetuate, an understanding of EU energy security that places great value on low energy prices and sees economic competitiveness as a product of EU energy security (see Fig. 4.4).

The economic competitiveness argument that the pro-fracking coalition advanced was so effective that even environmental NGOs began to research and include in their frame data on the limited economic benefits of shale gas extraction to counterbalance the industry frame. The pro-fracking coalition was more successful in adapting its frame to exogenous

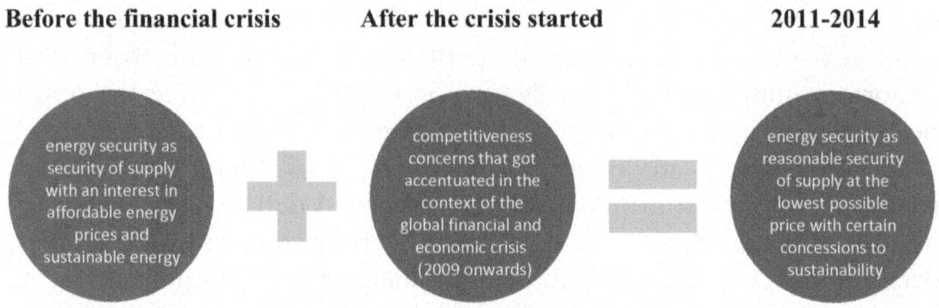

Fig. 4.4 Changes in the EU institutions' understanding of what EU energy security entails. (Source: Author)

factors such as the global financial and economic crisis, while the anti-fracking coalition entered the economic competitiveness debate later in the campaign, at a moment when in the policy subsystem there was already a strong association between fracking for shale gas and economic competitiveness. All these helped the pro-fracking coalition win the debate against the anti-fracking coalition.

A certain understanding of fracking for shale gas and its benefits spread in the policy subsystem through contagion. Both densely connected coalitions and strategically positioned actors in the policy subsystem support contagion. Brokers that were recognized by other actors as acting leaders of a coalition (the industry association, large oil and gas companies, and consultancies for the pro-fracking coalition; Food and Water Europe and Friends of the Earth Europe for the anti-fracking coalition) were more likely to influence opinions on fracking. When journalists in Brussels wrote on fracking for shale gas in the context of the debates taking place in the EP, they called the industry association or one of the NGOs leading the anti-fracking campaign (Food and Water Europe or Friends of the Earth Europe) and these were usually the two types of sources quoted in their articles (interview with policy officer at Food and Water Europe 2013). These organizations central to the subsystem had a greater ability to influence the shale gas debate and the understanding that interest groups, politicians, and public opinion develop on the issue.

Members of the pro-fracking coalition were numerous and occupied key positions in the policy subsystem working on fracking. Their high betweenness centrality shows that, through the reach that its members had in the broader policy subsystem, the pro-fracking coalition was in a good position to intermediate information exchanges and shape the understanding of the EU policy environment on the issue of fracking, shale gas, and in particular its benefits. At the same time, tight relations between its members indicated by a higher density gave the pro-fracking coalition a competitive advantage over the anti-fracking coalition.

The next two chapters will test if some of the hypotheses regarding the impact that resources, frames, and social structural factors have on coalition success are also confirmed by looking at the coalitions that advocated on the Southern Gas Corridor.

CHAPTER 5

The Southern Gas Corridor: Coalitions in Collision

In order to enhance its energy security, in addition to contemplating the exploitation of unconventional internal gas supplies, the EU is particularly interested in diversifying the external sources of gas supply that it resorts to and the routes that it uses to access these supplies. The EU has placed much emphasis recently on building the energy transport infrastructure that would enable source and route diversification, including transnational pipelines. Pipelines play an important role in determining trade patterns and energy flows; they link exporters and importers in interdependent trade relationships and are particularly important in the natural gas trade whose transport through pipelines is usually less expensive than transport by tankers (Proedrou 2012).

This chapter will explore the form that public-private interaction takes on EU energy policy topics by analysing developments around the Southern Gas Corridor, a system of pipelines meant to link the European Union with the gas-rich region of the Caspian Sea and the Middle East. It introduces the two advocacy coalitions clashing over the Southern Gas Corridor.

A.-M. Bocse, *International Networks, Advocacy and EU Energy Policy-Making*, Palgrave Studies in European Union Politics,
https://doi.org/10.1007/978-3-030-49505-3_5

The Southern Gas Corridor: Background and Developments

The idea of an EU-Caspian Region-Middle East Corridor (currently known as the 'Southern Gas Corridor') as a means of reducing EU energy insecurity was advanced by the European Union in 2003 under the name 'natural gas route 3' (NG.3) (European Parliament and the Council 2003b) and maintained in 2006 (European Parliament and the Council 2006c). As a response to a political and economic environment in which EU gas supply insecurity became a topic of increasing concern, in 2008 the project gained even more support, with the European Commission arguing that: 'A southern gas corridor must be developed for the supply of gas from Caspian and Middle Eastern sources, which could potentially supply a significant part of the EU's future needs. This is one of the EU's highest energy security priorities' (European Commission 2008, p. 4).

As discussed in greater detail in Chap. 2, several factors contributed to placing security of supply higher on the EU agenda. The EU enlargement of 2004–2007 incorporated into the EU Central and Eastern European countries with poorly developed energy infrastructure and which were highly dependent on Russian gas. The 2006–2009 Russo-Ukrainian gas disputes contributed to shaping the profile of Russia as an unreliable gas supplier in the perception of many Europeans. Interviews with key policy-makers indicate that EU enlargement and the 2009 Russo-Ukrainian gas crisis created the momentum for the development of the Southern Gas Corridor:

> the whole Southern Corridor wouldn't have started without the enlargement of 2004, and without the gas crisis, the whole issue of energy security as one of the driving forces of EU energy policy happened because of the enlargement. If there is no enlargement, energy security is not an issue. (interview with very senior Hungarian official 2014)

The EU energy agenda coincided with the interests of a few energy companies that began to work on connecting Europe with Turkey and the Caspian region in the early 2000s. One of these was the Austrian company OMV, which in 2002 was discussing with the Turkish company BOTAŞ the prospect of building a pipeline that would enable the transport to Europe of gas surplus on the Turkish market (interview with representative of OMV 2014). Two years later, the same companies advanced the idea of Nabucco,[1] a larger pipeline that would transport gas to Europe from multiple sources, including Iran as the main source, Iraq, and Azerbaijan, in response to the predicted increase in European gas demand (interview with representative of OMV 2014). In the early 2000s OMV even applied for a grant from the EU to conduct studies on how to bring gas across Turkey, before the European Commission advanced a formal policy on the Southern Gas Corridor (interview with European Commission official, DG Energy, working on energy markets 2013).

The concept of a Southern Gas Corridor was meant to be an inclusive one and at the same time independent of any specific pipeline project, including Nabucco, with which the Corridor was often associated in the public discourse. The fact that the natural gas route 3 (hereafter called the 'Southern Corridor') can be realized through a variety of pipelines and not just Nabucco was reaffirmed in the report that the coordinator of this gas route released in 2009 (van Aartsen 2009). In this way, the Commission hoped that, even if Nabucco failed to be realized, the idea of the corridor itself would not be compromised. As one senior EU official explains: 'we decided fairly early on that Nabucco might not work and we should replace it with a concept which was broader and non-specific, the phrase 'Southern Gas Corridor' came up here and it replaced the previous natural gas corridor 3 which was set up in 2003' (interview with senior European Commission official, DG Energy 2013).

Indeed, since 2008, several pipelines have been advanced by private and public entities as projects through which the Corridor could be realized, that is, the Interconnector Turkey-Greece-Italy (ITGI), Nabucco, and White Stream. The first two lost the first race to deliver gas from the Caspian region (from the Shah Deniz II field in Azerbaijan) in favour of the Trans Adriatic Pipeline (TAP). These pipelines were expected to transport together 60 to 120 billion cubic metres (bcm) of gas per year from the Caspian Sea and the Middle East to Europe. However, finding gas suppliers turned out to be more difficult than proposing pipeline projects. The sanctions against Iran and the political instability in Iraq left only

[1] Nabucco was named after the opera that gas executives attended the night before they met in Vienna to set up this project (Buchan 2009, p. 103). To highlight the importance of this pipeline for the EU diversification strategy, the EC appointed a special coordinator, Jozias van Aartsen, former Dutch Foreign Minister, who was expected to assist with the diplomacy involved in developing this project (Buchan 2009, p. 105). Jozias van Aartsen also pleaded for subsidizing some energy infrastructure projects, including Nabucco (Buchan 2009).

Azerbaijan as a feasible gas source in 2013. The main supplier of the Southern Gas Corridor in the near future will be the Shah Deniz consortium operating the Shah Deniz II field. The bid to transport gas from Shah Deniz II was won on 28 June 2013 by TAP over its rival pipeline Nabucco West—a restructured, shorter version of the initial Nabucco pipeline. Designed to transport annually 32 bcm of central Asian gas through Turkey into Austria, Nabucco project was downsized in 2012 when renamed Nabucco West. Nabucco West could transport only 16 bcm of gas from the Turkish border to Baumgarten, Austria, crossing Bulgaria, Romania, and Hungary on its way. It was shorter than Nabucco as it envisaged using the gas transport infrastructure already existing on Turkish territory rather than building new infrastructure. However, the 48 inches in diameter, 1329 km long Nabucco West could adapt its capacity for 10–23 bcm of gas, dependent on market demand.

Embracing a different route, TAP connects Italy with Turkey through Albania and Greece. In Turkey the pipeline meets the Trans-Anatolian Natural Gas Pipeline (TANAP). The transit of gas across Georgia is provided through an extension (South Caucasus Pipeline Expansion, SCPX) of the South Caucasus Pipeline[2] (SCP), which starts at the Sangachal terminal, near Baku, Azerbaijan, and which takes the Azeri gas to the border between Georgia and Turkey to meet the infrastructure provided by TANAP (interview with adviser, Mission of Georgia to the EU 2014; British Petroleum, BP 2015a).

After the Shah Deniz consortium chose TAP and signed the final investment decision on 21 December 2013, the EU became confident that the Corridor will be realized and gas will flow to Europe from Azerbaijan (interview with official in the EEAS 2 2013). Planned to become operational in 2020, TAP[3] pledged to offer in its first stage 10 bcm/year of gas to the European market. Through the Corridor, the EU will benefit from Caspian gas and in this way diversify its energy sources and routes.

Ten billion cubic metres is only a fraction of what the EU needs annually. Annual EU gas consumption is currently around 450 bcm/year. Additional gas sources in Turkmenistan or the Middle East can be accessed

[2] The South Caucasus Pipeline was developed with the support of the governments of Georgia, Azerbaijan, and Turkey and is a linchpin that makes possible the opening of the Southern Gas Corridor (interview with specialist in the Ministry of Energy of Georgia 2014).

[3] As of February 2020, on the TAP website, the pipeline will become operational in 2020 (TAP 2020).

in the mid to long term through the Southern Gas Corridor. However, even by delivering 10 bcm, experts inside and outside the European institutions argued that the Corridor will increase the leverage that EU Member States and companies have over gas exporters such as Russia when negotiating gas purchase prices. As one official pointed out:

> everybody wants to be able to tell the Russians that we can have different gas. Different gas in its physical state is good, it's a physical reality that gives you options, but it is even more important in its mental state because it gives you something to talk about and believe me it is not easy to talk to the Russians, particularly if they know that you do not have anything else to offer. … It is about competition, then you can choose the cheaper supplier. Russia is in a position to always be the cheaper supplier. It is fine if it is Russian gas, there is nothing wrong with it, it's just that you need to be in a market situation and in a competitive situation. (interview with official in the EEAS 1 2013)

This point of view is shared by experienced policymakers from outside the EU:

> so you can put pressure on Gazprom to make better deals with the Europeans, you have to put the conditions and stop them from looking down on you, stop them from dictating their conditions because this is the situation at this point in time. Gazprom is still so powerful and dominant, dominating the EU market because they can dictate their prices and dictate their conditions, but in the long run, probably they will have to be more flexible and I think they started showing a certain degree of flexibility, but it's not enough. (interview with senior Turkish official 2014)

In addition, the Corridor is meant to support the EU in developing its natural gas market and encourages more gas-on-gas competition.

Shah Deniz organized an official tender in order to select the pipeline through which they will deliver gas to Europe and received pipeline proposals until 1 October 2011. The Shah Deniz Consortium (comprising companies such as BP, TOTAL,[4] and the state-owned Azeri company SOCAR) chose TAP in June 2013, when assessing the two pipelines according to a set of commercial and political criteria. This decision was influenced by the change of position that the European Commission had

[4] French multinational oil and gas company.

regarding the best pipeline for the opening of the Southern Gas Corridor. Although initially the European Commission seemed to be more supportive of Nabucco, in the end it offered equal support to Nabucco West and TAP (interview with senior European Commission official, DG Energy 2013). As one EU official stated: 'from our point of view, the choice of TAP is equally important because at the end of the day the main objective, which was to open the Southern Corridor, is ensured' (interview with very senior European Commission official 2014).

The European Commission: A Target of Advocacy

The most active DG on the Southern Gas Corridor was DG Energy, in particular the Commissioner for Energy, Günther Oettinger (interview with European Parliament official 3 2013). Alongside the Commissioner for Energy, the President of the European Commission, José Manuel Durão Barroso, was also involved in developments taking place around the Southern Gas Corridor. Barroso personally attended the signing of the Nabucco Intergovernmental Agreement on 13 July 2009 and also undertook energy diplomacy visits in the Caspian region. In 2011 Barroso visited Azerbaijan and Turkmenistan in order to persuade these states to commit their gas to the Southern Corridor. At that point he credited the whole Southern Corridor with the accolade of: 'stepping stone in increasing European energy security' (Durão Barroso 2011). The President of the European Commission and the President of Azerbaijan, Ilham Aliyev, released a political declaration qualified by European Commission officials as extremely important:

> politically, this was a very important sign precisely to indicate that the Commission was behind this process and it was also very important to affirm that Azerbaijan was ready to be the enabler of the Southern Corridor, meaning that they were ready to supply at least the initial volumes of gas, to trigger the opening of the Southern Corridor. It remains to be seen whether there will be other suppliers, but it was very important indeed to put into writing the political commitment of Azerbaijan to actually supply the gas to the EU and the political commitment of the EU to actually take it up. (interview with very senior European Commission official 2014)

The decision on which pipeline project should win the bid to transport Azeri gas to Europe was made by the Shah Deniz consortium. BP and

SOCAR were identified by most interviewees as the key players behind Shah Deniz. BP operates the Shah Deniz field and has a 28.8% share in it. An important player in the Shah Deniz consortium was and remains SOCAR (16.7%), the state-owned oil and gas company of Azerbaijan.[5] BP and SOCAR were in charge of relations with political and public actors on behalf of the consortium, and they engaged in these relations both individually and jointly (interview with very senior Hungarian official 2014). So how did the European Commission become the target of advocacy?

The criteria on which the Shah Deniz consortium based its decision regarding the pipeline that it chose to deliver gas to Europe included not only economic and technical factors, such as commercial viability, project delivery, financial delivery, engineering design, alignment and transparency, operability, scalability, but also public policy considerations. These criteria were agreed upon in 2011 (Cook 2012a) and made public to the bidders and to the broader public. The importance of the political dimension of this project was stressed by BP officials both in the interviews I conducted (interview with representative of BP 2014) and in public declarations. The vice-president of Shah Deniz Development at BP, Alistair Cook, highlighted: 'We should make sure we satisfy two sides—the commercial side and the political side. Commercially, we should make sure that we have the right gas prices and the right transportation. Politically, we are looking for strong governmental support' (Cook 2012b). The public policy considerations were related to meeting the European Commission's objective of increasing European gas supply diversity and also referred to the potential of the pipeline to secure support from all relevant stakeholders, including the firm support of the states it will cross. The security of supply concerns that the Corridor addressed were high on the agenda particularly of new and smaller EU Member States (particularly countries from Central and Eastern Europe) rather than old and larger states that are more willing to conduct their energy diplomacy independently. Consequently, the supranational level represented by the European Commission took the lead on the Southern Gas Corridor rather than EU Member States (interview with industry consultant 1 2013). Given the political implications of this project, the European Commission

[5]Other partners in the mid-2010s were TPAO, the Turkish state oil and gas company (19%), Statoil, an integrated Norwegian oil and gas company (15.5%), Lukoil, the state-owned Russian oil company (10%), and the state-owned Iranian oil and gas company NIOC (10%) (BP 2015b).

became an important target of the advocacy conducted by the two contenders, Nabucco West and TAP.

Furthermore, to a certain degree Azeri support for any pipeline depended on the endorsement of the Commission and the EU States. Azerbaijan could influence the Shah Deniz decision through SOCAR. The Corridor is also a political and diplomatic instrument for Azerbaijan that is interested in cultivating closer relations with the EU. For Azerbaijan, the Southern Gas Corridor generates a connection with Europe which goes beyond economic and energy interests as it is a:

> sophisticated infrastructure project with its own political, commercial, and regulatory risks, and, if there are partners who choose to partner with Azerbaijan for that purpose, they have to share the commitment, the objectives, including the political ones, and of course they have to share the profit. (interview with Azeri official 2013)

In general, pipelines have the potential to foster relations between polities that go beyond cooperation in the field of energy. Pipelines establish a dependency relationship and generate political leverage (Kaysi 2011). The Southern Gas Corridor is no exception:

> such pipelines, you don't consider them as an economic tool only, you will always feel connected, your future will be linked so definitely such pipelines have more than their economic weight and their political ramifications and I think they enhance relations, like Baku-Tbilisi-Ceyhan. It's a kind of bridge between Azerbaijan, Georgia, and Turkey, it's like a bridge so everybody is making money and they feel that they are connected so, I repeat, that it has more weight than its economic weight. (interview with senior Turkish official 2014)

And:

> with the Southern Corridor, where you actually envisage a pipeline which comes from Azerbaijan via Turkey to the EU, I think it's also symbolically very important that there is this infrastructural link which goes beyond borders and crosses borders and clearly establishes a physical link between the countries involved. (interview with very senior European Commission official 2014)

Taking a final decision on Nabucco or TAP meant that the Southern Gas Corridor will be realized, that there will be a physical connection between Europe and the Caspian region.

The EU is not only a market for Azeri gas but can bring additional guarantees for the security of the country. Azerbaijan perceives itself as a European country squeezed between Russia and Iran: 'Azerbaijan is on the very east flank of Europe, a part of which we are, bordering as a gateway further to the East across the Caspian, a country which is sandwiched, squeezed in between hegemons' (interview with Azeri official 2013). At the same time, Azerbaijan is in open conflict with Armenia over the Nagorno-Karabakh province. Getting the EU interested in Azerbaijan through the Southern Gas Corridor might help Azerbaijan tackle security challenges posed by Russia and Armenia. According to Azeri sources, it could generate support for Azerbaijan in case the Nagorno-Karabakh dispute turns into a hot conflict:

> through these energy projects, that are blood lines of the EU energy system, Azerbaijan is trying to raise its importance in EU security strategy. The EU would care less about Azerbaijan if Azerbaijan had no energy. … Being energy supplier and potentially energy transit country from Central Asia, from Kazakhstan, Turkmenistan to the European Union, it increases Azerbaijan's importance, political importance to the European Union. (interview with representative of SOCAR 2014)

President Ilham Aliyev of Azerbaijan is reported to have stated: 'oil is about money and gas is about friends' (interview with senior European Commission official, DG Energy 2013). In recent years the European Commission has invested important policy and financial resources in the Southern Gas Corridor. Azerbaijan and SOCAR were very interested in supporting a pipeline that does not go against the public policy priorities of the European Commission or openly opposes any EU Member State.

To avoid getting involved in internal disputes between EU Member States over the Southern Gas Corridor, Azerbaijan seemed to favour interaction with the European Commission to bilateral interactions with EU Members involved in developing competing pipelines for the Corridor. The interviews I conducted indicated that Azeri officials were willing to go the extra mile not to show that they preferred one pipeline project over the other and to avoid offending any Member State that directly supported one project over the other:

> I am talking about the politics inside Europe about Azerbaijan, they have created such an environment of competition, of rivalry. We looked from outside as a potential investor and a potential supplier. We do not want to be part of that because we are not there, in the EU. We continue talking to the Commission. If it is about EU solidarity, you know better than us so please sort it out yourselves. I do not want to spoil any relations with any of the countries because everybody is equal. (interview with Azeri official 2013)

Beyond public political endorsement, the support of the EU and of national governments was perceived as essential to obtaining permits and exemptions for the pipelines, especially given their transnational nature:

> you have to cross so many borders to make one of these projects work. No matter how many private companies you've got, it is inherently, in some shape or form, a political agreement, because governments have to sign off on it. Once it gets into the EU then it will have to go for third party access rules or waiver of those rules, etc., so there is a lot of governmental involvement. (interview with official at the US Mission to the EU 2013)

EU internal market regulations require third party access to the energy infrastructure. However, exceptions can be made with the approval of national regulators and the European Commission when the exemptions support the development of major strategic infrastructure. Both Nabucco and TAP applied for exemptions from EU regulations. For instance, to become financially viable, TAP needed the Commission to approve a series of exemptions from EU law applicable in the EU countries that TAP would cross, that is, Italy and Greece:

> we are bound to respect a number of regulations including what is called third party access which is an important piece of legislation, and in order for TAP to become operational we needed to obtain from the European Union a third party access exception so that TAP would become profitable. (interview with senior Italian official 2014)

In May 2013, just a few weeks before Shah Deniz announced the winner of the competition between Nabucco West and TAP, the European Commission approved the TAP application for third party access exemption after the exemption was previously offered by national regulators in Italy and Greece (TAP 2013a). In the case of TAP, the Commission also approved exemptions from regulated tariffs on TAP's initial 10 bcm transit capacity, as well as on future expansion in capacity, and exemption from ownership unbundling[6] for 25 years (TAP 2013a). This put TAP in a better position to compete with Nabucco West.

For all the reasons presented in this section, the Commission became a target for the advocacy of coalitions emerging around TAP and Nabucco. EU support for the Southern Gas Corridor entailed diplomatic and political support, exemptions from EU law, as well as financial assistance for Nabucco from the European Commission and the European Investment Bank in the initial stages of the project. While the European Commission acted as an advocate with Azerbaijan, the European Commission was itself the target of the advocacy of two coalitions emerging around TAP and Nabucco.

Introducing the Clashing Coalitions

The advocacy coalitions approach helps understand the policy changes that took place in the Southern Corridor policy subsystem and the actors working on the Southern Gas Corridor and seeking to influence EU policy in this particular area. Two advocacy coalitions developed in the Southern Gas Corridor policy subsystem. The sociogram below (Fig. 5.1) offers an overview of the actors involved in this subsystem. The sociogram is based on analysis of the connections that actors in the policy subsystem of the Southern Gas Corridor declared they had established with other actors *vis-à-vis* the development of the Southern Gas Corridor. The sociogram aims to capture the interactions taking place in 2013.

The analysis in this chapter is performed at the level of policy subsystem inclusive of coalitions that emerged as clusters in the subsystem. This enabled me to generate a sociogram that presents the two coalitions (their members and links that bring them together), as well as the connections between each coalition and the policymakers that it aims to influence. The interviews with subsystem participants enabled recreation of a social structure that included 84 members connected through 288 unique edges (lines on the sociogram in Fig. 5.1).

[6]The EU Third Energy Package (legislation package for the EU gas and electricity market), which was proposed in 2007 and entered into force in September 2009, introduced the principle of ownership unbundling, preventing simultaneous ownership of generation and transmission networks by the same entity (Buchan 2010).

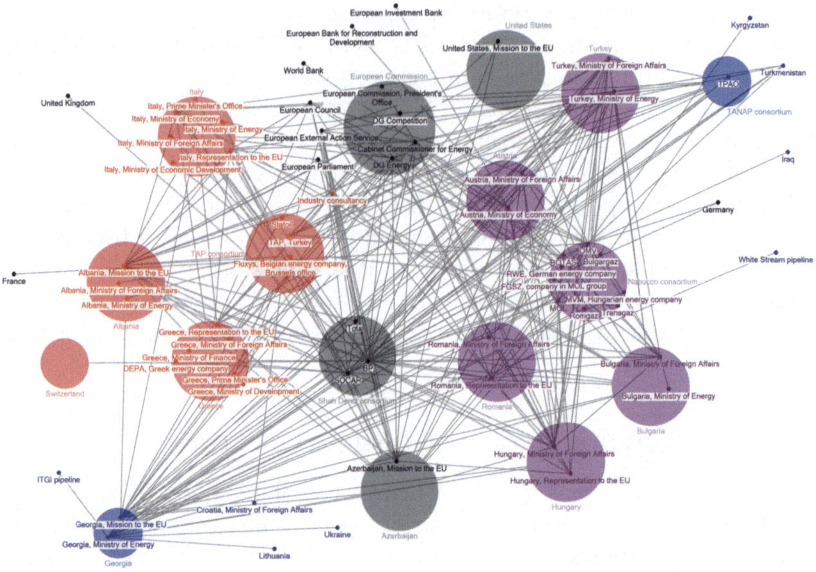

Fig. 5.1 Sociogram of the Southern Gas Corridor policy subsystem (generated with NodeXL). TAP Coalition: Red; Nabucco coalition: Purple; Targets of advocacy: Black; Other actors: Blue. (Source: Author)

As indicated in Fig. 5.1, the policy subsystem working on the Southern Gas Corridor includes representatives of governments and private energy companies, as well as a consultancy aiming to influence the European Commission. Two conflicting advocacy coalitions emerge out of this subsystem. Both coalitions worked towards the opening of the Southern Gas Corridor. However, the two coalitions differ with respect to the pipeline project they support:

> overall, this [opening the Southern Gas Corridor] was an objective which was shared as an EU objective, therefore the Commissioner could also count on the support of the Member States, who one or the other could have preferences for one or the other project. Obviously, those projects which would concern their own country, but the overall objective was really supported by all the Member States and endorsed even at the European Council level so these were the essential preconditions to help us come to a successful conclusion in the end. (interview with very senior European Commission official 2014)

The members of the coalition supporting TAP argued that TAP will make an important contribution to national and European energy security and will constitute a reliable source of revenue for investors in this pipeline project. Similar arguments were advanced by supporters of Nabucco, but in relation to the Nabucco pipeline.

At the level of each coalition, the motivation of actors to get involved varies. Governments and their representatives, on the Nabucco side or on the TAP side, are driven by energy security considerations, such as diversifying their access to energy sources or improving their energy transport infrastructure. Countries such as Turkey, Austria, and Italy also hoped that the additional gas would help them develop as gas hubs (interview with attaché at the Permanent Representation of Italy to the EU 2014; interview with senior official at the Ministry of Energy and Natural Resources of Turkey 2014). Energy companies are not primarily driven by energy security or public policy considerations, but by profit (interview with very senior Hungarian official 2014; interview with senior Turkish official 2014). Whilst often used by both Nabucco and TAP in their communication with public actors in order to make the case for their pipeline, energy security is not a priority for corporations investing in pipeline infrastructure. If they can generate energy security as a by-product of a successful business, energy companies will do so, but private energy companies and even state-owned companies are not interested in investing in projects that might not bring profit, no matter how strategically valuable they may be (interview with former Hungarian diplomat based in the US 2014; interview with senior Turkish official 2014). Even if not primarily driven by energy security and public goods, energy companies contribute to generating energy security. Energy security can be a positive externality of a profitable investment in energy infrastructure:

> having said that, we all take that into account when we develop these projects. Commercial imperative is a must, we can't get away from that, but if through its commercial imperative a project delivers all of those aspects of security of supply, diversification, etc., that's brilliant, that should be applauded. Companies all try to show that it does, so I think there's nothing wrong with that, but they won't be making decisions on that basis. (interview with TAP source 2013)

As a BP source highlighted:

> when you can make a good and profitable project and at the same time you can make a real positive contribution to the countries involved, where you go by happy coincidence, then I think we are really pleased to be able to do the two things at the same time. (interview with representative of BP 2014)

Successful projects are able to satisfy both public and private interests, as an energy expert based at the US Mission to the EU explains:

> so, it is both governments and it is private companies. Private companies try to figure out a way to navigate through all the governmental approval, to get a project put together that would make money and Member States are looking for transit fees, gas supply, construction contracts in their countries, etc. (interview with official at the US Mission to the EU 2013)

When a project simultaneously fulfils public policy considerations and the financial interests of energy companies, there is an opportunity for cooperation and coordinated activity between governments and energy corporations that leads to the emergence of coalitions including actors from both public and private sectors. This is the case with the Southern Gas Corridor, with the members of the Nabucco coalition in Fig. 5.2.

A web of dense connections emerged between governmental representatives and private actors advocating for Nabucco which led to the emergence of a coalition within the subsystem working on the Southern Gas Corridor. As one interviewee indicated: 'each government would be connected with their company and then the governments would connect and then the companies separately would be connected' (interview with representative of OMV 2014). This web of connections ensures a certain degree of coordination of activity between the governmental and corporate actors in the advocacy coalition.

The coalition supporting the Nabucco West pipeline included governmental representatives of Austria, Hungary, Romania, Bulgaria, and Turkey working with Nabucco Gas Pipeline International (also referred to in this book as the Nabucco consortium), set up on 24 June 2004 to develop, construct, and operate the Nabucco pipeline. Nabucco Gas Pipeline International and its officials were meant to speak on behalf of the project, defend its interests in relation to third parties, and act independently of its parent companies in the energy market.

The consortium developing the Nabucco pipeline included five parent companies: OMV (Austria); MOL (Hungary); Transgaz (Romania);

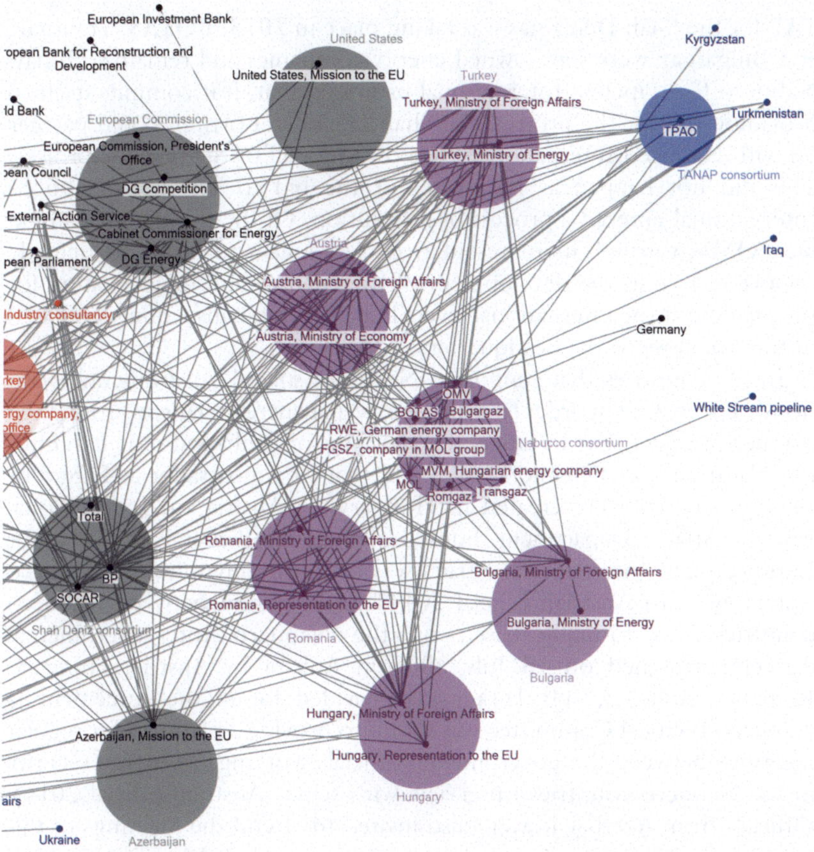

Fig. 5.2 Sociogram of the Nabucco coalition (in Purple). Nabucco coalition: Purple; Targets of advocacy: Black; Other actors: Blue. (Source: Author)

Bulgargaz (Bulgaria); and BOTAŞ (Turkey), each with an equal share in the project and Nabucco Gas Pipeline International (Jenkins 2012). The shareholder structure slightly changed at different times,[7] but these five companies held overall a lot of influence. The pipeline project was initiated by OMV (Austria) and BOTAŞ (Turkey) in 2002 and the other companies soon became involved in the project. At the moment when the bid against

[7] For a while it also included the German company RWE, which sold its shares to OMV in April 2013, and different subsidiaries of MOL.

TAP for the Shah Deniz gas was taking place in 2013, BOTAŞ, Transgaz, and Bulgargaz were state-owned energy companies and remain so today. Nabucco Gas Pipeline International promised that, if it commits itself to providing gas for the project, the Shah Deniz consortium could partner up with Nabucco International, thus owning half of the pipeline project. This did not happen as Nabucco lost the bid to TAP and Nabucco International entered a process of dissolution. Of the five parent companies, OMV, through its representatives, was meant to play a particularly important role in the development of the pipeline and in advocating for the pipeline at the international level. The Nabucco consortium was based in Vienna, close to the headquarters of OMV.

In the countries that supported Nabucco, special governmental positions were created in order to manage external energy relations around the Nabucco project. For instance, the positions of Ambassador-at-Large for the Nabucco Gas Pipeline Project and that of Ambassador-at-Large for Energy Security were created in Hungary. In Austria, an International Energy Affairs Department housed within the Federal Ministry for European and International Affairs was set up to advocate for Nabucco (interview with Austrian official 2014). Cooperation between Nabucco countries was formally based on the Nabucco Intergovernmental Agreement signed on 13 July 2009 in Ankara by Austria, Hungary, Romania, Bulgaria, and Turkey. As provided for in the agreement, a Nabucco Political Committee was set up to provide a platform for regular meetings between the governmental officials working on energy security in the Nabucco countries (interview with senior Austrian official 2014). Officials from Azerbaijan were also invited to attend the meetings of this Committee (Nabucco Gas Pipeline International 2012). The Political Committee was meant to facilitate cooperation between the Nabucco supporters.

The ambassadors for energy security of the Nabucco states met regularly to discuss developments around the Southern Gas Corridor, communicate their position, and coordinate their activities (interview with very senior Hungarian official 2014; interview with Hungarian governmental adviser on energy security 2014). The process of communication and coordination was more intense among Hungary, Romania, and Bulgaria (interview with very senior Hungarian official 2014). These three countries shared higher energy security concerns, while Austria and Turkey were also motivated by consolidating their position as energy hubs. Similar interests led to increased cooperation and confirm assumptions in social network theory regarding homophily. Homophily claims that similar network nodes are more likely to interact with each other (McPherson and Smith-Lovin 1987) and develop stronger social connections.

Even after Nabucco lost the bid against TAP and Nabucco Gas Pipeline International entered a process of dissolution, meetings between the representatives of the Nabucco countries around energy security continued.[8]

A second clique emerges on the sociogram, that advocating for TAP and against Nabucco for the Shah Deniz gas, as presented in Fig. 5.3.

The group advocating for TAP included governmental representatives from different ministries (Foreign Affairs, Energy, Economy) in Italy, Greece, Albania, as well as energy officers from the Permanent Representations to the EU of Italy and Greece and the Mission of Albania to the EU. The fieldwork conducted for this study indicated that these actors worked in close cooperation with officials of TAP AG (also referred to in this study as the TAP consortium), the company established to: 'plan, develop and build the TAP natural gas pipeline' (TAP 2015a). Great part of the advocacy with European institutions was performed by officials based in the Permanent Representations of Italy, Greece, and the Mission of Albania to the EU (interview with senior Albanian official 2014), and by a major Brussels-based consultancy (interview with TAP source 2013; interview with industry consultant 2 2014). In the words of a governmental official:

> for about one and a half year, there was very close cooperation with them [the Permanent Representations of Italy and Greece to the EU] and you know that our Mission was supposed to lobby for TAP since TAP was our gas pipeline. I mean Albania was part of that, just three countries, Greece, Albania, and Italy. These are the transit countries and so we worked hard with my Ambassador. You know that the energy issue in Europe is very sensitive and the competition was pretty intense. In this case the two final projects were Nabucco West and TAP. (interview with former attaché at the Mission of the Republic of Albania to the EU 2014)

[8] For instance, a seminar was organized at the Mission of the Republic of Hungary to the EU on 6 November 2013 to discuss the way forward for the countries that were involved in the development of Nabucco after this pipeline lost the bid against TAP. The first section of the event was moderated by the Ambassador-at-Large for Energy Security, Hungary. The event was attended by the ambassadors-at-large for energy security of Romania and Bulgaria (information collected through participant observation).

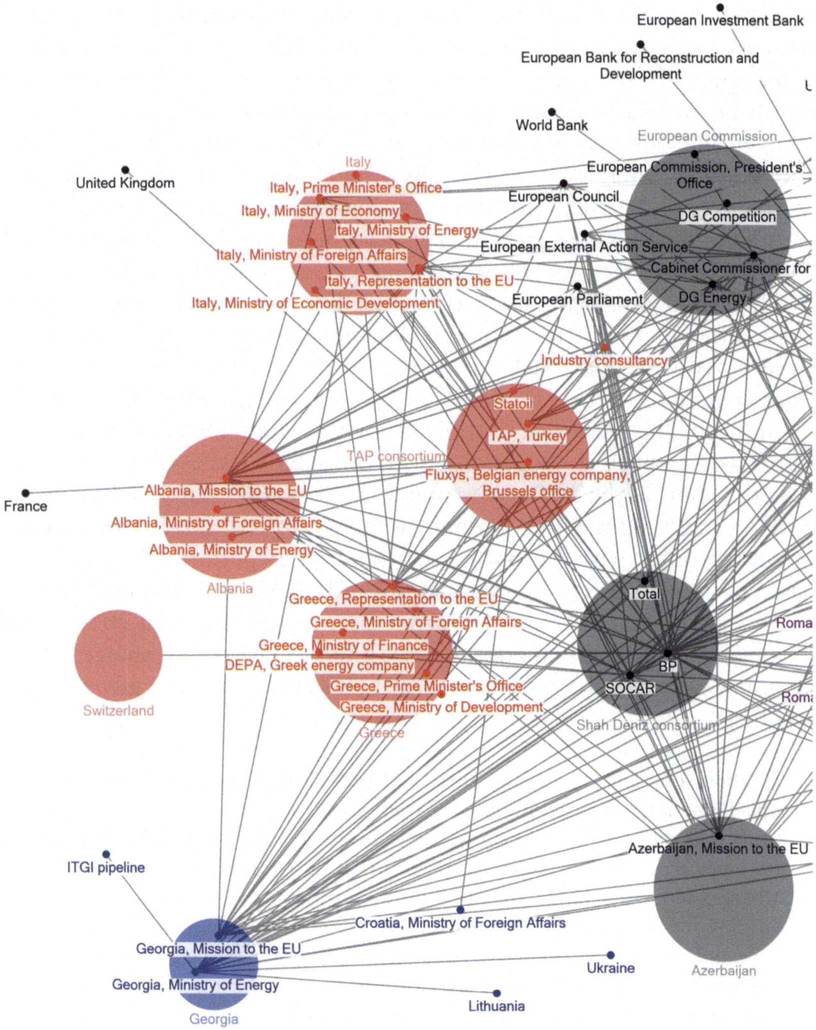

Fig. 5.3 Sociogram of the TAP coalition (in Red). TAP Coalition: Red; Targets of advocacy: Black; Other actors: Blue. (Source: Author)

As was the case with the countries involved in the development of Nabucco, the countries crossed by TAP signed international agreements. A memorandum of understanding was signed by Albania, Greece, and Italy in September 2012. An Intergovernmental Agreement on TAP was signed by the same countries in Athens, Greece, on 13 February 2013 (TAP 2013b, slide 21). A Political Committee was also established. In the words of a governmental official: 'that committee was not only political. It was political including the Minister of Foreign Affairs, the Minister of Energy, and so on, and then technicalities were dealt with at a technical level by specialists' (interview with former attaché at the Mission of the Republic of Albania to the EU 2014). The Committee ensured that governmental officials at various levels coordinated their activity: 'we sought through the intergovernmental agreement to establish a consulting committee, regular meetings with our Greek and Albanian friends, to work with the European Commission and so on' (interview with senior Italian official 2014).

At the time of the TAP bid against Nabucco for the Shah Deniz gas, the TAP shareholder structure included Axpo, Swiss energy company (42.5%), Statoil, Norwegian energy company (42.5%), and E.ON, German energy company (15%). In 2015 the TAP shareholders included BP (20%); SOCAR (20%); Statoil (20%); Fluxys (19%); Enagás (16%); and Axpo (5%). TAP offered participation in the pipeline project to BP and SOCAR, the companies investing upstream in the Shah Deniz gas field II. Companies that were involved in gas exploitation also became players in the TAP energy transport infrastructure and this justified its need for exemptions from the EU rules of ownership unbundling.

TAP began to seek opportunities to interact more with the European Commission and convince it of TAP's energy security policy merits (interview with industry consultant 1 2013; interview with industry consultant 2 2014). In this regard, in 2012 TAP employed a Brussels-based consultancy to help them manage relations with the European institutions (interview with industry consultant 1 2013; interview with industry consultant 2 2014). As one of the consultants working for the firm explains:

> the landscape in Brussels was particularly crowded with projects such as South Stream and Nabucco which was the flagship project for the European Union so they needed a reputation boost so to say. ... Following the initial two years of work in the communications sphere, we also pitched for the public affairs part of the business and so we also started collaborating on a

> regular basis with the Brussels institutions. (interview with industry consultant 2 2014)

In addition to the actors directly involved in the development of the Southern Gas Corridor, there were also those that played a more peripheral role. For instance, representatives of BP stayed in touch on the Southern Gas Corridor with the governments of Nabucco or the TAP transit countries, but also with those of Switzerland, Germany, and the UK. Switzerland backed the TAP project whose headquarters are based in Baar, Switzerland. Germany had an interest given its role as an important player in European energy security. Germany did not express a preference for one pipeline or another, but was interested in the Corridor opening (interview with representative of BP 2014). The UK took an interest given the involvement of BP in the development of Shah Deniz (interview with representative of BP 2014).

As can be observed in the sociogram mapping the actors that interacted on the Southern Gas Corridor, the supporters of TAP and those of Nabucco constitute two separate coalitions. The two coalitions were each aware of the position the competition took (interview with attaché at the Permanent Representation of Italy to the EU 2014), but beyond that exchanges were limited, including between governments involved with Nabucco or TAP (interview with senior official at the Ministry of Energy and Natural Resources of Turkey 2014). As one Nabucco supporter indicates, the interaction with government officials from Italy, Greece, Albania was reduced: 'we just met at conferences, but interactions, such as having joint discussions or joint projects, did not take place' (interview with representative of OMV 2014). The ongoing competition for the Azeri gas between the two projects prevented cooperation: 'No, I mean we had a competing project, we did not cooperate in this respect, didn't talk to each other' (interview with Nabucco source 2014). There was little interaction between the two coalitions in 2013. This led to a fracture in the policy subsystem working on the Southern Gas Corridor.

The advocacy coalition framework assumes a lack of trust between opposing coalitions and this study empirically confirms that lack of trust and suspicion develop. During interviews, the TAP supporters blamed, for instance, the supporters of Nabucco for tampering with the neutrality of the European Commission by sending advocacy letters to the Commissioner for Energy and to the President of the European Commission (interview with former attaché at the Mission of the Republic of Albania to the EU

2014), although TAP was engaging at the same time in advocacy. That the European Commission could take an open position of support for one project was construed by the TAP supporters as 'unfair':

> the TAP beneficiary countries didn't think and didn't use any kind of pressure on the Commission. They didn't try to influence the Commission to support TAP, but just to remain neutral and to play a fair game. The Commission did it so we have TAP in place. At that time, there were rumours that the Commission, but it was not true, that the Commission was going to support Nabucco because Bulgaria is a European Union Member, Romania is a European Union Member, Austria, Hungary, so many countries Members of the EU, but in TAP they had only Greece and Italy so weighting in terms of Members, Nabucco had more EU Member countries. (interview with former attaché at the Mission of the Republic of Albania to the European Union 2014)

The Silent Participants

As predicted by Sabatier, at a given point, in any subsystem there exist a series of entities that are not associated with any coalition (Sabatier 1998, p. 103). The subsystem working on the Southern Gas Corridor is no exception. Actors situated at the periphery of the sociogram have weak relations with the two coalitions. Some were part of a coalition initially and left it (for instance, the US was an open supporter of Nabucco in 2009). Some might be informal supporters of a coalition (Russia is believed to have favoured TAP, as revealed in an interview with Austrian official 2014). The social network analysis performed on the policy subsystem working on the Southern Gas Corridor in 2013 places the US towards the periphery of the policy subsystem and does not capture any direct Russian involvement.

Russia was known to be an opponent of the Southern Gas Corridor and out of the two pipelines objected to Nabucco the most. The Southern Gas Corridor constitutes an alternative to Russian gas entering the European market through the Brotherhood Pipeline, crossing Ukraine's territory. The Southern Gas Corridor and Nabucco, particularly, (as a pipeline that could transport 30 bcm/year, in its initial design) conflicted with Russian strategic and economic interests. The primary market for Russia is Central and Eastern Europe and Russia does not want additional gas, especially Azeri or Caspian gas coming to Central Europe.

EU officials are very suspicious when it comes to Russian intentions and practices (interview with European Parliament official 3 2013; interview with senior European Commission official, DG Energy 2013). According to sources based in the EU institutions, the Russian strategy to sabotage EU attempts to diversify its energy suppliers includes two elements visible also in the case of the Southern Gas Corridor, and particularly of the Nabucco pipeline:

> there are two strands. One strand is staggering the neighbours and preventing them from supplying gas through the Southern Corridor in Russia's sphere of influence so you need to build a sufficiency pipeline for the sources outside the sphere of influence of Russia. The second strategy is of course to build ties within Europe. They are very active, Berlusconi [the former Italian Prime Minister] has been a very good friend, Schröder [the former German Prime Minister] has been a very good friend. (interview with European Parliament official 3 2013)

None of the individuals interviewed could report direct contact with any Russian or Gazprom official or an attempt by Russia or Gazprom to influence the choice for one pipeline project or the other. That said, based on my own observation and interaction with Russian and Gazprom officials active in Brussels energy circles, Russia and its diplomats do have a rather secretive style of conducting policy. Some interviewees indicated that Russia might have had an impact on the choice between Nabucco and TAP indirectly through the leverage that it and its national companies have on Azerbaijan and SOCAR and on Bulgaria and Bulgargaz. Bulgaria is heavily dependent on Russian gas. Although not formally acknowledged, the fact that Russia tried to persuade Azerbaijan not to develop the Southern Gas Corridor would be hinted at in bilateral meetings between the EU and Azerbaijan (interview with official in the EEAS 2 2013). A governmental official interviewed also claimed that: 'concerning Nabucco, we are quite convinced that Russia has exerted some influence in order to make sure that the smaller pipeline [TAP] is built' and that they have evidence that Russia influenced the choice of Shah Deniz (interview with Austrian official 2014). The interview with a senior Bulgarian official indicates that the Bulgarian government was also, at least indirectly, influenced by the Russian pipeline preference for the Southern Gas Corridor and reluctantly showed its support for the Corridor:

> to the Bulgarian government, the Southern Gas Corridor was right from 2009, let's say, an unavoidable evil. If the EU was going for such an option, the Southern Gas Corridor, of course Bulgaria would join in the efforts, but it did so with some hesitation and this has continued throughout three governments. ... These three governments in particular have believed much more in South Stream than in the Southern Corridor. Besides, they have seen perhaps too big an irritation for Russia. ... Russia and the Russian lobby which particularly under this government have a strong hold in Bulgaria, they have always had it, they would simply dismiss Nabucco without much argument and this is what the Bulgarian government, a series of Bulgarian governments bought into. (interview with very senior Bulgarian official 2013)

Official sources speaking on behalf of Azerbaijan have, however, denied that Russian preferences ultimately tilted the balance towards TAP (interview with Azeri official 2013). BP and SOCAR representatives did not confirm any Russian pressure either.

The US has always been a supporter of the Southern Gas Corridor, but its direct involvement with it, as well as the support offered to Nabucco, has fluctuated. The idea of the Southern Gas Corridor benefited from the support of the US as a result of the implications that the Corridor might have for the energy security of Europe and for the economic independence of the states in the Caspian region. As a senior official from the US Mission to the EU explained:

> we have an interest in European energy security and in the states of the former Soviet Union and the Caspian having an independent outlet for their natural resources to competitive markets in order to avoid being controlled by the Russians, going through Russian infrastructure [in order to sell their gas]. Basically, we want to get them to have some economic independence, more than they had, going back to the definition of energy security. You want reliability of supply. The Russian gas has been a very reliable supply, but you want to have diversity of supply because having everything supplied through a single provider just inherently creates risks. (interview with official at the US Mission to the EU 2013)

Several interviewees mentioned the important role played by the US in the development of the Southern Gas Corridor (interview with representative of SOCAR 2014; interview with senior Turkish official 2014). The US supported the Corridor through the dialogue it had with governments in the Caspian Region (Azerbaijan, Georgia), Turkey, and the EU Member States (interview with official at the US Mission to the EU 2013). Support was offered by the US through foreign policy choices and the appointment in Azerbaijan of American ambassadors with an interest in energy security and a good understanding of Eastern Europe (interview with former Hungarian diplomat based in the US 2014; interview with representative of an energy company 2014; interview with representative of BP 2014). However, unlike in the case of the Baku-Tbilisi-Ceyhan oil pipeline in which the US played a leading role, in the case of the Southern Gas Corridor the US expected the EU to play the leading role (interview with senior Georgian official 2014).

US support for the Southern Gas Corridor decreased during the early years of the Obama administration. This was in large part due to the reset in US-Russian relations (interview with senior European Commission official, DG Energy 2013; interview with former Hungarian diplomat based in the US 2014). The 'reset' policy was one adopted by US President Barack Obama at the beginning of his mandate and aimed to: 'engage the Russian government to pursue foreign policy goals of common interest' (The White House 2010). The reset in US-Russian relations triggered American reluctance to alienate Russia by supporting a pipeline system that worked against Russian energy and economic interests.

The US position has fluctuated from one of firm and open support for Nabucco in 2009, when a US delegation attended the signing of the 13 July 2009 Intergovernmental Agreement between the Nabucco countries, to one of neutrality regarding the right pipeline in 2013. The official position that the US took was that pipeline projects need to be built based on their commercial feasibility and that the commercial case for Nabucco declined from 2009 to 2013 (interview with official at the US Mission to the EU 2013). In any case, the recognition of the US as an international power with an interest in the energy dynamics of the Caspian Sea determined a dialogue between the US and European actors working on the Southern Gas Corridor:

> we made a number of presentations of the TAP project in the United States just to explain what it was about, the role it played in the security of energy supplies, and so on, but they did not have a specific say on that. As a friend and ally, we kept them informed, we discussed with them and so on, but the decision was a sovereign decision by the EU and the concerned countries. (interview with senior Italian official 2014)

Overall, in 2013 the US did not seem to play a central role in the development of the Southern Gas Corridor. This meant that the European Commission was the main political actor shaping developments around the Southern Gas Corridor, including the outcome of the competition between Nabucco and TAP. The next chapter will discuss in more detail the strategies through which advocacy coalitions and in particular the TAP coalition gained access to the European Commission and changed its preferences in relation to the Southern Gas Corridor.

CHAPTER 6

The Southern Gas Corridor: The Power of Resources, Words, and Structure

This chapter continues the analysis of policy developments around the Southern Gas Corridor and of the actions coalitions undertook in order to alter the position of the EU Commission. Chapter 1 hypothesizes that a coalition is more likely to be successful ***if it possesses and makes good use of material and informational resources; if it develops a broad, timely, and dynamic frame; and if it is well interconnected and includes members who are central to the policy subsystem working on a particular issue.*** Here I will show that the TAP coalition surpassed the Nabucco coalition on many of these aspects and this accounts for its success in changing the mindset of the European Commission from one of support for Nabucco to a position of neutrality regarding which pipeline is selected to open the Southern Gas Corridor.

Until 2013, the European Commission had a strong record of publicly supporting Nabucco. On 13 July 2009 the Nabucco Intergovernmental Agreement was signed in Ankara, Turkey, in the presence of a European Commission delegation led by the President of the Commission, José Manuel Durão Barroso, and the then EU Commissioner for Energy, Andris Piebalgs.[1] At the signing of the Intergovernmental Agreement backing Nabucco, the President of the European Commission showed his open support for Nabucco: 'Nabucco will provide energy security to

[1] A US delegation also attended the event. The signing of the Intergovernmental Agreement on TAP in 2013 did not benefit from the presence of high EU officials.

A.-M. Bocse, *International Networks, Advocacy and EU Energy Policy-Making*, Palgrave Studies in European Union Politics,
https://doi.org/10.1007/978-3-030-49505-3_6

Turkey, to South East Europe and to Central Europe. Nabucco is thus a truly European project' (Durão Barroso 2009, p. 2). Durão Barroso also added that 'Gas pipes may be made of steel, but Nabucco can cement the links between our people' (Durão Barroso 2009, p. 2), indicating the political importance of this project, that went beyond energy policy considerations. Although Nabucco would have made a contribution to the EU gas supply, it could not cover more than 5–10% of its gas demand. However, the pipeline was an important symbol of the EU effort to diversify its gas supply and transport routes (European Parliament 2009b). It was also a signal that the EU is willing to develop deeper political and economic relations with Turkey and the countries of the Caspian region. For a long time, Nabucco was considered by the European Commission to be 'the flagship project' of the Southern Gas Corridor. Nabucco would often pride itself for having the endorsement of the European Commission. For instance, the CEO of Nabucco Gas Pipeline International, Reinhard Mitschek, stated that:

> Nabucco is a truly European project. The Commission has identified Nabucco as a preferential corridor. Therefore the project is listed within the EEPR [European Energy Programme for Recovery] framework for direct funding of up to 200 million euro. Our shareholders, and our route, are drawn from EU member states. Nabucco will benefit Europe, of course, in terms of diversification of energy supply, diversification and will offer freedom of choice to customers. (Mitschek 2013c)

Nabucco benefited from exemptions from EU law, and from EU funding of 200 million euro for 2009–2012 through the European Energy Programme for Recovery (European Energy Programme for Recovery 2013). However, the European Commission withdrew its considerable support for Nabucco which was very prominent in the late 2000s and publicly claimed starting with spring 2013 that it has no particular preference for Nabucco or TAP, as long as the European Union gains access to the Azeri gas through a pipeline (interview with senior European Commission official, DG Energy 2013; interview with very senior European Commission official 2014). In the words of an EU official:

> we supported both projects equally. As you know, we were more vocal in supporting maybe Nabucco for a long time, but then we delivered on TAP because in the weeks prior to the decision it was the European Commission

who granted exemptions, for instance, to make this project viable and put it on an equal footing with Nabucco. (interview with official in the EEAS 2 2013)

This chapter will offer an overview of the European Commission interaction with the two advocacy coalitions (emerging around Nabucco and, respectively, TAP) that explains this change of position. In the next section I argue that the resources coalitions possess help them gain access to policymakers and influence policy. I show that the TAP coalition benefited from better access to the European Commission than the Nabucco coalition.

The Power of Resources

This section will show that informational and financial resources are very useful to gaining access to the European Commission. This access provides coalitions with an opportunity to receive, at turn, strategic information from the Commission and to influence its position through the information they share with it and through the frames they generate. The study of the fracking for shale gas campaigns presented in Chap. 4 reveals that actors use, in particular, technical knowledge to gain access to European institutions and in this way shape EU energy policy choices. In the case of the Southern Gas Corridor, coalitions gain entry and leverage given the technical, economic, and political knowledge their members possess, but especially through the financial power of their corporate members.

Possessing Information

EU institutions are highly dependent on outside information concerning various aspects of energy exploitation and transport. The nature of the information exchanged by actors involved in shaping large infrastructure projects varies. Exchanges between the two coalitions and the Commission took place in the process of awarding exemptions to both TAP and Nabucco. Both consortia engaged in a technical conversation with regulators in the transit countries and with the European Commission (interview with representative of OMV 2014). The information exchange was specialized, concerning the field of EU law and economics. The European Commission wished to make sure that the pipeline projects complied with

EU law. Sometimes the Commission simply wished to check on the progress of a project or wanted to hear the opinions of corporations on regional energy politics:

> the Commission was interested in the development of the project, especially in the last year, where we are, did we make some technical design, how is the project progressing, for example, the exemptions. There was some initiative of the European Commission to ask for our opinion on, for example, this initiative that they have with the World Bank for the Trans-Caspian Pipeline. They were interested in what we think about it, if this was possible. (interview with representative of OMV 2014)

In addition to expert knowledge, the two advocacy coalitions provided the European Commission with 'Information about the Domestic Encompassing Interest (IDEI)'[2] (Bouwen 2002, p. 369). This 'concerns the needs and interests of a sector in the domestic market' (Bouwen 2002, p. 369). They provided the European Commission with information on national political and energy policy preferences. The EU Commission needed to take into consideration the arguments and preferences of its Member States, as energy security is an area of shared competence between the EU and its Members.

Both coalitions included EU Member States that threw their political weight behind Nabucco or TAP. The meetings that took place between the governmental supporters of TAP and the European Commission and the governmental supporters of Nabucco and the European Commission confirm the fact that the Commission found value in interacting with the governments backing both these projects. The TAP coalition, for instance, included government representatives from Greece, Italy, and Albania who could provide first-hand knowledge of the political and financial situation in these countries.

Governments involved in the development of the Southern Gas Corridor, and supporting one pipeline project or another, communicated among themselves and with the European Commission at different levels. Usually a message of support was offered at a high level, as a result of a meeting between the governmental parties involved in a pipeline project. Several energy summits dedicated to the opening of the Southern Gas

[2] IDEI is developed by Bouwen in relation to corporate lobbying, but it can be applied also to advocacy conducted by coalitions encompassing both public and private actors.

Corridor took place at the end of the 2000s and were attended by high governmental officials: the Budapest Nabucco Summit on 27 January 2009; the Sofia Energy Summit on 25 April 2009; and the Prague Southern Corridor Summit on 8 May 2009. In addition, meetings between heads of state marked the signing of the intergovernmental agreements on which both Nabucco and TAP were based. The European Commission was often present through its representatives at these events. Bilateral meetings and talks also took place and individual and joint messages were released as a result.[3] These summits and meetings gave the public, the media, and the European Commission a signal that there is political support from the EU Members for Nabucco (in the case of Bulgaria, Romania, Hungary, and Austria), or for TAP (in the case of Greece and Italy).

Possessing Financial Resources

Energy corporations in the coalitions are purchasers of gas and investors in the pipeline infrastructure. Governments and the EU can play a role in facilitating such investments:

> I would believe it [the European Commission] has been not just helpful, but essential to do this work, to pave the way politically for the companies to come to their investment decisions, but obviously we cannot replace the companies in such decisions. Obviously, we cannot commit to buy the gas or to build the pipelines, but we can assist by really opening the way, establishing the network at government level, establishing good contacts, sometimes supporting financially as we've done with various programmes, the European Economic Recovery Programme and other instruments, so I think it is a necessary tandem and one does not replace the other. (interview with very senior European Commission official 2014)

Relations between the European Commission and energy companies in opening the Southern Gas Corridor are described as a 'necessary tandem'. The companies need the political support of the Commission as much as the European Commission needs companies on board. Companies develop

[3] In addition to high-level public declarations, communication at the middle level took place, on more technical aspects, meetings with the Commission, Member States, and companies. At a later stage, if needed, high officials were asked to make a political statement that consolidated what was discussed at these meetings (interview with attaché at the Permanent Representation of Romania to the EU 2014).

and in great part finance large infrastructure projects such as Nabucco and TAP. The cost of the entire Southern Gas Corridor (stretching over 3500 km) is estimated at 40 billion euro and it comprises several energy transport projects, including TAP (TAP 2015b). The construction of TAP alone is estimated at 1.5 billion euro. The TAP consortium also approached the European Bank for Reconstruction and Development and the European Investment Bank, as well as various Export Credit Guarantee agencies to help fund the pipeline (TAP 2013b, slide 17).

In order for the Southern Gas Corridor to be realized, energy corporations on one gas route or another (Nabucco or TAP) needed to commit to buying gas. Energy companies negotiate gas purchase agreements and they were in at least weekly contact with Shah Deniz in order to negotiate the gas purchase terms (interview with representative of OMV 2014). Their economic power gives companies access to governmental officials and treatment similar to that of senior officials:

> there is a lot of interaction at the level of embassies, companies on the ground, the government companies, state-companies relations develop. This shows that this is a project which is so important politically, where states are not the only actors and you see big companies certainly playing a very important role. When you see the interactions, they are on the same level, you know, they are received in the same way, the top guys from the companies, almost treated like the state officials, they all have government relations departments. (interview with senior Georgian official 2014)

Being able and willing to allocate resources to face-to-face advocacy conducted by government relations departments can increase a coalition's advocacy success. The supporters of TAP attribute their effectiveness in making a strong case for their pipeline to extensive face-to-face engagement with a wide range of actors, including the European Commission (interview with TAP source 2013). This implied extensive travel to several European capitals for the TAP team (interview with industry consultant 2, 2014; interview with senior Italian official 2014). Keeping the information flow alive through personal engagement brought TAP a competitive advantage over Nabucco.

Consortia such as TAP and Shah Deniz often organized events in Brussels to which they invited representatives of governments involved in the Southern Gas Corridor to participate and circulated statements and newsletters to all the parties that had an interest in the Corridor (interview with senior Albanian official 2014). The public affairs consultancy that the TAP consortium employed in Brussels played an important role in organizing media, networking and advocacy events and meetings. In addition, exchanges between the two coalitions and policymakers took place in more neutral venues, provided by the European institutions. The European Parliament, for instance, regularly organized events on the Southern Gas Corridor. Government officials advocating for one project or the other interacted in the framework of the European Commission and Council working groups (interview with attaché at the Permanent Representation of Italy to the EU 2014).

Choosing to engage European decision-makers and advocate personally at events and through private meetings was advantageous to the TAP coalition as personal communication is central to European energy policymaking (as shown also in previous chapters). Within the broader system working on the Southern Gas Corridor, communication took place mainly in person, although some information was also exchanged in a mediated manner (email, phone, and teleconference). Mail (formal letters that are archived) is still used in communications between governments and state-owned energy companies (interview with representative of TANAP 2014).

Despite advances in technology, face-to-face communication remains very important and its value was also highlighted by energy corporations engaged in the development of the Southern Gas Corridor. As a key BP official working on the Southern Corridor explains, the most important exchanges took place in person, despite the fact that the Southern Gas Corridor involved actors from dozens of countries and corporations scattered all over the world:

> a huge amount of face-to-face. For all this modern technology and you can Skype people and have video conferences, most of it was done like you and I here in this room today [in person, like the interview for this research]. (interview with representative of BP 2014)

Experts based in public affairs and consultancy firms also agreed that face-to-face communication was essential for a consistent exchange of information on the Southern Gas Corridor. As a consultant working at the firm hired by TAP indicates:

> for daily interactions, I mean for ad-hoc interactions, I would say email and telephone, but for a consistent exchange of information it's 90% face-to-face

> meetings. It's a completely different picture if you send somebody an email with some bullet points and then if you have the opportunity to sit down with that person and flesh out all the implications around that development or concept, I think it's much more enlightening and useful for both parties. (interview with industry consultant 2, 2014)

Information and communication technology (ICT) is helpful in preparing the setting for the personal communication: 'in a way you prepare the ground through the ICT and then you reap the fruits by individual meetings' (interview with senior Italian official 2014). But ICT cannot replace personal communication:

> when two persons communicate there is a lot of verbal communication and a lot of non-verbal communication. Now ICT only transmits a part of communication, mainly verbal, little bit of non-verbal communication. You communicate by videoconference for instance, but not everything so the ICT conveying of message is partial, always partial. You can get the whole picture, the whole communication both verbal and non-verbal, only with physical meetings. (interview with senior Italian official 2014)

European institutions also seemed to prefer face-to-face interaction to other forms of communication. Both mediated (phone, email, etc.) and face-to-face communication was used by the European Commission in the process of developing the Southern Gas Corridor. However, personal interaction remains essential for senior EU officials:

> all of it is important, of course, the personal contact is very important. It's not by chance that Commissioner Oettinger since the beginning of his mandate as Energy Commissioner was five or six times in Azerbaijan, for example, so obviously the personal contact is extremely important. I would say that I personally do not think that we will come to a stage where technology fully replaces personal contact. Personal contact remains very important and the sitting at the table with your counterpart is probably much more efficient than just the contact by emails which remain rather impersonal, or phone, for that matter. (interview with very senior European Commission official 2014)

As with the interaction between the private and public actors when it came to shaping EU policy concerning the extraction of shale gas, communication between the EU institutions and the corporate sector on the

Southern Gas Corridor was not unidirectional. The two coalitions also received valuable information from the public sector, particularly the European Commission, that helped them in their advocacy work. Meeting with policymakers provided advocates and lobbyists with the opportunity to receive information on EU Commission priorities, as well as political and diplomatic developments around the Southern Gas Corridor:

> some people in the Commission provided useful information on various policy developments that were relevant for us or relevant ongoing diplomatic developments so yes, I cannot put a percentage on how much it was TAP providing information, how much were the institutions, but it was a two-way process definitely. (interview with an industry consultant 2 2014)

Coalitions used information from the institutions to reshape their advocacy strategies. As one key interviewee noted, when proposing a large energy infrastructure project, you want to make sure that you have: 'the people that influence the decision on your side, you know what is their thinking on the issue' (interview with former Hungarian diplomat based in the US 2014). Consortia also received information and guidance from the Commission in the process of securing exemptions from EU competition law (interview with representative of OMV 2014).

As entities that have considerable material resources, companies have the ear of the European Commission and of DG Energy. They also have extensive technological and economic knowledge on energy issues. The two coalitions were also able to communicate the energy policy preferences of EU Member States to the European Commission. These types of information gave coalitions access to the European Commission as they constitute 'access goods' (Immergut 1992; Bouwen 2002). The TAP coalition seems to have been more successful in engaging in communication processes with the European Commission and other stakeholders by prioritizing exchanging information in person and by organizing advocacy events. But how do these goods translate into influence? In the case of the Southern Gas Corridor, access triggered a bidirectional information flow, from advocates to the Commission and the other way around. The information received from the Commission enabled TAP advocates to conduct a more effective campaign. At the same time, access enabled the two coalitions to present the European Commission arguments in favour of the pipeline that each supported. The next section will show how the two coalitions tried to build a case for their pipeline by resorting to framing.

The Power of Words

The previous section showed that information exchanges were central to interactions between the two coalitions and the European Commission. The information that the two coalitions chose to pass on to the European Commission was filtered so that it supported their case. In this section I argue that coalitions resorted to framing in order to alter the position of the European Commission on the Southern Gas Corridor. In this process, they also redefined EU energy security.

As already hypothesized, frames are more likely to make an impact if: ***(1) They are broad and resonate with many actors; (2) They respond to exogenous unfolding events, and (3) They respond effectively to opposing frames.*** The coalitions working on the Southern Gas Corridor amended their frames in order to enhance their impact. TAP and its supporters framed TAP as a project that meets the energy interests of the EU better than Nabucco in the year 2013, at the moment when the Shah Deniz Consortium was choosing a pipeline for its gas. I argue that TAP's advocacy success is explained to an important degree by the TAP coalition articulating a broad frame that responded very well to exogenous events and that effectively engaged and built on the frame advanced by Nabucco.

The TAP consortium was aware of the European Commissions' long-term support for Nabucco when they entered the direct race for the Shah Deniz gas against this pipeline (interview with TAP source 2013). The Commission was mainly interested in supporting the project with the highest policy benefits, particularly for EU energy security. The European Commission helped develop the Southern Gas Corridor in an attempt to diversify the sources of energy that the EU has access to, as well as the energy routes to existing (Azerbaijan) and potential future sources of gas (for instance, Iraq and Iran). As discussed in more detail in Chap. 2, for the EU energy security entails the diversification of energy sources and energy routes.

TAP seemed to have a stronger business case than Nabucco. By 2013, Nabucco became less profitable owing to a series of factors. It became clear that investment in a large (30 bcm/year capacity) pipeline is risky given that only 10 bcm/year of gas was available from Azerbaijan. The global gas market shifted dramatically from 2011 as the shale gas revolution took place in the US and made a lot of cheap coal that was no longer needed in the US available to the European market reducing temporarily the demand for gas on the market (interview with Nabucco source 2014). The 10 bcm TAP seemed to respond better to the new market conditions. However, TAP was perceived by certain governments and by the European Commission as weaker from a diversification policy and geostrategic point of view (interview with industry consultant 1 2013; interview with very senior Bulgarian official 2013). TAP had, therefore, the difficult task of persuading the European Commission that their project is as politically relevant as Nabucco.

To secure the support of the European Commission, TAP was aware that they need to bring policy benefits at the centre of their discourse. Governments talk policy and companies talk business. In order to be persuasive, the supporters of TAP needed to highlight especially those TAP benefits that were more likely to make an impact on the audience, in this case, the European Commission: 'of course you would tailor your messages according to the audience' (interview with industry consultant 2 2014). In order to convince the European Commission, TAP representatives stressed the public policy benefits of the project: 'all projects try to position themselves in a race. The more they could present themselves as meeting EU policy objectives, the more support one got politically' (interview with TAP source 2013).

Successful lobbying and advocacy entailed responding to the policy interests of the European Commission and EU Members and showing that TAP is 'strategic':

> if you are dealing with governments, you have to speak in their language and about policy. It was all about the strategic policy benefits that TAP could bring, underpinned by a commercially viable project that is not reliant on subsidies given the crisis faced by many of us in Europe, so underpinning the strategic value of a project that in Greece alone will create something like 2.000 direct jobs and 10.000 indirect jobs, and create value, you know, from taxes, etc. Greece needs that money, Greece needs to show that it can attract foreign direct investment. This is strategic for Europe. (interview with TAP source 2013)

Broad Frame and Resonating with Many Actors

In arguing for the policy benefits of its project, the TAP coalition has successfully engaged in a process of frame amplification, defined in Chap. 1 as 'the clarification and invigoration of an interpretive frame that bears on a particular issue, problem or set of events' (Snow et al. 1986, p. 469). Like the Nabucco coalition, the TAP coalition presented its project as a pipeline that will contribute to the energy security of the EU and particularly to that of some of its Member States that are more challenged when it comes to security of supply.

Several states that joined the EU in 2004–2007 display a high degree of dependence on Russian gas (Bulgaria, Poland, etc.) and some of them have since the mid-2000s very actively supported EU internal and external policies meant to reduce this dependence. In the context of the 2009 Russo-Ukrainian gas crisis, energy security goals developed around security of supply and gaining more independence from Russia and Russian gas. Maltby argues that:

> in contrast to the period before, the gas supply disruptions of 2006/2009 provided a window for the Commission to act as an energy security policy entrepreneur, contributing towards a shift in the perception of Union gas supplies from secure to insecure, and dependency on gas imports on a small number of suppliers (particularly Russia) from positive to negative. (Maltby 2013, p. 441)

Nabucco had a reputation with European officials and in terms of public opinion as the project that can help the EU meet its energy security goals, especially as defined in late 2000s, mainly in terms of security of supply. It aimed to increase access to gas supply for new EU members from Central and Eastern Europe. According to its self-declared strategic goals, Nabucco aimed: 'to contribute to the security of supply for all [Nabucco] partner countries and for Europe as a whole' (Nabucco Gas Pipeline International 2013b). According to its developers, Nabucco would bring freedom of supply choice to European gas consumers by diversifying the gas offer available to Europe with gas from the Caspian Sea and from other sources (Nabucco Gas Pipeline International 2013a). The Nabucco consortium referred to its project in public communications and interaction with the European institutions as 'the new gas bridge from Asia to Europe and the flagship project in the Southern Corridor'

(Nabucco Gas Pipeline International 2013c), in this way reinforcing its leading role in opening the Southern Gas Corridor.

The promoters of Nabucco also claimed that the project would help the EU gain its independence from Russian gas. Nabucco Gas Pipeline International argued that Nabucco will make: 'an important contribution to energy security and diversification in these countries, which are all heavily dependent on gas from Russia' (Nabucco Gas Pipeline International 2013c). The pipeline aimed to cater to the energy needs of countries that are highly dependent on Russian gas, for instance, Bulgaria. In addition to bringing gas to Central and Eastern Europe, whose security of supply is dependent on Russia, Nabucco also claimed to improve the energy transport infrastructure in a region lacking interconnectors:

> it starts with the argument that I already mentioned, if you have all the infrastructure, linking Romania, Bulgaria, Hungary, then the security of supply was given, this interconnectivity is still a big issue for these countries and security of supply with gas for industries is extremely important. (interview with Nabucco source 2014)

Countries such as Bulgaria found the Southern Gas Corridor to be an opportunity to develop the national transit grid (interview with Bulgarian energy expert 2014). Nabucco was designed in such a way that it offered off-take points in all the EU countries it would transit.

In addition, in its initial stage, Nabucco also included a segment crossing Turkish territory and this was very much welcomed by the European Commission. All Nabucco, including this segment of the pipeline, would have been built according to EU law and owned mainly by European companies, giving Europeans extensive legal and economic control over it (interview with senior European Commission official, DG Energy 2013).

TAP reinvigorated the frame advanced by the coalition behind Nabucco. Similarly to Nabucco, TAP supporters made the argument that, by contributing to opening the Southern Gas Corridor, their pipeline would enhance EU energy security. The 2013 TAP presentation argues that TAP will offer 'diversity and security of energy supply for Europe' (TAP 2013b, slide 4), and that TAP supports: 'the EU's initiative to enhance Europe's energy security by connecting to new sources of natural gas in the Caspian Sea' (TAP 2013b, slide 4). Unlike Nabucco, which mainly targeted the Eastern and Central European markets, TAP claimed to make a difference in the South-Eastern and Western European energy markets: '10 bcm annually initially available from Shah Deniz will be able to supply 7 million households in South Eastern and Western Europe' (TAP 2013b, slide 4).

TAP promised to increase the energy security of the Western Balkan countries that were in the process of acceding to the EU. In this way, the project claimed to contribute to EU energy security in the long term. As a key interviewee argued, the TAP team:

> have worked very hard with countries in South Eastern Europe to set up several agreements with the Western Balkan countries, Albania, Montenegro, Bosnia and Herzegovina, Croatia, Slovenia, etc., in trying to see how we could facilitate, not actually build or construct any pipelines, but facilitate gas delivery there. (interview with TAP source 2013)

As a partner and transit country for TAP and member of the TAP coalition, Albania was in direct contact with the European Commission and argued that the construction of TAP will impact on both its economic situation and that of the Balkan countries in times of economic crisis, as well as on the energy security of the Balkans (interview with former attaché at the Mission of the Republic of Albania to the EU 2014). In its interaction with European institutions, Albania made a case for the whole region:

> our role was just to show them why TAP was helpful and very much needed for our countries and just arguing with figures not only for Albania, but for the entire region, for the entire Western Balkans. ... The Balkan countries someday will join the EU and they will introduce a huge problem within the EU in terms of energy supply so the sooner these countries work for the energy mix, the better for the EU once these countries join the EU. That was the main, let's say, argument we were using. (interview with former attaché at the Mission of the Republic of Albania to the EU 2014)

In addition to that, TAP promised that it will not disregard the Bulgarian situation, the most energy dependent on Russian gas of the countries that would have been covered by Nabucco, and will make sure that, even if Nabucco is not realized, Bulgaria will receive gas from Shah Deniz II. All in all, supporters of TAP argued that both TAP and Nabucco create important benefits for Bulgaria (interview with senior Italian official 2014).

The TAP coalition also drew attention to the situation of energy dependence on Russia that Greece finds itself in and the alleviation of such dependence that will be provided by TAP. TAP advocates claimed that Greece is more dependent on Russian gas than countries whose energy security would benefit from the competitor to TAP, Nabucco:

> we always forget that Greece is heavily dependent on Russian gas, more dependent on Russian gas than Hungary, than Romania, than Austria. Bulgaria and Greece are the two most vulnerable countries in that sense. (interview with TAP source 2013)

Overall, TAP adopted the energy security frame that Nabucco used so effectively in the past and reinvigorated it by claiming that Southern European and Western Balkan energy security should also be catered for and that TAP can do this, alongside covering the energy shortage of Bulgaria, the most vulnerable Central and Eastern European state that will benefit from the Nabucco pipeline. In this regard, TAP made sure that it responds to concerns regarding energy justice related to energy accessibility and tackling energy poverty, which is more prominent in less developed European states, such as Bulgaria. In generating accessibility, the pipeline contributed to developing 'an energy system that gives people an equal shot of getting the energy they need, energy systems that generate income and enrich lives' (Sovacool and Dworkin 2014, pp. 15–16). Access to energy can help close the gap between economically more developed countries in Western Europe and those less developed or strongly hit by the 2008 financial crisis in Central, Eastern, and Southern Europe, as well as bring revenues to transit countries through transit fees. At the same time, access to gas dislocating coal in the energy mix can help EU Member States reduce their GHG emissions and fight climate change. Overall, TAP successfully extended the frame of energy security as security of supply that Nabucco advanced, as indicated by Table 6.1:

This section shows that, when it comes to the security of supply dimension, the TAP frame was slightly broader than that of TAP and this frame included other dimensions on which TAP had a competitive advantage. In addition, TAP proved its political entrepreneurship by bringing elements related to energy pricing and economic competitiveness to the frame it advanced, as indicated by Table 6.2.

Table 6.1 Elements of the Nabucco and TAP frames presented in a comparative way: the energy security as security of supply dimension

	Benefits generated				
Coalition	*Security of supply*				
	Security of the EU	Security of Central and Eastern Europe	Security of vulnerable Bulgaria	Security of Greece	Security of the Western Balkans, future EU members
Nabucco	X	X	X		X (but very late in the debate)
TAP	X		X	X	X

Source: Author

Responding to Exogenous Unfolding Events

In the frame developed by TAP the accent was placed not only on secure supply but also on reduced gas transit tariffs and commercial feasibility, important arguments in an EU that was in 2013 struggling to recover from the 2008 global financial and economic crisis. At the same time, TAP claimed to make a difference to the recovery of the EU country most severely hit by the economic crisis, Greece. As indicated in Chap. 1, changing policy requires: '(a) significant perturbations external to the subsystem (e.g. changes in socio-economic conditions, system-wide governing coalitions, or policy outputs from other subsystems) and (b) exploitation of those opportunities by the heretofore minority coalition within the subsystem' (Jenkins-Smith and Sabatier 1994, p. 179). The 2008 financial and economic crisis was such a perturbation in socio-economic conditions that TAP, initially a minority coalition and the underdog, exploited more effectively than the coalition behind the more established Nabucco project.

The TAP coalition responded through its frame better than Nabucco to the exogenous factor constituted by the 2008 crisis. The economic crisis brought an additional focus on energy prices and a stronger argument for developing a pipeline that can deliver gas at the lowest price, although it might not be the most strategic project in the long term. TAP argued that the project they propose: 'is the most cost-effective solution in the Southern Gas Corridor' (TAP 2013b, slide 27). TAP implied lower construction costs and a higher guarantee that investors will get a return on their investment (interview with representative of an energy company

Table 6.2 Elements of the Nabucco and TAP frames presented in a comparative way

	Benefits generated							
	Energy security						*Economic benefits*	
Coalition	*Security of supply*					*Best possible gas price*	*European economic recovery from the crisis*	
	Security of the EU	Security of Central and Eastern Europe	Security of vulnerable Bulgaria	Security of Greece	Security of Western Balkans, future EU members		European economic growth	Greek economic recovery
Nabucco	X	X	X		X (but very late in the debate)		X	
TAP	X		X	X	X	X	X	X

Source: Author

2014; interview with official at the US Mission to the EU 2013). A cheaper pipeline meant lower gas transit costs.

The advocacy the TAP coalition conducted with BP also paid off through the indirect impact that it had on the Commission. BP ended up supporting the TAP coalition in their argument that reduced pipeline costs are more important than geostrategic considerations. The European Commission and Nabucco were receiving signals from BP that the project they will eventually select needs to bring profit to investors and that relying on meeting political objectives is not enough. As one interviewee mentioned: 'I think the interests just cannot be, things cannot be just political, which were in the case of Nabucco, Nabucco was just so much a political project' (interview with representative of an energy company 2014). A BP source added:

> what we wanted to communicate to the European Union was the limits of what we could do whilst keeping Shah Deniz profitable so we wanted to make it very clear to them that it was fundamentally important that the companies involved make a good enough return on the huge investments they put in. Then, if you take that kind of boundary, that understanding of what their aims are and our aims are, the majority of the discussions and the information exchanges were about trying to overlap those two so that we could get at a win-win for the companies and the European Commission. (interview with representative of BP 2014)

This strengthened the argument made by TAP. Under the impact of the economic crisis, energy costs became a more central dimension of the vision that the Commission had on EU energy security as a result of its interaction with corporate actors and particularly TAP coalition:

> where previously under Commissioner Piebalgs it was always clear that Nabucco is going to be the main priority because this would enable essentially the weaker Bulgaria, Romania, and others to be more independent, under Oettinger it changed very clearly and it came down more or less to the opinion that it doesn't matter which project, it must be economically viable. You can see the influence of the economic crisis a little in this argument as well. (interview with Nabucco source 2014)

In addition, in their interaction with European institutions, the TAP consortium and government representatives (those of Italy, Greece, and Albania) argued that TAP would benefit the Southern European EU countries, severely hit by the economic crisis and suffering from a lack of economic competitiveness. TAP was presented as a project that will benefit the Greek economy (interview with attaché at the Permanent Representation of Greece to the EU 2014; interview with TAP source 2013). TAP promised that the realization of the project will bring major foreign direct investment (FDI, 1.5 billion euro) and employment to Greece and in this way support the economic recovery of the Eurozone (TAP 2013b, slide 9). Italy also made a strong case by arguing that having TAP crossing its territory will benefit its economic well-being and help Italy develop into a gas hub for Europe:

> we want to diversify our sources. That's why the Azeri gas is important and so we fully support the development of a Southern Corridor bringing gas into Italy, because we need gas. But also because we are in a position to become a gas hub for Europe, importing gas from other countries and directing it towards the rest of Europe. So the Azeri gas is ideal for us from these two points of view, domestic consumption, and to help us develop our role of gas hub for the rest of Europe. (interview with senior Italian official 2014)

TAP was very successful in integrating the economic argument in its frame and hoped that, if the Commission is persuaded of the importance of the economic merits of a project, TAP will also secure the Commission's support. As the section below will show, in the final stages of the selection process Nabucco also attempted to build an economic case for its project.

Responding Effectively to Opposing Frames

Each coalition attempted to present its gas interconnector as the best option among those available to the Southern Corridor. The two coalitions were aware of each other's frames and engaged in a dialogue. As we have seen, TAP did not develop its frame in isolation. It borrowed the energy security argument from Nabucco and reinvigorated it by claiming that it can provide for the energy security not only of vulnerable Bulgaria, but also of the Western Balkans and Greece. As a key interviewee explains: 'I am sure Romania, Hungary speak about energy security so TAP had to talk about energy security, how they bring energy security' (interview with representative of an energy company 2014).

In its turn, Nabucco borrowed from TAP in making a case that it will make a difference for Balkan countries beyond Bulgaria. The Nabucco Gas Pipeline International CEO declared at a meeting in May 2013 in Bucharest that: 'Nabucco is the shortest route to the markets of South Eastern Europe, and remains the best option to open the Southern Gas Corridor' (Mitschek 2013b). A key interviewee shed some light on the dynamics of this process:

> at the beginning of this year [2013], TAP started to talk about how they are going to be great for the Balkans because from TAP it will be easy to deliver gas to Croatia, Bosnia, Macedonia, etc. This is a discussion they started to advertise TAP more. What Nabucco had to do was to make a whole new presentation on how Nabucco is great for the Balkans, from Nabucco you can deliver to all these countries and even more. This is a clear example of how in such a situation you sell your product with whatever helps to sell it. If you need to talk about diversification, you talk about diversification, ... You need to make sure that your product sells the best and for that you claim it can even do things it might not be able to do, but you say it does. (interview with official in the European External Action Service, EEAS 1 2013)

In the last stages of the pipeline selection process (early 2013), also the supporters of Nabucco tried to integrate the economic argument in their frame. According to its developers, Nabucco West constitutes the best option for transporting gas from Azerbaijan to the very heart of Europe at limited costs, given that no expensive offshore sections are incorporated in the project. However, overall the project remained more expensive than TAP (costing around 1.5 billion euro). Nabucco West's costs were estimated at 5 billion euro in November 2012 (Bloomberg Business 2012). Nabucco's CEO, Reinhard Mitschek, claimed that the pipeline will boost economic growth, particularly in the countries it transits, by attracting investment and by generating revenues and taxes (Mitschek 2013a). However, its economic case was weaker than the one of TAP. Nabucco could contribute to the economic growth of poor EU countries such as Romania and Bulgaria, but would contribute less than TAP to the recovery of Greece, a Member of the Eurozone. TAP responded better to the EU's need to financially stabilize Greece, a top priority for the EU for several years.

The TAP coalition seems to be the victor in the 'framing contest' (Ryan 1991, pp. 75–94) that the two coalitions engaged in, drawing on and expanding the energy security as security of supply frame that Nabucco advanced and, through its frame also responding better to the global economic crisis. The TAP coalition's interpretation of the world and what constitutes an energy security priority differed from the interpretation articulated by the supporters of Nabucco. They tended to emphasize the need to diversify the supply of the countries in Central and Eastern Europe that Nabucco crossed rather than the benefits that a new pipeline might bring to Southern Europe and the Western Balkans. Members of different coalitions interpret reality in different ways and might draw different conclusions from the same data (Sabatier 1998). Starting from the same political and economic reality, the members of the two coalitions made different claims in an attempt to maintain or gain the support of the European Commission. The quality of the frame they articulated was very important in this process, as well as the web of connections linking actors in the policy subsystem.

The Power of Structure

The TAP coalition was successful in changing the position of the European Commission from one of open support for Nabucco to a neutral one. I will argue that this outcome was triggered in part by the role of broker that the TAP consortium played in the policy subsystem. This chapter draws upon social network analysis to calculate coalition-level metrics and individual actor metrics. I start by looking at coalition connectedness.

Interconnected Coalition

Using the group metrics function in NodeXL, I calculated the density and geodesic distance for both coalitions, and for the whole subsystem. The results are included in Table 6.3.

Looking at measures such as the coalitions' density and geodesic distance provides some quantitative data on the overall level of connectedness of actors in a coalition. The coalition density[4] is calculated by dividing the number of total edges (connections) between the coalition members by the maximum number of possible edges among the same members. As the numbers of members in the social structure increases, the density tends to decrease. It was, therefore, predictable that the density of the whole

[4] Also known in social network analysis jargon as 'graph density'.

Table 6.3 Including the coalition level metrics and the subsystem level metrics for the Southern Gas Corridor study

Graph metrics	*TAP coalition*	*Nabucco coalition*	*Whole subsystem*
Nodes/members	24	25	84
Number of ties/connections between members (excluding duplicate ties)	30	62	288
Density	0.112	0.223	0.093
Maximum geodesic distance (diameter)	3	4	4
Average geodesic distance	1.968	1.834	2.488

Source: Author

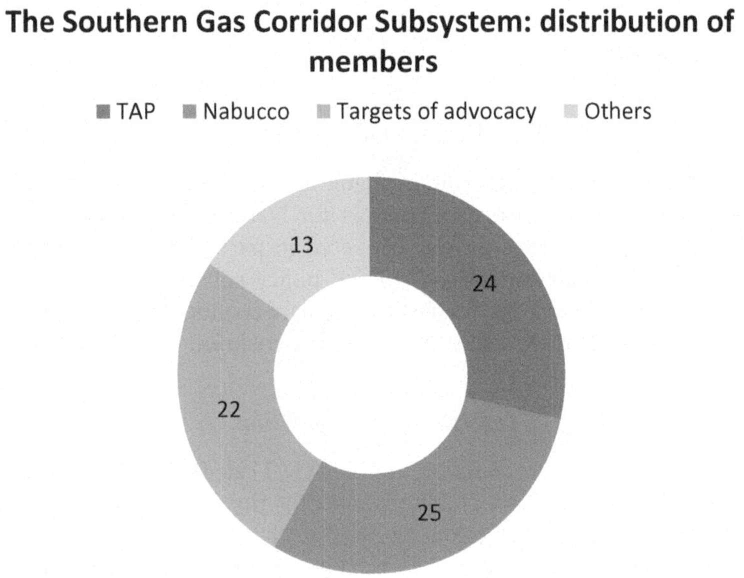

Fig. 6.1 The Southern Gas Corridor subsystem's distribution of members. (Source: Author)

subsystem (0.093) is lower than that of the two coalitions (0.112 for TAP and 0.223 for Nabucco). As the two coalitions are of relatively equal size, the TAP coalition has 24 members and Nabucco 25 members (Fig. 6.1), we can compare their density and diameter without fear of bias.

As shown in Table 6.3, the Nabucco coalition density (0.223) is higher than that of the TAP coalition (0.112). Based on connections they reported during interviews, the members of the Nabucco coalition were better connected among themselves than members of the TAP coalition. A high density means that information exchanges and synchronization of advocacy frames could take place with greater ease in the Nabucco coalition. There were more ties through which information could pass and through which communication on joint advocacy campaigning could take place than in the TAP coalition.

In an ideal world, everybody in a coalition is in direct contact with everybody in the same coalition and the geodesic distance between any two coalition members is 1. In reality, this is rarely the case and communication between two coalition members is mediated by other members. Table 6.3 shows that, on average, in order to reach another member, a member of the TAP coalition would go through 1.968 nodes, while a member of the Nabucco coalition would go through 1.834. Given that these figures are very close, it is hard to claim that they had a major impact on the success of one coalition or another. The maximum geodesic distance is lower in the case of the TAP coalition (with a value of 3) than in the case of Nabucco (with a value of 4). This means that no TAP coalition member had to cross more than 3 other members in order to reach everybody in the coalition. This should have supported the exchange of resources, information, and frames in the TAP coalition better than maximum geodesic distance did in the case of Nabucco.

From the analysis at the coalition level we can conclude that the Nabucco coalition was denser and that the TAP coalition, although less dense, has its members concentrated in a smaller social space. The aim of the two coalitions was to influence the European Commission so influencing the understandings of the Southern Gas Corridor emerging at subsystem level was important for each coalition. The next section looks in particular at actors that emerged as brokers at the subsystem level. Conducting the analysis at the subsystem level also enables me to capture indirect advocacy actions that, as this research will show, were important tools used by the TAP consortium.

Including Nodes Central to the Subsystem

This section will look at the leaders of the two coalitions, the Nabucco and TAP consortia, and compare their relational power as revealed by their degree and betweenness centrality in order to determine if this might have given one coalition an advantage over the other coalition in its advocacy work. As already noted in Chap. 5, the Nabucco and TAP consortia were set up to speak on behalf of the projects, defend their interests in relation to third parties, and act independently of parent companies on the energy market. Therefore, these entities had a strong formal mandate to advocate on behalf of the two projects and to represent them in relation to the European Commission. Supported by national governments in their advocacy role, they were nevertheless expected to take a leading role in this. Both interview data and the SNA confirm that the Nabucco and TAP consortia acted as brokers in the Southern Gas Corridor subsystem (Fig. 6.2).

The TAP consortium built an extensive network in 2012–2013 in the policy subsystem working on the Southern Gas Corridor, according to the testimony of the subsystem participants. The social network analysis run

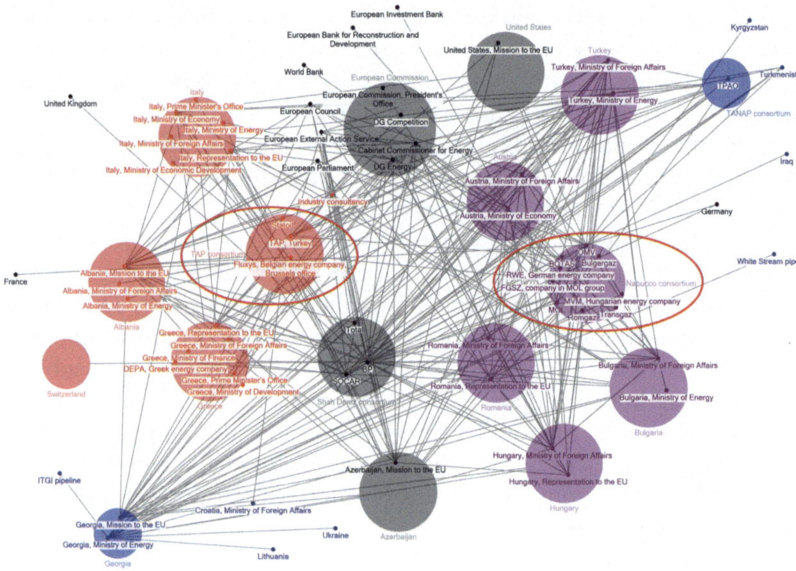

Fig. 6.2 Brokers in the Southern Gas Corridor subsystem. TAP Coalition: Red; Nabucco coalition: Purple; Targets of advocacy: Black; Other actors: Blue. (Source: Author)

on the connections[5] established between actors working on the Southern gas Corridor in 2013 indicates that the TAP and the Nabucco consortia were well connected in the Southern Corridor subsystem.

The two coalitions clashing over the Southern Gas Corridor were of roughly the same size (the Nabucco coalition had 25 members while TAP had 24 members). Unlike in the case of fracking for shale gas, degree centrality could be calculated for each coalition and the results compared without fearing that the difference in coalition size might distort the degree centrality scores.

The degree centrality in Table 6.4 is topped by BP, the TAP consortium, the Nabucco consortium, and SOCAR in a subsystem including 84 entities. BP and SOCAR were the operators of the Shah Deniz and key decision-makers on the pipeline that would open the Southern Gas Corridor. This made them the target of much interaction and contributed to their high degree centrality. The TAP consortium had the same degree centrality score as Nabucco, that is, 29, so based on this we cannot explain why one coalition was more successful than the other.

The situation is slightly different when it comes to betweenness centrality. Betweenness centrality is a good indicator of the reach that an actor has in the broader policy subsystem as it captures the ability of a network actor to act as a broker between otherwise disconnected segments of the network.

[5] The connections on which the social network analysis was run are those identified as connecting actors working on the Southern Gas Corridor in interviews. More details on the steps and conventions used for the social network analysis presented in this chapter can be found in Chap. 1.

Table 6.4 Degree centrality scores of actors in the Southern Gas Corridor subsystem (top 5 scores)

Policy actor	*Degree centrality*	*Coalition that it belongs to*
BP	36	–
TAP consortium	29	TAP coalition
Nabucco consortium	29	Nabucco coalition
SOCAR	22	–
OMV	20	Nabucco coalition

Source: Author

Table 6.5 Betweenness centrality scores of actors in the Southern Gas Corridor subsystem (top 5 scores)

Policy actor	*Betweenness centrality*	*Coalition that it belongs to*
TAP consortium	877.269	TAP coalition
BP	566.361	–
Georgia, ministry of energy	491.360	–
Nabucco consortium	441.144	Nabucco coalition
OMV	307.733	Nabucco coalition

Source: Author

According to Table 6.5, TAP had the highest betweenness centrality score in the network (877.269), while Nabucco occupied a less strategic position in the network according to its betweenness centrality score (441.144). Its high betweenness centrality recommends TAP as the top broker in the policy subsystem. Given its high betweenness centrality, TAP was in a better position to access information, send information, and present policymakers with the frame adopted by the TAP advocacy coalition. This shows that, whilst entering the Southern Gas Corridor competition later, TAP consortium was very effective in building up connections in the policy subsystem and in placing itself in a position to diffuse a frame that would highlight the benefits of the TAP project for decision-makers in the European Commission.

Interview data also revealed that the TAP consortium played a very important role in bringing together its supporters and in diffusing information to all the parties interested in the Southern Gas Corridor, including representatives of the TAP governments and the European Commission:

> I would emphasize the significant role that the TAP consortium played in keeping informed all beneficiary countries, organizing round-tables, organizing, let's say, meetings and keeping always and every week beneficiary countries informed, and all other, let's say, beneficiaries and interest groups. (interview with former attaché at the Mission of the Republic of Albania to the EU 2014)

TAP consortium seemed to be very well connected to several ministries and high officials in the TAP countries. Below is a list of contacts:

Italy, Prime Minister's Office
Italy, Ministry of Foreign Affairs

Italy, Ministry of Energy
Italy, Ministry of Economic Development
Albania, Ministry of Foreign Affairs
Albania, Ministry of Energy
Greece, Prime Minister's Office
Greece, Ministry of Foreign Affairs
Greece, Ministry of Development
Greece, Ministry of Finance

TAP consortium worked with officials from the TAP governments in promoting TAP with European institutions and international partners. Government officials from the TAP transit countries were mobilized by the TAP consortium to support the TAP pipeline not only at a national level, but also to take a proactive attitude in advocating for the pipeline within the EU:

> I think the External Affairs Director and his team did an absolute stellar job convincing the governments of the host countries, Greece, Italy, and Albania that, if you do not put your full weight behind TAP, gas is not going to reach your markets. ... So I think they did an absolutely phenomenal job in this, in this regard, bringing the governments of the host countries on board and then, I think, to some extent exerting some sort of pressure on Brussels. (interview with industry consultant 2 2014)

A senior Italian official gave some insight into the advocacy work that the TAP countries conducted in relation to the European Commission:

> we made our position very clear that we want a level playing field with them [Nabucco], we stated that repeatedly, as it is our duty to do, as an important Member State of the European Union. Our Greek friends did exactly the same and in the end the European Commission took an equal stance .... But it is true, we had conversations, discussions, technical meetings with the European Commission which is quite normal. ... I participated in a number of meetings in Brussels, with representatives of the Commission together with members of my government so I do not deny that the work was intense, but it was always very correct and in the end we are satisfied with the outcome, which is what matters. (interview with senior Italian official 2014)

When Ministers of Foreign Affairs from the TAP countries attended the Council of the European Union they met with other Ministers and the EU

Commissioner for Energy and asked the Commission to remain neutral on the matter (interview with former attaché at the Mission of the Republic of Albania to the EU 2014).

The TAP consortium attributes its success to this broad reach in the policy subsystem that enabled it to influence opinions on the best option for opening the Corridor:

> I believe in part we were successful because we engaged not only with the Italian, the Albanian, the Greek governments, but we engaged with the Azeri government, with the US government. ... In terms of the policy debate, the information flows, we tried to contribute hugely to that, we targeted a whole range of actors, of key stakeholders. (interview with TAP source 2013)

In this way TAP supporters reached out not only to the European Commission, but also to other policy actors that were part of the subsystem and could advocate with the Commission on behalf of TAP. The TAP consortium seems to have placed more value upon building a wide social network among actors that might have a stake and a say in the Southern Gas Corridor than the Nabucco consortium did. Interview data revealed that representatives of the TAP consortium engaged in extensive travel in order to promote TAP (interview with TAP source 2013; interview with industry consultant 2 2014). A charismatic and engaged representative who establishes with ease connections with other policymakers can make a difference in a policy field in which policy contacts matter a lot:

> for me, for example, it is amazing to see how much actually depends on personal contacts. In a sense, you have certain procedures that you have to follow and certain communication channels that are established. For example, if you have the different working groups from the Council of the European Union, the different ministerial Councils, you have working groups that prepare those councils. But apart from that it really depends so much on the person who talks to people, who asks questions. Most meetings are just with people who know you, people like you, and, next time they get some information that they find interesting, they forward it to you. Maybe there is a network that is built. (interview with Austrian official 2014)

Some policy actors are aware of the networked structure of the policy world in which they are active. Hafner-Burton et al. claim that: ‘As agents, nodes comprehend the power that inheres in network structure, however, they may over time attempt to influence that structure' (2009, p. 573). Faul also argues that:

> there is more to networked power than structural position alone: it is also important to consider the ways in which policy actors may exercise agency in order to change their network and also to wield more influence over other actors and over the policy arena more broadly. (Faul 2013, p. 290)

Network members might alter their network ties in order to occupy a more influential position in the network and in this way they change the structure of the network (Faul 2013). They also alter their degree or betweenness centrality this way. The process is known in the literature as *rewiring* a network (Faul 2013, pp. 290–291).

The TAP consortium is an example of such an actor that sought in early 2013 to increase the degree and reach of its ties in the Brussels policymaking environment and ended up affecting policy outcomes on the Southern Gas Corridor. TAP consortium was aware that the existing social structure might favour Nabucco and engaged in a process of rewiring the social structure, of making it work to its advantage. In this regard, TAP even resorted to a specialized public affairs consultancy that played an important role in helping the consortium expand its policy contacts, especially in Brussels:

> so we were working for TAP, we mainly supported them in building their network, maintaining their network here. For them, it was really important especially in the beginning when the Commission was very supportive of Nabucco. They didn't know TAP so well. They really gained trust and got to know who TAP is. (interview with industry consultant 1 2013)

And:

> then, yes, starting in 2012 we had the role of following relevant policy developments in Brussels and then, yes, organizing their agenda and advising them on the best people to meet when they were coming for Brussels meetings. (interview with industry consultant 2 2014)

Nabucco and its supporters also offered presentations to policymakers based in Brussels: 'we had of course presentations, we had a lot of information rounds, the MEPs were very convinced of the Southern Gas Corridor pipeline and they were very much, I think, overall, in sympathy with it' (interview with Nabucco source 2014). However, overall, TAP seemed to have a more prominent presence internationally and in Brussels in 2012–2013. Nabucco was more established and seemed to be the favourite of the European Commission so its advocates felt less pressure to impress policymakers.

The Nabucco consortium had a lower betweenness centrality than the TAP consortium. Interview data also indicated that the consortium office in Vienna did not have a particularly intense exchange with key government officials working for the Nabucco member countries. Apparently, the communication between the Nabucco consortium and the Nabucco governments was rather difficult overall and contacts in the national governmental sector did not go as far as they did in the case of TAP with governments of countries this pipeline crossed:

> there was a total lack of information, misinformation on the consortium part, on the part of headquarters, they said one thing then the Shah Deniz said another. ... Just coordination, but it's important, many times you don't even know the other's position. I give you an example, the head of the Nabucco consortium was asking me for the email addresses of my Romanian and Bulgarian counterparts who have been in their positions for three years before me, he called me because he didn't have them. (interview with very senior Hungarian official 2014)

In addition, none of the countries that supported Nabucco emerged as a coalition leader that took initiative and ensured that coordination meetings were held without delays (interview with very senior Hungarian official 2014). Leadership also failed to come from the corporate segment of the coalition (interview with very senior Bulgarian official 2013). Diplomatic sources from the Nabucco countries confessed that they would have liked the Nabucco consortium to be more aggressive in pursuing its interests, but the consortium included many corporate actors and they were not always successful in harmonizing all their opinions (interview with former Hungarian diplomat based in the US 2014).

Formally, the Nabucco consortium and the signatories of the Nabucco Intergovernmental Agreement were in contact, as well as the Nabucco governments among themselves. In practice, those connections were not always used efficiently for communication and cooperation in the coalition. Leadership was missing in the Nabucco coalition and betweenness centrality scores show that the Nabucco consortium had a more limited reach in the policy subsystem than TAP. The role of leading broker that the TAP coalition's leader, the TAP consortium, played in the policy subsystem helps explain the success of this advocacy coalition.

Conclusion

This chapter looks at three types of factors (resources, frames, and structure) that can explain why the TAP coalition was successful in determining the European Commission to withdraw its support for Nabucco and embrace a position of neutrality regarding the pipeline chosen for the opening of the Southern Gas Corridor. When the European Commission took this position, the two projects became equals as regards political criteria and this enabled the decision made by Shah Deniz to be based on commercial criteria. This tilted the balance in favour of TAP. Commercially, TAP seemed to make a stronger case than Nabucco. The pipeline was cheaper to build and it provided a more attractive tariff for gas transport (interview with TAP source 2013). In addition, the companies involved in TAP were more willing to share the downstream benefits with the upstream companies developing Shah Deniz by offering a more attractive price for Shah Deniz gas (interview with senior European Commission official, DG Energy 2013; interview with representative of SOCAR 2014). The European Commission itself contributed in the end to the financial case for the TAP project by offering exemptions from EU law (interview with official in the EEAS 2 2013).

Based on the evidence presented in the chapter, we can conclude that TAP's advocacy success was the result of a successful framing process supported by the right resources and a favourable social structure (as revealed also by Fig. 6.3).

This study brings additional evidence for the argument that energy corporations have economic leverage; they decide on trade routes and pipelines, contract quantities of energy supplied, and so forth, and are often able to lobby governments successfully (as argued also by Jaffe et al. 2006). Resources also provide coalitions, of which companies are part, with an opportunity to transmit their message and vision of EU energy security to the European institutions through framing. Resources bring access.

In the case of the policy subsystem working on the Southern Gas Corridor, as was also the case with the policy subsystem working on fracking, a frame is successful when frame alignment takes place (be it through

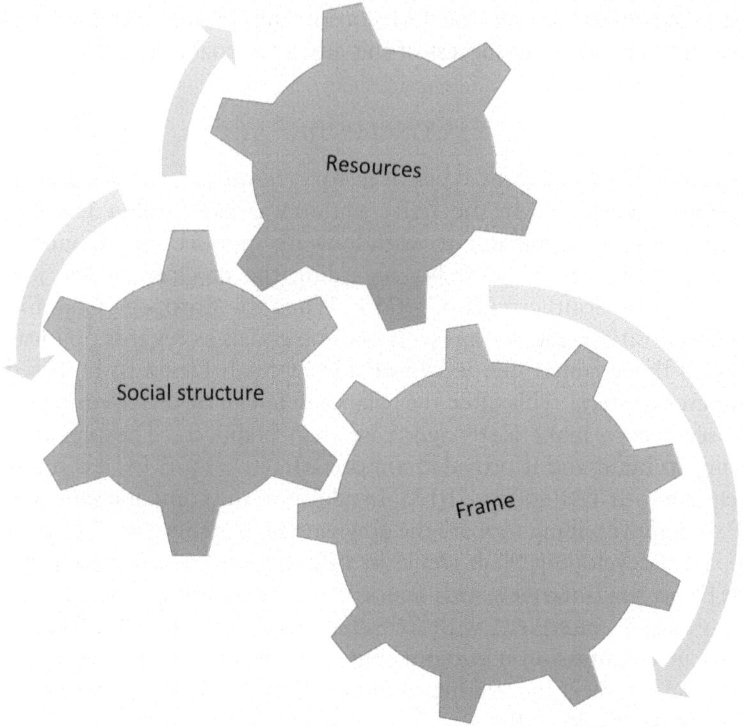

Fig. 6.3 Interplay between resources, frame, and structure in determining the success of the TAP coalition. (Note: the size of the figures reflects their relative contribution. Source: Author)

frame extension or frame amplification), when it takes properly into account the political and economic context, and it interacts successfully with the competitive frame advanced by the opposing advocacy coalition. The TAP coalition did not limit itself to reproducing the frame used by the Nabucco coalition, but also reinvigorated it. TAP claimed that it will improve the energy security situation not only in Greece but also in the countries of the Western Balkans, future EU Members (interview with energy executive 2013). In the discourse developed by TAP, the accent falls not only on secure supply, but also on gas pricing (interview with official in the EEAS 1 2013). The frame that the TAP coalition articulated was successful in convincing the European Commission, as the audience at which it targeted its frame, that both Nabucco and TAP have the same policy merits.

The debate around the Southern Gas Corridor also contributed to a redefinition of what EU energy security entails. The Commission had to accept that measures targeting EU energy security and EU energy independence in relation to Russia need to be supported by economic reasoning and private investors will not foot the bill for energy security if they do not make a return on their investment. As an official who followed closely the developments around the Southern Gas Corridor stated:

> that whole project shows that politics on its own is not enough. You either find the right time to team up with the market players and you have the companies behind you, then you can push politically, but if politics goes on its own, it won't be able to get such a large project up and running. You need the market and the companies behind it. (interview with very senior Hungarian official 2014)

The European Commission and the public sector can influence outcomes in the energy security field only to a certain degree. The European Commission can set general policy guidelines and regulate the activity of energy companies, but at the end of the day companies have the final word on what they invest in. Companies are interested in obliging and generating public goods, but not if this might mean losing money, no matter how often they mention EU energy security in their public declarations and on their websites.

Developments around the Southern Gas Corridor show that excessive politicization or securitization of a project with deep economic implications does not always produce the desired policy effects. In the end, the Commission abandoned the idea of building a pipeline first and foremost for political reasons. As one interviewee points out: 'They switched. At the beginning it was also clear that they wanted this pipeline for political reasons, to enable the independence of these countries [Central and Eastern European countries]' (interview with Nabucco source 2014). By 2013, energy security became, even in the eyes of the Commission, less about the security of supply defined as independence from Russian gas and more about accessing gas at affordable prices and through smaller pipeline

Fig. 6.4 Changes in the EU Commission's understanding of what EU energy security entails. (Source: Author)

systems, interconnectors, rather than through large pipeline projects.[6] The Commission did not change its point of view in isolation, but through interaction with advocacy coalitions (such as the one behind TAP) in the context of the global financial and economic crisis.

As Fig. 6.4 shows, under the impact of the global financial and economic crisis the interest in security of supply diminished and the price element became increasingly important. Gas consumption was reduced in Europe during the recession and the shale gas revolution in the US reduced the US demand for coal and made a lot of coal available for the European market, coal that could substitute gas. With enough liquidity, enough gas on the market, accessing gas supplies at high commercial costs was not a priority.

This chapter also shows that structural factors account for differences in advocacy success. The TAP consortium occupied a central position in the policy subsystem working on the Southern Gas Corridor. Its high betweenness centrality indicates that, through the reach that it had in the broader policy subsystem, the consortium was placed in a good position to mediate information exchanges and shape the understanding that the EU policy environment had on TAP's benefits. The TAP consortium was very

[6] The Commission published a list of projects of common interest on 18 October 2013. Grants were made available even for interconnectors targeting only two EU countries as long as they contribute to the integration of the networks in these countries. As the Southern Gas Corridor was identified as one of the priority corridors in terms of diversification of supply, many of these projects are situated along the Corridor.

active in building connections with key members of the TAP coalition and the broader policy subsystem. A Brussels-based consultancy also contributed to enhancing the reach of the TAP consortium in the policy subsystem and especially with the European Commission. The Nabucco consortium displayed a lower betweenness centrality than the TAP consortium and implicitly a lower ability to disseminate information, project its frame, and collect information from the policy subsystem.

If in the fracking for shale gas case study the denser coalition was also the most successful coalition, this was not the case here. Nabucco was a denser coalition or at least its members reported more connections among themselves. On the other hand, judging connectedness based on coalition diameter, TAP seemed to be in a better position than Nabucco. These mixed results do not allow me to draw a conclusion on the relation between coalition connectedness and coalition success in the case of the Southern Gas Corridor.

The next chapter will draw a few conclusions regarding the implications of the findings in this book for EU energy policy and policy networks literature, will discuss the methodological and policy implications of its findings, and will indicate a few research avenues to complement the research conducted here.

CHAPTER 7

Further Discussion and Conclusions

This chapter focuses in its first and second sections on the contribution that the book makes to the scholarship on EU energy policy, policy networks, particularly advocacy coalitions, and governance. This book looked at opposing advocacy coalitions emerging around regulating fracking for shale gas in the EU and the development of the Southern Gas Corridor. It showed that advocacy coalitions can reshape EU energy policy outcomes. Policy networks are credited as important actors in international governance and energy governance is no exception. The third section of this chapter discusses the methodological innovations that this research brings to the study of policy networks and EU energy policy. The fourth section builds on the substantial findings of this study to make several policy recommendations, especially to European institutions. The final section acknowledges the limitations of this study and uses them as a springboard to discuss avenues that future research on EU energy policy and policy networks might embrace.

Contribution to EU Energy Policy Literature

Empirically, this study has generated new data through fieldwork and interviewing on the expanding field of EU energy policy which remains understudied. Unlike other studies on EU energy policy, this study does not attempt to explain developments in this field by focusing only on the work of European institutions and EU governments (for instance, such

A.-M. Bocse, *International Networks, Advocacy and EU Energy Policy-Making*, Palgrave Studies in European Union Politics,
https://doi.org/10.1007/978-3-030-49505-3_7

studies are the ones of Buchan 2010; Maltby 2013). Maltby, for instance, acknowledged that his focus on the European Commission's work in explaining EU energy policy development is a research limitation and that: 'further work is needed to investigate the constellation of shifting power and authority within this multi-level governance policy sphere, in which supranational institutions, national energy champions and private energy companies all play a role in steering the development of EU energy policy' (Maltby 2013, p. 442). This research also avoids excessively focusing on Russia or EU-Russia relations in the study of EU energy policy (a focus that is not always justified by the wide range of developments in EU energy policy that do not include Russia and often pass unnoticed) to include other actors that have a stake in EU energy policy and particularly energy security policy: energy companies (state-owned or private), NGOs, consultancies, and governmental actors situated outside the EU, for instance in North America or in the Caspian region.

This choice was determined in great part by the policymaking reality I encountered in Brussels through extensive fieldwork. The fieldwork revealed that policy outcomes in EU energy policy and particularly energy security policy are a product of the interaction between European institutions, governments, and the private sector. The research confirmed that assumptions in the governance literature such as 'policy choices are shaped and refined in bargaining between a diverse range of actors, including some who are non-governmental, all of whom have an interest in what policy is chosen' (Peterson 2010, pp. 107–108) apply to the EU energy policymaking environment.

In answering the first research question: *What shape does public-private interaction take in the field of EU energy policy?* by looking at the issue areas of fracking for shale gas and the Southern Gas Corridor, I found that this interaction can take the shape of complex subsystems inclusive of advocacy coalitions. They display a networked form of organization and engage in extensive (predominantly informational) resource exchanges with European institutions. These coalitions are embedded in the broader Brussels energy policymaking environment and some actors are part of two coalitions by working both on fracking for shale gas and on the Southern Gas Corridor.

This research showed that the pro-fracking and TAP coalitions were successful in projecting their preferences at the level of the European Parliament and the European Commission, respectively, and as a result they influenced policy outcomes. The framing process that the coalitions presented in this study engaged in impacted understandings of EU energy security, including that of European institutions. In early 2010s, the EU understanding of EU energy security and the means to achieve it changed. Coalitions working on fracking and the Southern Gas Corridor contributed to changing the discursive focus from energy security as security of supply to energy security as access to cheap energy so that the competitiveness of the European economy could be maintained in the aftermath of the 2008 global financial and economic crisis.

For instance, the TAP supporters argued that a gas pipeline's commercial merits come before political priorities in the context of the global crisis and, as Chap. 6 shows, by 2013 the European Commission seemed to adopt this point of view. The global financial and economic crisis that began in 2008 had a great influence on EU energy policy debates after 2010. The cheap gas that entered the US energy market as a result of the US shale gas revolution made the energy-intensive American industry more competitive. This study agrees with the existing literature on EU energy policy according to which external factors and crises play an important role in EU energy policy developments (Buchan 2010), but argues that this depends on the degree to which policy actors make reference to them and highlight their consequences for the EU policy. The members of the pro-fracking and TAP coalitions often mentioned the economic crisis in an attempt to build a stronger argument for their advocacy case.

This research shows that developments around large energy transport infrastructure projects such as the Southern Gas Corridor, even if they have an important geopolitical stake, cannot be explained only by looking at EU preferences, state preferences, or geopolitics. Developing large infrastructure projects such as the Southern Gas Corridor is dependent on a symbiosis between public and private actors. Economic considerations influence policy outcomes when it comes to energy policy. As one policy actor involved in developments around the Southern Gas Corridor indicated: 'at the end of the day I think it's the commercial case and relationship that is going to make a project see the light of day' (interview with industry consultant 2 2014). An advocacy coalition approach helps explain policy outcomes in complex multi-level subsystems involving a wide variety of public and private actors situated at both the national and supranational levels and this renders it very suitable for looking at energy and energy security policy.

As discussed in Chap. 1, the ACF can shed light on policy initiatives in different areas (in different policy subsystems), as well as their interdependencies and potential causal relations (Sabatier 1998; Rozbicka 2013). Feindt shows, for instance, how changes in the EU Common Agricultural Policy between 1970 and 2000 were connected to deeper EU integration in the field of environmental policy (Feindt 2010). My case studies reveal interdependencies between EU energy policy and EU security and foreign policy. The Southern Gas Corridor study highlights the clash between the EU Member States that make up the two advocacy coalitions. The competition between TAP and Nabucco created an additional divide among EU Member States, who have in the past often failed to align their foreign and energy policy objectives, especially in relation to Russia.

At the same time, the Southern Gas Corridor presented the European Commission with the opportunity to interact on behalf of EU countries with the countries of the Southern Caucasus and in this way engage in its most consistent acts of energy diplomacy so far. The Southern Gas Corridor entails not only building gas pipelines to support commercial relations, but also establishing political and diplomatic relations with various suppliers. It has broader political and security implications for the EU, as well as for the Southern Caucasus. Debates around fracking at the EU level triggered close cooperation and exchanges with the American and Canadian governments, as well as with regulators in these countries. Be it to secure gas or valuable regulatory expertise, European policymakers engaged in a dialogue with international partners to enhance EU energy security.

In addition to non-state actors, this study explores the role of another neglected actor in European energy scholarship, the European Parliament. Kohler-Koch predicted a shift in the EP towards a US Congress type of legislature, given changes in the function of the Parliament and its interaction with interest groups (Kohler-Koch 1997). This research showed that the European Parliament is increasingly perceived as an important player in debates on controversial topics that can attract public opposition, such as fracking. The European Parliament's opinion on fracking for shale gas in the EU was considered key in framing the debate on fracking in Europe. This and other studies found that the European Parliament was at the very centre of the fracking for shale gas debate and policymaking (for instance, Wyciszkiewicz 2013 is calling the European Parliament the 'shale gas battleground').

The literature on governance claims that: 'policy networks can narrow options and shift the agenda' (Peterson 2010, pp. 107–108). The advocacy coalitions targeting the European Parliament, especially the pro-fracking coalition through its input in the European Parliament resolution, narrowed the policy options that the European Commission had in later stages of the policymaking process. The findings of this research question claims in previous studies according to which the European Commission is more interested than the Parliament in interacting with companies and business associations in order to receive expert knowledge (Bouwen 2002, p. 380, 2004b, p. 345; Dür and Mateo 2012, p. 969). This study shows that advocacy coalitions supply technical information that is valued by officials and civil servants in the Parliament. The Parliament has less in-house expertise on energy and energy security than the European Commission (Maltby 2013). This makes the European Parliament even more dependent on external technical expertise than the European Commission. At least this seems to be the case with policymaking concerning technical fields such as environment and energy and with cases in which the European Parliament is the first EU institution to take a position on an issue, as it was the case with fracking.

This research also shows that EU energy security policy is characterized by a considerable degree of informality. The European Parliament consulted advocacy coalitions on fracking despite the absence of formal provisions in this regard as MEPs, MEP advisers, and European Parliament staffers acknowledge their limited technical knowledge of fracking and the need to learn more about this field from specialized NGOs and companies directly involved in shale gas exploration and exploitation. Advocacy coalitions were also consulted on the Southern Gas Corridor by the European Commission, as they could provide insight into the technical, financial, and political implications of large energy transport infrastructure projects. Furthermore, the study also argued that the EU indirectly impacts on the energy mix of its Member States although the mix falls outside its formal competences. In the EU integration history, EU action on a certain issue has often preceded the formalization of the EU mandate through treaties in that area. As an emerging area of European integration, the field of EU energy security seems to be no exception. This study shows that informal practices complement formal arrangements and offer a more important role in policymaking to non-state actors (that form advocacy coalitions) and to the European Parliament. Advocacy coalitions take advantage of the informality of this field in order to shape policy.

Based on the arguments advanced in this section of the chapter, it can be concluded that the range of actors that have an impact on EU energy policy and EU energy security policy is broad. Non-state actors play an important role as part of broad advocacy coalitions, although they benefit from little attention, especially in the studies that analyse EU energy policy developments from an International Relations or European Studies angle. In addition, my study complements the limited number of studies analysing these actors in interaction (Kreutler 2014; Bomberg 2017), as part of networked social structures that limit or enable their work. The implications of these findings for future policy and research are discussed in the last two sections of this chapter. Now I move to discussing the implications of my findings for the advocacy coalition literature.

Contribution to the Advocacy Coalition and Governance Literatures

Beyond its implications for the literature on EU energy policy, this research aims to address the literature on advocacy coalitions as specific types of policy networks and the one on governance. In previous chapters, I discussed in detail the factors that contribute to the success of an advocacy coalition. The influence of interest groups has been only marginally covered by the advocacy literature, mainly because it is considered very difficult to assess their impact (see Mahoney 2008; Dür 2008).[1] This research attempts to remedy this by studying coalition impact and by advancing and testing hypotheses with the aim of developing a theoretical model that can help us understand what factors determine the success of an advocacy coalition, as well as the way in which these factors interact in enabling the coalition to succeed. In developing this theoretical model, the research draws on an original combination of policy networks/advocacy coalitions' literature, studies of framing, and on social network theory. The existing literature on advocacy coalitions, in general, and coalitions operating in the EU context, in particular, often fails to capture interactions between opposing advocacy coalitions and the effects they might have on their opposition (for instance, the work of Mahoney 2008; Kreutler 2014). Particularly as regards controversial topics, often advocacy coalitions will emerge in opposition to other coalitions. The table below presents in a comparative way the factors that contributed to the success of the

[1] An important part of the literature on advocacy and lobbying has focused on coalition-formation, campaign organization, and strategies or advocacy access (Mahoney 2008, p. 183).

pro-fracking and TAP coalitions presented in Chaps. 3, 4, 5, and 6 in the attempt to answer my second research question: *What explains the success of advocacy coalitions operating in the field of EU energy policy?*

The findings presented in Table 7.1 show that possession of resources, a broad, timely, and dynamic frame, and structural factors, as well as the way in which all these interact, contribute to the success of an advocacy coalition. The in-depth investigation of the cases allowed to process-trace the factors behind the success of the coalitions studied. It allowed to determine that the wording of the European Parliament resolution was impacted by advocacy activity. It also allowed to control for other factors that might have influenced it, but did not emerge as relevant during the actual extensive fieldwork. Such factors could have included: the intervention of Member States fearing that the resolution will limit their prerogatives in the energy field, public opinion, or media in the Member States or the Members of the European Parliament (MEPs) interacting with industry and NGOs at the national rather than the EU, supranational level. Similarly, extensive data collection supporting process tracing indicated that the switch in the position of the European Commission from one of support for Nabucco to one of neutrality regarding what pipeline project is chosen by Shah Deniz was generated by the effective TAP advocacy. This advocacy brought Nabucco and TAP on a par as far as the political criteria set by Shah Deniz are concerned. However, it cannot be denied that in the end the final decision was taken by Shah Deniz also taking into consideration the commercial criteria and Nabucco was not helped by its larger costs and uncertainty regarding the availability of large enough volumes of gas needing transportation infrastructure.

My findings testify to the fact that new governance conditions fragmented decision-making and increased interdependence between government and non-state actors (Rhodes 1997; Bache 2008; Eikeland 2011). Resource (informational, financial, political, etc.) interdependence is often used to explain: 'why governmental and non-governmental organizations are bound together in networks' (Eikeland 2011). Information is the most important resource that energy policy actors exchange in the cases studied by this research. Advocacy coalitions gain access to European institutions given the high technical expertise of their members in energy exploration, exploitation, and transport and the environmental implications of these processes. The coalitions that emerged around TAP and Nabucco provided the European Commission with information on the technological and economic aspects of pipeline development, as well as energy

Table 7.1 Factors that contributed to the success of a coalition

Name of the coalition	*Factors*							
	Resources		*Frame*				*Structural factors*	
	Information/technical expertise	*Financial resources*	*Developed a broad frame*	*Reinvigorated successfully an old frame*	*Effectively integrated exogenous factors in the frame*	*Engaged in a dialogue with the frame of the opposing coalition*	*Coalition connectedness*	*Included actors central to the subsystem*
Pro-fracking coalition	Yes	Yes	Broader than the opposing coalition	–	Yes	Yes	Slightly denser than the opposing coalition	Yes (more than the opposing coalition)
Anti-fracking coalition	Yes	Not much	Narrower than the opposing coalition	–	Less effectively than the opposing coalition	Yes	Slightly less dense than the opposing coalition	Yes (less than the opposing coalition)
TAP coalition	Yes	Yes	Broader than the opposing coalition	Yes	Yes	Yes	–	Yes (better connected than the opposing coalition)
Nabucco coalition	Yes	Yes	Narrower than the opposing coalition	No, made a limited attempt in this regard	Less effectively than the opposing coalition	Yes	–	Yes (less connected than the opposing coalition)

Source: Author

preferences of various EU Member States and the impact of certain EU energy infrastructure projects on the economic development of EU Members.

This book shows that information supply often works as an access tool that enables the successful conduct of advocacy work. European institutions are mostly at the receiving end, but they can also communicate information on political preferences or procedures. This information can be used by a coalition to secure the support of MEPs for fracking or to develop a pipeline project by benefiting from the EU's political support and exemptions from EU rules. This dialogue seems to be at the very core of advocacy/lobbying processes taking place in the EU and forms part of the political response to advocacy and lobbying.

This study also shows that possessing financial resources might shape the amount of informational resources that one has and how certain actors use their informational resources. The financial resources that energy companies possess enable them to employ more people (in-house experts or specialized consultancies) to engage in advocacy or to compile information and conduct research that will support the advocacy work. The same resources enable them to organize events (or hire consultancies to organize events) that facilitate their interaction with policymakers. This is particularly important because, similarly to other studies (Rogers and Beal 2008, p. 159), this research found that personal contact is important in the decision-making process.

Personal contact is more likely to make a difference particularly on topics that are highly controversial, such as fracking, or that generate opposition among EU Member States, such as the Southern Gas Corridor. It supports persuasion. As argued in the literature: 'personal contact may have greater effectiveness in the face of resistance or apathy on the part of the communicatee' (Rogers and Beal 2008, pp. 159–160).

Possessing informational and material resources might increase a coalition's access to European institutions, but it still has to develop a persuasive argument to gain institutional support. Chapters 4 and 6 show that the most successful coalitions were those that developed a broad/reinvigorated frame that responded effectively to the economic concerns raised by the global financial and economic crisis and that dealt effectively with issues raised by the opposing coalition. In discussing framing processes, this research sheds light on how interest groups gather information (particularly of a scientific nature), make sense of it, and transmit it to policymakers. Systematic studies on information processing are missing, although the importance of information in the EU policymaking process has been widely acknowledged in the literature (Chalmers 2012). Both the advocacy coalition and the epistemic community approach indicate that: 'the information is thus neither guesses nor "raw" data; it is the product of human interpretations of social and physical phenomena' (Haas 1992a, p. 4). For instance, the two coalitions working on fracking developed opposing frames starting from the same empirical reality by choosing to integrate in their frame scientific data that supported their argument and to neglect other scientific evidence.

In explaining the success of certain advocacy coalitions, this research embraces an original approach by drawing on social network theory and social network analysis. The research responds to a need highlighted in the literature on international networks to expand the scholarship that seeks to investigate the connection between the network function and the network structure (Maoz 2012). I used SNA to investigate the structure of the coalitions studied. SNA was employed to calculate coalition metrics (density, geodesic distance) and subsystem/coalition member metrics (degree centrality, betweenness centrality). The research shows that the inclusion in the coalition of actors well connected in the policy subsystem can help explain the coalition's success against opposition.

The study responds to the calls in social sciences and humanities literature to move beyond identity-based explanations of social action and embrace explanations drawing on: 'commonality, connectedness, and groupness' (Brubaker and Cooper 2000, p. 20). The agent's social capital depends on: 'the size of the network connections he can effectively mobilize and on the volume of the capital (economic, cultural or symbolic) possessed in his own right by each of those to whom he is connected' (Bourdieu 1986, p. 249). My research found that certain policy subsystem actors emerged as subsystem brokers. This provided them with greater access to resources held by other actors in their coalition (material and informational resources) or in the subsystem (information that the European institutions could provide).

This study also offers insight into the process through which the connections (ties) in a policy subsystem can be established and through which brokers might emerge. In the Southern Gas Corridor subsystem, for instance, the TAP consortium resorted to a specialist consultancy to help them establish additional contacts in Brussels-based policymaking circles and particularly with the European Commission. TAP was aware of the advantages that contacts with key policymakers, placed at the very centre of the policy subsystem, can bring them. Such tie formation processes altered the structure of the policy subsystem and brought TAP towards its centre. As argued by previous studies: 'strategic tie management may also enable the *repositioning* of a node within the network, thus changing the network structure through agency' (Faul 2013, p. 286). Whilst they depend on structure, policy actors are not the prisoners of structure. They can affect structure in order to move towards the centre of a particular policy subsystem and reap the policy benefits of such a move.

The presence of brokers in coalitions and in the subsystem challenges the assumption that international governance through networks relies on non-hierarchical social structures. This study showed that the relational power that brokers concentrate is higher than that of other actors in the policy subsystem. They can exercise control over the flow of resources (including informational resources) bound for other actors and can contribute to shaping their preferences. This is in contradiction to the claim that policy networks are horizontal structures (Peterson 2010). Keck and Sikkink stated that networks are: '(in)voluntary, reciprocal, and horizontal patterns of communication and exchange' (1998, p. 8). Others claim that the concept of 'governance' implies the horizontal dispersion of authority among a broad number of actors (Hix 1998; Eising and Kohler-Koch 1999; Krahmann 2003a). A governance approach assumes a flat, non-hierarchical, and inclusive policymaking system in which actors have equal chances of reaching policymakers. Evolution in the field of social media and communication technology is supposed to make this possible (Keck and Sikkink 1998). However, as this research showed, key advocacy communication often takes place in person.

This study confirms claims advanced in the literature according to which, at the European level: 'the business lobby is better resourced and better connected to key decision-makers' (Burns and Carter 2012, p. 516). Similar claims are made by official publications released by the European institutions, for example, the European Parliament study on lobbying EU institutions (Library of the European Parliament 2013). This is not surprising given that financial resources can be used to build ties and improve one's standing in broader social networks. But the empirical investigation also shows that organizations such as Friends of the Earth Europe and Food and Water Europe are as well connected as large oil and gas companies in the policy subsystem working on fracking for shale gas. Networking skills can compensate for the lack of material resources. Having discussed the contribution to the literature on advocacy coalitions and governance through networks, I now briefly highlight the methodological contribution of this study.

Contribution to Methodology

This research draws upon a large set of interviews with policy elites working on fracking and the Southern Gas Corridor, as well as on participant observation. Through its choice of data collection and analysis methods, the research design embraced brings to the forefront the voices of contemporary energy and energy security policy actors in order to capture their formal and informal policymaking and networking practices. This provides the study with an insider, detailed perspective on coalition development, dynamics, and strategies. This research examines policy networks that work on topics central to the EU and global energy policy debates, networks with a European focus but a global membership.

To capture the connection between social structures and meaning, this research employs an original combination of social network analysis and frame analysis. It acknowledges that informational and material resources, as well as the positions occupied in the social structure, do not in themselves explain policy outcomes. Developing persuasive frames that do not necessarily mirror the material interests of certain policy actors can be equally effective as they generate credibility for their developers. A frame's ability to make an impact depends, however, to a significant degree on the position that actors promoting it occupy in the policy subsystem. This explains why certain frames are more successful than others and why frames articulated by NGOs might never become dominant in energy policy subsystems in which the industry occupies a central position.

The study also contributes methodologically, by employing SNA, to an area of security that has been less investigated through this method. SNA has been applied so far to empirical case studies involving particularly terrorism and transnational crime networks (Baker and Faulkner 1993; Krebs 2002; Kenney 2009; Kahler 2009b) or the development of network-centric warfare (Dekker 2002). SNA is used by Mérand et al. 2011 to map the complex interaction characterizing the European Common Security and Defence Policy (CSDP) (Mérand et al. 2011). My study shows that SNA can be a valuable tool with which to investigate the interaction between government and non-state actors aiming to provide security in areas such as energy and the environment.

The original application of this methodological tool to the study of energy policy advocacy coalitions made possible the study of policy interactions, the resulting subsystems and coalition structures, and the relative positions of actors in those structures. The research innovatively combines group metrics (for instance, coalition density) and individual actors' metrics (for instance, betweenness centrality) to determine the structural factors that might shape the success of an advocacy coalition. Such a methodological approach can be replicated in other studies. In addition, unlike other studies that run SNA on secondary data (Hafner-Burton and Montgomery 2009), SNA is applied here to an original data set collected through extensive fieldwork.

Through the methodology that I adopted, this study aims to ground empirically the network metaphor that in recent years has occupied a central place in the process of theorizing about contemporary society and politics (Castells 1996). The 'network society' (Castells 1996) is a concept that has benefited from a lot of interest from both academia and the media, but it still has to prove its empirical grounding. The data collected here, in depth and in a systematic manner, on coalitions opposing each other on the issue of fracking and the Southern Gas Corridor captures a section of this 'network society'. SNA performed with specialized software can be very helpful in generating sociograms mapping the 'network society'. The network metaphor is used in many studies, but the reader rarely gets the opportunity to see what the network looks like, who its members are, and how they connect. Software packages such as NodeXL can help study and present complex networks, but they are rarely used. The sociograms in most literature remain very basic. My research draws upon cutting-edge research software to make the study of complex social structures more manageable and provides a model that can be used in future studies.

In particular, the study provides a solid methodology for studying opposing coalitions that interact with each other. Most of the studies on policy networks examine, perform SNA, and generate sociograms on a single policy network (examples include the studies conducted by Kenney et al. 2012; Faul 2013). In addition, by simultaneously studying the two policy subsystems working on fracking and the Southern Gas Corridor, I found that they share common actors: the US Mission to the EU, consultancies, and so forth. Such findings provide empirical evidence of the networked nature of contemporary politics and society.

In recreating the structure of policy subsystems and advocacy coalitions, this research innovatively combines SNA and participants' descriptions of policy subsystems and advocacy coalitions provided in interviews. Interviews enabled me to track the process through which certain actors ended up occupying a particular position in the policy subsystem, revealed by SNA. The final position was often the result of the deliberate strategy and agency of other coalition members. For instance, in the case of fracking for shale gas, the pro-fracking oil and gas companies adopted a frame broad enough to bring in their coalition the chemical industry. In this way, this research responds to recent calls in the literature to embark on: 'the simultaneous examination of agency and structure of networks of global governance' (Faul 2013, p. 291).

This section discussed the methodological innovations that this study introduces: combining a network analysis approach with a frame analysis approach in the exploration of networks' advocacy strategies; looking also at group SNA metrics rather than only at individual actor SNA metrics; and studying advocacy coalitions in interaction especially when they are in opposition. In a nutshell, this research used innovative combinations of data collection and analysis tools to study the presence and influence of advocacy coalitions and to understand how influence is brokered. The next section of this chapter discusses the policy lessons that might be drawn from the findings presented in this book.

Policy Recommendations

Several recent events seem to indicate that energy will continue to occupy an important place on the EU agenda. They include the tense relations between the EU and Russia in the context of the Russian annexation of Crimea in 2014, the EU sanctions that followed, and the climate commitments made by the EU at the Paris summit in December 2015 triggering a firmer commitment to greening the energy system. In such a context, the findings presented here are not only academically valuable, but also relevant for policy making.

The advocacy coalitions analysed in this study are international structures relevant for regional and international governance. One of the challenges that policymakers are confronted with is to properly integrate the non-state sector in the regional and global energy governance system and to make sure that material resources are not the only factor that determines whose voice gets heard. This research shows that, when it comes to energy policy, corporate actors (given their resources, framing capabilities, and position in social structures) are often better equipped to influence policy outcomes than NGOs. European institutions might consider creating some mechanisms through which the energy policymaking space becomes more inclusive. Particularly high-level European officials are less accessible to environmental NGOs. Interviewed sources reported that a company such as Gazprom would meet with the Energy Commissioner as often as three times a year (interview with public affairs consultant working for Gazprom 2013), while leading European environmental NGOs would not secure a single meeting during a year at the Commissioner Cabinet level (interview with policy officer at Food and Water Europe 2013; interview with policy officer at Friends of the Earth Europe 2013).

EU institutions can only benefit in their policymaking work from a wider variety of perspectives and varied expertise. A way of reaching this goal is to provide EU grants for NGOs and civil society groups that would enable them to conduct campaigns and to improve their skills in communicating to an institutional audience. The EU has a few such programmes in place. Another option would be to engineer the structure of policy subsystems and advocacy coalitions. European institutions could take the initiative to build ties with actors that are peripheral to the policy subsystem. In this regard, the EU institutions would contribute to a more energy-just world defined 'as one that is fair in how it treats people and communities in energy decision-making' (Sovacool and Dworkin 2014, p. 5). Two important pillars of procedural justice applicable to the field of energy are 'access to information, access to and meaningful participation in decision-making' (Walker and Day 2012, p. 72), stress Walker and Day in their work focusing on fuel poverty. Previous literature also found that principles of procedural justice (identified by Gross 2007 particularly as 'appropriate participation, the ability of voice to be heard, adequate information, being treated with respect, and unbiased decision-making', p. 2736) can increase the local acceptance of controversial energy projects and infrastructure.

Peripheral actors themselves might seek to engage in rewiring processes in order to ensure that they occupy a more central position in the subsystem and have more opportunity to influence policy. There is emerging literature that suggests that, after becoming aware of the geography of the social structure they are part of, actors can alter it and better position themselves (Kilduff and Krackhardt 2008; Hafner-Burton et al. 2009; Faul 2013). Participants in policymaking have an idea of the social structure underpinning it based on their daily experience, but a systematic study such as this might offer a more comprehensive image of the architecture of a policy subsystem.

In the case of the Southern Gas Corridor, better coordination among the Nabucco consortium and governments that were part of the Nabucco Intergovernmental Agreement could have led to other policy outcomes. Relations among Central and Eastern European states that supported Nabucco are historically marked by border disputes and regional rivalry and these countries need to learn to work effectively together and push for common goals especially when such goals bring them in opposition to older and larger EU Member States, such as Italy. The Central and Eastern European Members, their governmental representatives, as well as MEPs coming from here, do not have a lot of experience with lobbying EU institutions and building effective advocacy connections (interview with European Affairs consultant 2014).

Currently, EU energy security policy as regards key energy infrastructure projects has limited effectiveness given the limited role that the Commission plays in policy implementation and infrastructure financing. It is expected that these projects will be financed by private sources. Return on investment is a priority for private investors in gas pipelines and drilling projects, while energy security is a priority for the EU Commission and EU governments. The EU Commission needs to find new ways to incentivize investment in the projects it considers strategic. Having formulated a series of recommendations mainly for European institutions, but also for other actors involved in energy security policy, I now discuss the limitations of my research and potential future research directions for the field of EU energy policy and international policy networks.

Research Limitations and Additional Research Avenues

This section of the chapter acknowledges the limitations of this research and makes recommendations for future research at the methodological and substantive levels. Such recommendations are meant to address the limitations of this study and to contribute to the development of the scholarship on European energy policy and on policy networks.

A challenge and limitation of any research that is reliant on interviews is that subjects might forget or willingly not mention who they interacted with in policymaking. In the case of this study, such errors were reduced by triangulating among the large number of interviews I conducted, with data obtained through fieldwork observation, and with data in publicly available written sources.

Another potential limitation of the research is that its findings can be generalized only to a certain degree. The findings on coalitions advocating the EU are embedded in the specificity of this polity. In addition, whilst networks display similar structural characteristics which might indicate that similar social processes take place within them, each network is ultimately unique in its structure. That said, this research looks in great depth at two cases, each encompassing two opposing coalitions. Looking at more than one case enabled me to capture certain patterns of public-private interaction and factors that influence the advocacy coalition success that are more likely to be valid across cases. The level of detail offered on the two cases also meets the requirements of 'transferability' that some authors recommend as a replacement for 'generalizability'. Transferability is based on: 'the ability of the researcher to provide sufficient rich detail that a reader can assess the extent to which the conclusions drawn in one setting can transfer to another' (King and Horrocks 2010, p. 161).

As mentioned, the sociograms included in this work capture a network at a certain point in time. Most social network analysis 'examines a single network at a time' (Faust and Skvoretz 2008, p. 191), despite the fact that networks are fluid social structures. Changes in the structure of the fracking for shale gas subsystem most likely occurred since my data was collected. Collecting data on the structure of the subsystem during a new advocacy campaign and in this way conducting a longitudinal case study will enable the dynamic study of network transformations and can constitute the object of future research. That said, this research looks at ties between network members that were maintained over several months of advocacy campaigning and were reported as such during the interviews. This research has the advantage of assessing stable patterns of interaction that are more relevant to understanding social interaction (Wasserman and Faust 1994, p. 57) than, for instance, studies of networks capturing the interaction at a singular policy event.

This study has focused mainly on information exchanges that take place in advocacy coalitions and between advocacy coalitions and the targets of their advocacy. Exchanges involving financial resources and staff were not central to the work of the coalitions studied here. As financial exchanges would be illegal between MEPs and EU officials, on the one hand, and interest groups, on the other, it is hard to ascertain if indeed they took place. Such studies are beyond the means of an academic researcher. That said, research projects developed in partnership with law enforcement bodies might indeed provide additional insight into the circulation of resources in policy subsystems. Such partnerships could also provide further information on the degree to which energy extraction companies that might lose their gas market share in the case of a shale gas revolution in Europe (such as Gazprom) have financially supported the anti-fracking movement in Europe. Other actors that were not explored by the book are the media. Although certain advocacy coalitions' members[2] had an interest in making sure Brussels-based media and public opinion is on their side, media played a limited role in the actual advocacy campaigns; at least, the extensive exploration of advocacy coalitions through fieldwork did not indicate that media actors played a key, central role.

This research contributes through the case study on fracking for shale gas to the literature that discusses the increasing role of the European Parliament in European policymaking. However, this research is limited to the field of energy policy. The recent increase in the number of energy interest groups, public affairs and lobbying firms specializing in energy, and energy consultancies in Brussels seems to indicate that the Brussels advocacy and lobbying sector is moving closer to the American model.

Additional research is needed on the concept of 'energy security' and its significance in relation to Europe. This research has attempted to define energy security from the EU perspective and to capture the alterations that this concept has undergone in the context of the financial and economic crisis. I argue that the perception of European institutions on what energy security entails has changed in interaction with advocacy coalitions as a result of information and frame exchange processes taking place at the level of policy subsystems.

In 2012–2013 energy pricing was an important dimension of EU energy security. The European Commission seemed to agree that the 'strategic' merits of a pipeline project cannot compensate for a pipeline not fulfilling commercial criteria to the degree its competition does. The annexation of Crimea by Russia in 2014 and the EU sanctions that followed indicate a reconfiguration of relations between the EU and its main

[2] For example, in 2010 TAP employed a Brussels-based consultancy to handle their communication with Brussels-based media (interview with industry consultant 1 2013; interview with industry consultant 2 2014).

gas supplier, Russia. It would be worth studying what kind of impact this change has had on the way in which the EU is configuring its energy security priorities. Most likely, the findings will show that the EU is prioritizing again 'strategic' choices over infrastructure investment that makes the most commercial sense. The fact that on 19 January 2016 the Commission dedicated 179 million euro (out of 207 million euro available for 15 key gas interconnectors) to an interconnector that will contribute to reproducing the route of Nabucco is an indicator in this regard. The Commission is funding this pipeline almost alone.

However, all in all, it remains unclear, even for the European Commission, if energy security is a public good. Energy security is not a conventional commodity and EU free market and competition rules might not apply fully to the energy sector. Additional academic work should be conducted to define what energy security is and what it should be in the European context in order to help the EU develop more consistent and efficient energy security policies.

Glossary

Acronym/[1] *Abbreviation*	*Definition*
ACF	Advocacy coalition framework
ALDE	Alliance of Liberals and Democrats for Europe, political group in the European Parliament; liberal-centrist group, supported free market economics
Bcm	Billion cubic metres
BOTAŞ	Oil and gas pipeline and trading company, Turkey
BP	British Petroleum, British multinational oil and gas company
Bulgargaz	Large Bulgarian gas distribution company
BUND	'Bund für Umwelt und Naturschutz Deutschland', translated as 'Association for the Environment and Nature Conservation, Germany'
CEP	Common Energy Policy
DEPA	'Δημόσια Επιχείρηση Παροχής Αερίου', translated as 'Public Gas Supply', a publicly owned Greek natural gas supply corporation
DG	Directorate-General, European Commission
ECR	European Conservatives and Reformists, political group in the European Parliament; center-right group, interested to reform the EU based on euro-realism and respecting national sovereignty
EEAS	European External Action Service
EEPR	European Energy Programme for Recovery
EFD	Europe of Freedom and Democracy, political group in the European Parliament; right-wing group committed to protecting national sovereignty

(*continued*)

[1] The Glossary also includes abbreviations in the graphics and figures of this book.

A.-M. Bocse, *International Networks, Advocacy and EU Energy Policy-Making*, Palgrave Studies in European Union Politics,
https://doi.org/10.1007/978-3-030-49505-3

(continued)

Acronym/ Abbreviation	*Definition*
EP	European Parliament
EPP	European People's Party, political group in the European Parliament; centre-right group, committed to a competitive and democratic Europe
EU	European Union
Euratom	European Atomic Energy Community
Eurogas	An association representing the European gas industry
FDI	Foreign direct investment
FGSZ	'Foldgazszallito Zrt', translated as 'Natural Gas Transmission Ltd.', a Hungarian natural gas transmission company
Gazprom	'Gazovaya promyshlennost', translated as 'Gas industry', a large Russian gas company
GMF	(The) German Marshall Fund
Greens/ EFA	Greens/European Free Alliance, political group in the European Parliament; group promoting fundamental human rights and environmental justice
ICT	Information and communication technology
IEA	International Energy Agency
ITGI	Interconnector Turkey-Greece-Italy
ITRE	Committee on Industry, Research and Energy, European Parliament
MEP	Member of the European Parliament
Mln	Million
MOL	'Magyar OLaj- és Gázipari Részvénytársaság', translated as 'Hungarian Oil and Gas Public Limited Company', a Hungarian multinational oil and gas company, headquartered in Budapest
MVM	'Magyar Villamos Művek', translated as 'Hungarian Power Companies', Hungarian energy consortium
NATO	North Atlantic Treaty Organization
NGO	Non-governmental organization
NIOC	'National Iranian Oil Company', state-owned Iranian oil and gas company
OGP	(The) Organization of Oil and Gas Producers
OMV	'Österreichische Mineralölverwaltung', translated as 'Austrian Oil Management', an international oil and gas company based in Vienna
Romgaz	A Romanian natural gas company
RWE	'Rheinisch-Westfälisches Elektrizitätswerk', translated as 'The Rhine-Westphalia Power Plant', a German electrical utilities company
SCP	South Caucasus Pipeline
SCPX	South Caucasus Pipeline Expansion
SNA	Social network analysis

(*continued*)

(continued)

Acronym/ Abbreviation	*Definition*
SOCAR	State Oil Company of the Republic of Azerbaijan
Statoil	Norwegian petroleum company
S&D	Progressive Alliance of Socialists and Democrats, political group in the European Parliament; the group has a social-democratic political orientation and, in general, shows interest for environmental concerns
SMO	Social movement organization
TANAP	Trans-Anatolian Natural Gas Pipeline
TAP	Trans Adriatic Pipeline
TPAO	Turkish Petroleum Corporation
Transgaz	The technical operator of the Romanian natural gas transmission system
UK	United Kingdom (of Great Britain and Northern Ireland)
US	United States (of America)
WWF	World Wildlife Fund

References

Primary Sources

Interviews: *Fracking for Shale Gas Case Study*

Interview with European Affairs consultant (2014) the interview took place in Brussels, at the consultancy office.

Interview with European Commission official, DG Clima (2014) the interview took place in Brussels, at DG Clima.

Interview with European Commission official, DG Energy (2013) the interview took place in Brussels, at DG Energy.

Interview with European Commission official, DG Enterprise and Industry (2014) the interview took place in Brussels, at DG Enterprise and Industry.

Interview with European Commission official, DG Environment (2014) the interview took place in Brussels, at DG Environment.

Interview with European Parliament official 1 (2013) the interview took place in Brussels, at the European Parliament.

Interview with European Parliament official 2 (2013) the interview took place in Brussels, at the European Parliament.

Interview with European Parliament official 3 (2013) the interview took place in Brussels, at the European Parliament.

Interview with European Parliament official 4 (2013) the interview took place in Brussels, at the European Parliament.

A.-M. Bocse, *International Networks, Advocacy and EU Energy Policy-Making*, Palgrave Studies in European Union Politics, https://doi.org/10.1007/978-3-030-49505-3

Interview with former officer at the German Marshall Fund, Brussels office (2013) the interview took place in Brussels, at Cafe Elvis.
Interview with former policy officer at the World Wildlife Fund Europe (2013) the interview took place in Brussels, at Cafe Karsmakers.
Interview with former researcher at the German Marshall Fund, Brussels office (2013) the interview took place via Skype.
Interview with industry consultant 1 (2013) the interview took place in Brussels, at the consultancy office.
Interview with journalist at a trade specialised publication (2014) the interview took place in Brussels.
Interview with journalist at an influential Brussels-based media outlet (2013) the interview took place in Brussels, in the European headquarter.
Interview with official at the Mission of Canada to the European Union (2013) the interview took place in Brussels, at the Mission.
Interview with official at the United States Mission to the European Union, EU (2013) the interview took place in Brussels, at Librairie Filigranes.
Interview with policy adviser to a Committee on Industry, Research and Energy, ITRE, Member of the European Parliament (2013) the interview took place in Brussels, at the European Parliament.
Interview with policy adviser to a Liberal Member of the European Parliament (2013) the interview took place in Brussels, at the European Parliament.
Interview with policy adviser to a Polish Conservative Member of the European Parliament (2014) the interview took place in Brussels, at the European Parliament.
Interview with policy adviser to a Polish Member of the European Parliament (2013) the interview took place in Brussels, at the European Parliament.
Interview with policy adviser to a Polish Member of the European Parliament, member of the European People's Party (2013) the interview took place in Brussels, at the European Parliament.
Interview with policy adviser to the European Conservatives and Reformists in the European Parliament (2013) the interview took place in Brussels, at the European Parliament.
Interview with policy adviser to the European People's Party in the European Parliament (2013) the interview took place in Brussels, at the European Parliament.
Interview with policy adviser to the Greens/European Free Alliance in the European Parliament (2013) the interview took place in Brussels, at the European Parliament.
Interview with policy officer at Food and Water Europe (2013) the interview took place in Brussels, at the organization office.
Interview with policy officer at Friends of the Earth Europe (2013) the interview took place in Brussels, at the organization office.

Interview with policy officer at Friends of the Earth France (2015) the interview took place in Paris, at the organization office.
Interview with policy officer at Greenpeace European Unit (2013) the interview took place in Brussels, at the organization office.
Interview with Polish official (2013) the interview took place in Brussels.
Interview with public affairs consultant working for Gazprom (2013) the interview took place in Brussels.
Interview with representative of a Dutch energy company (2013) the interview took place in Brussels.
Interview with representative of a French energy company (2014) the interview took place in Brussels.
Interview with representative of a Norwegian energy company (2014) the interview took place in Brussels.
Interview with representative of an American energy company (2013) the interview took place in Brussels.
Interview with representative of an Italian energy company (2014) the interview took place via Skype.
Interview with representative of chemical industry association (2014) the interview took place in Brussels.
Interview with representative of industry association (2014) the interview took place in Brussels, at Cafe Elvis.
Interview with representative of the US Chamber of Commerce (2014) the interview took place in Brussels, at the US Chamber of Commerce.
Interview with Russian academic and energy law expert (2013) the interview took place via Skype, Brussels/Moscow.
Interview with senior policy adviser to the Greens/European Free Alliance in the European Parliament (2013) the interview took place in Brussels, at the European Parliament.
Interview with source in the gas industry (2014) the interview took place in Brussels.

Interviews: *Southern Gas Corridor Case Study*

Interview with adviser, Mission of Georgia to the European Union (2014) the interview took place in Brussels, at the Mission.
Interview with adviser on international security to the President of Romania (2013) the interview took place in Romania.
Interview with attaché at the Permanent Representation of Greece to the European Union (2014) the interview took place in Brussels.
Interview with attaché at the Permanent Representation of Italy to the European Union (2014) the interview took place in Brussels.

Interview with attaché at the Permanent Representation of Romania to the European Union (2014) the interview took place in Brussels.

Interview with Austrian official (2014) the interview took place in Vienna.

Interview with Azeri official (2013) the interview took place in Brussels.

Interview with Bulgarian energy expert (2014) the interview took place via Skype, Brussels/Sofia.

Interview with Deputy Assistant Secretary General of NATO (2014) the interview took place in Brussels, at the NATO headquarters.

Interview with energy executive (2013) the interview took place via Skype, Brussels/Ankara.

Interview with energy section official, NATO (2015) the interview took place in Brussels, at the NATO headquarters.

Interview with European Commission official, DG Energy, working on energy markets (2013) the interview took place in Brussels, at DG Energy.

Interview with former attaché at the Mission of the Republic of Albania to the European Union (2014) the interview took place via Skype, Brussels/Tirana.

Interview with former Hungarian diplomat based in the US (2014) the interview took place in Budapest.

Interview with Hungarian governmental adviser on energy security (2014) the interview took place in Budapest.

Interview with industry consultant 2 (2014) the interview took place in Brussels, at the restaurant 'Le Pain Quotidien'.

Interview with Nabucco source (2014) the interview took place via Skype.

Interview with official in the European External Action Service, EEAS 1 (2013) the interview took place in Brussels, at the EEAS headquarters.

Interview with official in the European External Action Service, EEAS 2 (2013) the interview took place via Skype.

Interview with official in the European External Action Service, EEAS, Network on Energy Diplomacy (2013) the interview took place in Brussels, at the EEAS headquarters.

Interview with representative of an energy company (2014) the interview took place in Brussels.

Interview with representative of British Petroleum (2014) the interview took place in the UK.

Interview with representative of OMV (2014) the interview took place via Skype, Brussels/Vienna.

Interview with representative of SOCAR (2014) the interview took place in Brussels.

Interview with representative of TANAP (2014) the interview took place via Skype, Brussels/Ankara.

Interview with Russian official based in Brussels (2013) the interview took place in Brussels.

Interview with senior Albanian official (2014) the interview took place in Brussels.
Interview with senior Austrian official (2014) the interview took place in Vienna.
Interview with senior European Commission official, DG Energy (2013) the interview took place in Brussels, at DG Energy.
Interview with senior Georgian official (2014) the interview took place in Brussels.
Interview with senior International Energy Agency official (2015) the interview took place in Paris, at the International Energy Agency headquarters.
Interview with senior Italian official (2014) the interview took place via Skype, Brussels/Oslo.
Interview with senior official at the Ministry of Energy and Natural Resources of Turkey (2014) the interview took place via Skype, Brussels/Ankara.
Interview with senior Turkish official (2014) the interview took place in Paris.
Interview with specialist in the Ministry of Energy of Georgia (2014) the interview took online Cambridge/Tbilisi, Georgia.
Interview with TAP source (2013) the interview took place via Skype.
Interview with very senior Bulgarian official (2013) the interview took place via Skype, Brussels/Sofia.
Interview with very senior European Commission official (2014) the interview took place in Brussels, in the Berlaymont building.
Interview with very senior Hungarian official (2014) the interview took place in Budapest.

Documents and Media

Azernews (2013) *European Commission grants legislation exemptions for TAP and Nabucco West*, 17 May 2013, available at: http://www.azernews.az/oil_and_gas/54024.html, accessed 15 May 2015.
Bloomberg Business (2012) *Nabucco gas pipe's cost to fall on shorter route, Mitschek says*, available at: http://www.bloomberg.com/news/articles/2012-11-15/nabucco-gas-pipe-s-cost-to-fall-on-shorter-route-mitschek-says, accessed 1 May 2014.
British Petroleum, BP (2015a) *South Caucasus pipeline*, available at: http://www.bp.com/en_az/caspian/operationsprojects/pipelines/SCP.html, accessed 14 April 2015.
British Petroleum, BP (2015b) *Shah Deniz*, available at: http://www.bp.com/en_az/caspian/operationsprojects/Shahdeniz.html, accessed 15 April 2015.
Carrington, Damian (2015) 'David Cameron rejects call for fracking ban', *The Guardian*, 26 January 2015, available at: http://www.theguardian.com/environment/2015/jan/26/david-cameron-rejects-fracking-ban-shale-gas, accessed 15 December 2015.
Cook, Al (2012a) quoted in the interview of Natural Gas Europe and TAP, *Caspian gas for Europe: Trans Adriatic Pipeline and Shah Deniz on delivering*

different parts of the Southern Gas Corridor, 29 April 2012, available at: http://www.naturalgaseurope.com/trans-adriatic-pipeline-southern-gas-corridor, accessed 15 May 2015.

Cook, Al (2012b) quoted in the report of *Olgu Okumuş*, *The selection criteria of Shah Deniz*, 26 November 2012, available at: http://www.naturalgaseurope.com/the-selection-criteria-of-shah-deniz, accessed 15 May 2015.

Council of the European Union, Foreign Affairs Council (2015) *Council Conclusions on Energy Diplomacy and EU Energy Diplomacy Action Plan*, available at: http://data.consilium.europa.eu/doc/document/ST-10995-2015-INIT/en/pdf, accessed 30 October 2019.

Directorate-General for Energy (2013) *EU energy, transport and GHG emissions. Trends to 2050. Reference scenario 2013*, available at: http://ec.europa.eu/energy/sites/ener/files/documents/trends_to_2050_update_2013.pdf, accessed 15 November 2015.

Directorate-General for Energy (2014) *Enforcement of laws*, available at: http://ec.europa.eu/energy/en/topics/enforcement-laws, accessed 15 November 2015.

Directorate-General for Energy (2015) *EU energy in figures. Statistical pocketbook 2015*, available at: https://ec.europa.eu/energy/sites/ener/files/documents/PocketBook_ENERGY_2015%20PDF%20final.pdf, accessed 1 December 2015.

Directorate-General for Energy (2019) *EU energy in figures. Statistical pocketbook 2019*, available at: https://op.europa.eu/en/publication-detail/-/publication/e0544b72-db53-11e9-9c4e-01aa75ed71a1/language-en?WT.mc_id=Searchresult&WT.ria_c=37085&WT.ria_f=3608&WT.ria_ev=search, accessed 18 February 2020.

Durão Barroso, José Manuel (2009) *Remarks by Commission President José Manuel Barroso upon the signature of the Nabucco intergovernmental agreement*, SPEECH/09/339, available at: http://europa.eu/rapid/press-release_SPEECH-09-339_en.htm, accessed 10 May 2013.

Durão Barroso, José Manuel (2011) *Joint Declaration on the Southern Gas Corridor of José Manuel Durão Barroso (President of the European Commission) and Ilham Aliyev (President of the Republic of Azerbaijan)*, 13 January 2011, Baku, the Republic of Azerbaijan, available at: http://ec.europa.eu/energy/infrastructure/strategy/doc/2011_01_13_joint_declaration_southern_corridor.pdf, accessed 8 May 2013.

Euractiv (2013) *South Stream bilateral deals breach EU law, Commission says*, available at: http://www.euractiv.com/energy/commission-south-stream-agreemen-news-532120, accessed 5 July 2015.

European Commission (2000) *Green Paper: Towards a European strategy for the security of energy supply*, COM(2000) 769 final, available at: http://iet.jrc.ec.europa.eu/remea/sites/remea/files/files/documents/com_2000_769_enegy_security.pdf, accessed 15 May 2014.

European Commission (2006) *Green paper: A European strategy for sustainable, competitive and secure energy*, COM(2006) 105 final, available at: europa.eu/documents/comm/green_papers/pdf/com2006_105_en.pdf, accessed 15 November 2012.

European Commission (2007) *An energy policy for Europe: Commission steps up to the energy challenges of the 21st century*, available at: http://europa.eu/rapid/press-release_MEMO-07-7_en.htm, accessed 15 November 2012.

European Commission (2008) *Communication from the European Commission to the European Parliament, the Council, the European Economic and Social Committee and the Committee of the Regions, EU energy security and solidarity action plan: 2nd strategic energy review*, COM/2008/781, available at: http://aei.pitt.edu/39567/1/COM_(2008)_781.pdf, accessed 2 July 2015.

European Commission (2009a) *Directive 2009/28/EC of the European Parliament and of the Council of 23 April 2009 on the promotion of the use of energy from renewable sources and amending and subsequently repealing Directives 2001/77/EC and 2003/30/EC*, available at: http://eur-lex.europa.eu/legal-content/EN/TXT/?uri=CELEX:32009L0028, accessed 15 May 2013.

European Commission (2009b) *Commission staff working document accompanying document to the proposal for a Regulation of the European Parliament and of the Council concerning measures to safeguard security of gas supply and repealing Directive 2004/67/EC, The January 2009 Gas supply disruption to the EU: an assessment*, SEC(2009) 977 final, available at: http://eur-lex.europa.eu/legal-content/EN/TXT/?uri=CELEX:52009SC0977, accessed 15 December 2012.

European Commission (2010) *Communication from the Commission to the European Parliament, the Council, the European Economic and Social Committee and the Committee of the Regions, Energy 2020: A strategy for competitive, sustainable and secure energy*, COM(2010) 639, available at: http://www.eumonitor.eu/9353000/1/j4nvhejn9d40zzo_j9vvik7m1c3gyxp/vikqhoxu3pzn, accessed 2 July 2015.

European Commission (2011) *Communication from the Commission to the European Parliament, the Council, the European Economic and Social Committee and the Committee of the Regions: Energy roadmap 2050*, COM(2011) 885, available at: http://ec.europa.eu/transparency/regdoc/?fuseaction=list&coteId=1&year=2011&number=885&language=EN, accessed 15 December 2012.

European Commission (2012a) *Directive 2012/27/EU of the European Parliament and of the Council of 25 October 2012 on energy efficiency, amending Directives 2009/125/EC and 2010/30/EU and repealing Directives 2004/8/EC and 2006/32/EC*, available at: http://eur-lex.europa.eu/legal-content/EN/TXT/?qid=1399375464230&uri=CELEX:32012L0027, accessed 15 May 2015.

European Commission (2012b) *Codecision*, available at: http://ec.europa.eu/codecision/stepbystep/text/index_en.htm, accessed 16 March 2015.

European Commission (2013) *Communication from the Commission: Annual Growth Survey 2014*, COM(2013) 800 final, available at: http://ec.europa.eu/europe2020/pdf/2014/ags2014_en.pdf, accessed 1 July 2014.

European Commission (2014a) *Communication from the Commission to the European Parliament and the Council: European Energy Security Strategy*, COM(2014) 330 final, available at: http://eur-lex.europa.eu/legal-content/EN/TXT/PDF/?uri=CELEX:52014DC0330&from=EN, accessed 1 June 2014.

European Commission (2014b) *Commission Recommendation of 22 January 2014 on minimum principles for the exploration and production of hydrocarbons (such as shale gas) using high-volume hydraulic fracturing*, (2014/70/EU), available at: http://eur-lex.europa.eu/LexUriServ/LexUriServ.do?uri=OJ:L:2014:039:0072:0078:EN:PDF, accessed 24 January 2014.

European Commission (2014c) *Communication from the Commission to the European Parliament, the Council, the European Economic and Social Committee and the Committee of the Regions on the exploration and production of hydrocarbons (such as shale gas) using high volume hydraulic fracturing in the EU*, COM(2014) 23 final/2, available at: http://eur-lex.europa.eu/legal-content/EN/TXT/?uri=CELEX:52014DC0023R%2801%29, accessed 10 May 2015.

European Commission (2014d) *European Commission recommends minimum principles for shale gas*, Press release, available at: http://europa.eu/rapid/press-release_IP-14-55_en.htm, accessed 24 January 2014.

European Commission (2015a) *Communication from the Commission to the European Parliament, the Council, the European Economic and Social Committee, the Committee of the Regions and the European Investment Bank, Energy Union package: A framework strategy for a resilient Energy Union with a forward-looking climate change policy*, COM(2015) 80 final, available at: http://eur-lex.europa.eu/resource.html?uri=cellar:1bd46c90-bdd4-11e4-bbe1-01aa75ed71a1.0001.03/DOC_1&format=PDF, accessed 5 July 2015.

European Commission (2015b) *Priorities*, available at: http://ec.europa.eu/priorities/index_en, accessed 30 November 2015.

European Commission (2016) *European Energy Programme for Recovery*, available at: http://ec.europa.eu/energy/eepr/projects/, accessed 15 January 2016.

European Commission and the Secretary General for the European Council/the High Representative for Common Foreign and Security Policy (2006) *An external policy to serve Europe's energy interests*, available at: www.consilium.europa.eu/uedocs/cmsUpload/st09971.en06.pdf, accessed 15 November 2012.

European Council (2007) *Brussels European Council 8/9 March 2007. Presidency conclusions*, 7224/1/07, REV 1, available at: http://www.consilium.europa.eu/uedocs/cms_Data/docs/pressdata/en/ec/93135.pdf, accessed 15 November 2012.

European Energy Programme for Recovery (2013) *Nabucco*, available at: http://ec.europa.eu/energy/eepr/projects/files/gas-interconnections-and-reverse-flow/nabucco_en.pdf, accessed 11 November 2013.

European External Action Service (EEAS) (2016) *A Global Strategy for the European Union's Foreign and Security Policy*, available at: https://eeas.europa.eu/sites/eeas/files/eugs_review_web_0.pdf, accessed 29 October 2019.

European Parliament (2008) *European Parliament resolution of 20 February 2008 on the Treaty of Lisbon*, P6_TA(2008)0055, available at: http://www.europarl.europa.eu/sides/getDoc.do?type=TA&reference=P6-TA-2008-0055&format=XML&language=EN, accessed 12 March 2014.

European Parliament (2009a) *European Parliament resolution of 17 September 2009 on external aspects of energy security*, P7_TA(2009)0021, available at: http://www.europarl.europa.eu/sides/getDoc.do?type=TA&reference=P7-TA-2009-0021&format=XML&language=EN, accessed 15 March 2014.

European Parliament (2009b) *MEPs debate Caspian gas and Saharan solar energy*, REF.: 20090915STO60688, available at: http://www.europarl.europa.eu/portal/en/search?q=20090915STO60688, accessed 10 April 2013.

European Parliament (2012a) *European Parliament resolution of 21 November 2012 on industrial, energy and other aspects of shale gas and oil*, P7_TA(2012)0444, available at: http://www.europarl.europa.eu/sides/getDoc.do?type=TA&reference=P7-TA-2012-0444&language=EN, accessed 15 February 2013.

European Parliament (2012b) *Report on industrial, energy and other aspects of shale gas and oil*, A7-0284/2012, available at: http://www.europarl.europa.eu/sides/getDoc.do?type=REPORT&reference=A7-2012-0284&language=EN, accessed 15 December 2012.

European Parliament (2012c) *European Parliament resolution of 21 November 2012 on the environmental impacts of shale gas and shale oil extraction activities*, P7_TA(2012)0443, available at: http://www.europarl.europa.eu/sides/getDoc.do?type=TA&reference=P7-TA-2012-0443&language=EN, accessed 15 December 2012.

European Parliament (2015) *Employment*, available at: http://www.europarl.europa.eu/atyourservice/en/20150201PVL00046/Recruitment, accessed 30 November 2015.

European Parliament and thee Council (1996) *Directive 96/92/EC of the European Parliament and of the Council of 19 December 1996 concerning common rules for the internal market in electricity*, available at: http://eur-lex.europa.eu/LexUriServ/LexUriServ.do?uri=CELEX:31996L0092:EN:HTML, accessed 15 March 2014.

European Parliament and the Council (1998) *Directive 98/30/EC of the European Parliament and of the Council of 22 June 1998 concerning common rules for the internal market in natural gas*, available at: http://app.vlex.com/#vid/37420939, accessed 15 March 2014.

European Parliament and the Council (2000) *Directive 2000/60/EC of the European Parliament and of the Council establishing a framework for the Community action in the field of water policy*, available at: *eur-lex.europa.eu/legal-content/EN/TXT/?uri=CELEX:32000L0060*, accessed March 2013.

European Parliament and the Council (2003a) *Directive 2003/30/EC of the European Parliament and of the Council of 8 May 2003 on the promotion of the use of biofuels or other renewable fuels for transport*, available at: http://iet.jrc.ec.europa.eu/remea/directive-200330ec-european-parliament-and-council-8-may-2003-promotion-use-biofuels-or-other, access 10 December 2013.

European Parliament and the Council (2003b) *Decision no 1229/2003/EC of the European Parliament and of the Council of 26 June 2003 laying down a series of guidelines for trans-European energy networks and repealing Decision No 1254/96/EC*, available at: http://www.eihp.hr/english/pdf/l_17620030715en00110028.pdf, accessed 20 October 2013.

European Parliament and the Council (2006a) *Regulation (EC) No 1907/2006 of the European Parliament and of the Council of 18 December 2006 concerning the Registration, Evaluation, Authorisation and Restriction of Chemicals (REACH)*, available at: http://eur-lex.europa.eu/legal-content/EN/TXT/?uri=CELEX:02006R1907-20140410, accessed 15 November 2015.

European Parliament and the Council (2006b) *Directive 2006/32/EC of the European Parliament and of the Council of 5 April 2006 on energy end-use efficiency and energy services and repealing Council Directive 93/76/EEC*, available at: http://eur-lex.europa.eu/legal-content/EN/TXT/?uri=URISERV:l27057, accessed 10 December 2013.

European Parliament and the Council (2006c) *Decision no 1364/2006/EC of the European Parliament and of the Council of 6 September 2006 laying down guidelines for trans-European energy networks and repealing Decision 96/391/EC and Decision No 1229/2003/EC*, available at: http://ec.europa.eu/ten/energy/legislation/doc/2006_09_22_ten_e_guidelines_2006_en.pdf, accessed 20 October 2013.

European Parliament and the Council (2009) *Directive 2009/73/EC of the European Parliament and of the Council of 13 July 2009 concerning common rules for the internal market in natural gas and repealing Directive 2003/55/EC*, available at: www.energy-community.org/pls/portal/docs/1164181.PDF, accessed 10 June 2015.

European Parliament and the Council (2010) *Regulation (EU) No 994/2010 of the European Parliament and of the Council of 20 October 2010 concerning measures to safeguard security of gas supply and repealing Council Directive 2004/67/EC*, available at: www.urso.gov.sk/sites/default/files/NEP_994-2010_20-10-2010_en.pdf, accessed 15 March 2014.

European Parliament and the Council (2012) *Regulation (EU) No 670/2012 of the European Parliament and of the Council of 11 July 2012 amending Decision No 1639/2006/EC establishing a Competitiveness and Innovation Framework Programme (2007–2013) and Regulation (EC) No 680/2007 laying down general rules for the granting of Community financial aid in the field of the trans-European transport and energy networks*, available at: http://eur-lex.europa.eu/LexUriServ/LexUriServ.do?uri=OJ:L:2012:204:0001:0010:EN:PDF, accessed 10 November 2015.

European Union Member States (1986) *The Single European Act*, available at: http://ec.europa.eu/archives/emu_history/documents/treaties/singleuropeanact.pdf, accessed 15 April 2013.

European Union Member States (2009a) *The Treaty of Lisbon*, available at: http://eur-lex.europa.eu/legal-content/EN/TXT/PDF/?uri=OJ:C:2007:306:FULL&from=EN, accessed 12 March 2013.

European Union Member States (2009b) *The Treaty on European Union*, available at: http://www.lisbon-treaty.org/wcm/the-lisbon-treaty/treaty-on-european-union-and-comments.html, accessed 12 March 2013.

European Union Member States (2009c) *The Treaty on the Functioning of the European Union*, available at: http://www.lisbon-treaty.org/wcm/the-lisbon-treaty/treaty-on-the-functioning-of-the-european-union-and-comments.html, accessed 12 October 2012.

Grzyb, Andrzej, Bogdan Marcinkiewicz, Marian-Jean Marinescu, Paul Rübig, Alejo Vidal-Quadras (2010) *Written declaration on the possibility to utilise gas from alternative sources in Europe*, P7_DCL(2010)0067, 6 September 2010, available at: http://www.europarl.europa.eu/sides/getDoc.do?pubRef=-%2f%2fEP%2f%2fNONSGML%2bWDECL%2bP7-DCL-2010-0067%2b0%2bDOC%2bPDF%2bV0%2f%2fEN, accessed 15 November 2013.

Harvey, Fiona (2014) 'Russia "secretly working with environmentalists to oppose fracking"', *The Guardian*, 19 June 2014, available at: http://www.theguardian.com/environment/2014/jun/19/russia-secretly-working-with-environmentalists-to-oppose-fracking, accessed 15 March 2015.

Higgins, Andrew (2014) 'Russian money suspected behind fracking protests', *The New York Times*, 30 November 2014, available at: http://www.nytimes.com/2014/12/01/world/russian-money-suspected-behind-fracking-protests.html?_r=0, accessed 15 March 2015.

International Energy Agency (2008) *IEA Energy policies review: The European Union*, available at: http://www.oecd-ilibrary.org/docserver/download/6108191e.pdf?expires=1437520777&id=id&accname=oid007055&checksum=BB1A67E4B8B2AA716B09B1FCD9864528, accessed 10 July 2015.

International Energy Agency (2015) *World Energy Outlook*, available at: http://www.worldenergyoutlook.org/, accessed 10 December 2015.

Library of the European Parliament (2013) *Lobbying the European institutions*, Library Briefing, 18/06/2013, on file with the author.

Ministerial Council (2009) *Regulation (EC) No 715/2009 of 13 July 2009 on conditions for access to the natural gas transmission networks and repealing Regulation (EC) No 1775/2005*, available at: www.energy-community.org/pls/portal/docs/2938031.PDF, accessed 10 June 2015.

Mitschek, Reinhard (2013a) *Nabucco will diversify gas supplies, boost economic growth: CEO Reinhard Mitschek*, Press release, available at: http://www.nabucco-pipeline.com/portal/page/portal/en/press/NewsText?p_item_id=DD63B218D39B006AE040A8C001011C1D, accessed 15 May 2013.

Mitschek, Reinhard (2013b) *Governments commit to develop further interconnections for Southern Gas Corridor*, Press release, available at: http://www.nabucco-pipeline.com/portal/page/portal/en/press/NewsText?p_item_id=DD39C138D7B77EA8E040A8C00101276C, accessed 15 May 2013.

Mitschek, Reinhard (2013c) *Nabucco is a truly European project: an interview with Reinhard Mitschek*, available at: http://www.nabucco-pipeline.com/portal/page/portal/en/press/NewsText?p_item_id=D5B123EC7483C3B0E040A8C001016635, accessed 15 May 2013.

Mombaur, Peter Michael (2003) *Report on a proposal for a Directive of the European Parliament and the Council concerning measures to safeguard security of natural gas supply*, Final A5-0295/2003, available at: http://www.europarl.europa.eu/sides/getDoc.do?pubRef=-//EP//TEXT+REPORT+A5-2003-0295+0+DOC+XML+V0//EN&language=en, accessed 2 July 2015.

Nabucco Gas Pipeline International (2012) *Second Nabucco Political Committee concludes in Vienna with resounding declaration of political support*, available at: www.naturalgaseurope.com/content/8350/Nabucco10Oct2012.pdf, accessed 14 May 2015.

Nabucco Gas Pipeline International (2013a) *Environmental impact assessment—Objectives*, available at: http://www.nabucco-pipeline.com/portal/page/portal/en/safety/esia_concept, accessed 14 May 2013.

Nabucco Gas Pipeline International (2013b) *Strategic goals*, available at: http://www.nabucco-pipeline.com/portal/page/portal/en, accessed 14 May 2013.

Nabucco Gas Pipeline International (2013c) *The Project*, available at: http://www.nabucco-pipeline.com/portal/page/portal/en/Home/the_project, accessed 12 May 2013.

Sampol, Célia (2009) 'Lisbon treaty: Lisbon strengthens Parliament's powers', *Europolitics* (daily in English).

Saryusz-Wolski, Jacek (2007) *Report on towards a common European foreign policy on energy*, available at: http://www.europarl.europa.eu/sides/getDoc.do?pubRef=-//EP//NONSGML+REPORT+A6-2007-0312+0+DOC+PDF+V0//EN, accessed 12 March 2014.

Shale Gas Europe (2015) *Shale gas and the environment*, available at: http://shalegas-europe.eu/shale-gas-explained/shale-gas-and-environment/, accessed 15 December 2015.

The Energy Charter Treaty Signatory States (1994) *The Energy Charter Treaty*, available at: http://www.energycharter.org/fileadmin/DocumentsMedia/Legal/1994_ECT.pdf, accessed 15 May 2015.

The White House (2010) *U.S.-Russia relations: 'Reset' fact sheet*, available at: https://www.whitehouse.gov/the-press-office/us-russia-relations-reset-fact-sheet, accessed 5 May 2015.

Trans Adriatic Pipeline, TAP (2013a) *Trans Adriatic Pipeline secures third party access exemption*, available at: http://www.tap-ag.com/news-and-events/2013/05/17/trans-adriatic-pipeline-secures-third-party-access-exemption, accessed 15 April 2015.

Trans Adriatic Pipeline, TAP (2013b) *TAP's Corporate Presentation*, available on file, document send by a TAP official to me via email on 9 December 2013.

Trans Adriatic Pipeline, TAP (2015a) *About us*, available at: http://www.tap-ag.com/about-us, accessed 10 April 2015.

Trans Adriatic Pipeline, TAP (2015b) *Southern Gas Corridor*, available at: http://www.tap-ag.com/the-pipeline/the-big-picture/southern-gas-corridor, accessed 10 May 2015.

Trans Adriatic Pipeline, TAP (2020) *TAP project schedule*, available at: https://www.tap-ag.com/the-pipeline/project-timeline#35, accessed 17 February 2020.

van Aartsen, Jozias, European Coordinator (2009) *Activity report: project of European interest n° NG 3*, available at: http://ec.europa.eu/energy/infrastructure/tent_e/doc/axis/2009_axis_linking_activity_report_2007_2009.pdf, accessed 20 October 2013.

Welle, Klaus (2014) *Total quality management along the whole legislative cycle—A fresh look at better law-making*, Speech by Klaus Welle at the Association of European Chambers of Commerce and Industry (Eurochambres) Conference, Brussels, 30 January 2014, available at: http://www.europarl.europa.eu/the-secretary-general/resource/static/files/2014/2014-01-30_Klaus_Welle_eurochambres_conference_at_EP.pdf, accessed 15 June 2015.

Secondary Sources

Ahmadov, Ingilab (2010) 'The Southern Corridor and Nabucco—A Promising Challenge for Caspian Countries' in Kristin Linke and Marcel Vietor (eds) *Beyond Turkey. The EU's energy policy*, a publication of Friedrich Ebert Stiftung, pp. 15–19, available at: library.fes.de/pdf-files/id/07553.pdf, accessed 15 February 2014.

Alford, Robert and Roger Friedland (1985) *Powers of theory: capitalism, the state and democracy* (Cambridge: Cambridge University Press).

Atkinson, Michael and William Coleman (1992) 'Policy networks, policy communities and the problems of governance', *Governance*, 5:2, pp. 154–180.

Bache, Ian (2008) *Europeanization and multilevel governance: cohesion policy in the European Union and Britain* (Plymouth: Rowman & Littlefield).

Baker, Wayne and Robert Faulkner (1993) 'The social organisation of conspiracy: illegal networks in the heavy electrical equipment industry', *American Sociological Review*, 58:6, pp. 837–860.

Barke, Richard and Hank Jenkins-Smith (1993) 'Politics and scientific expertise: scientists, risk perceptions, and nuclear waste policy', *Risk Analysis*, 13:4, pp. 425–439.

Behrens, Arno and Christian Egenhofer (2008) '*Energy policy for Europe: identifying the European added-value*', *Centre for European Policy Studies Task Force Report*, 6 March 2008, available at: http://aei.pitt.edu/9530/, accessed 15 September 2015.

Belova, Maria (2010) 'The Southern Corridor—Not without Russia?' in Kristin Linke and Marcel Vietor (eds) *Beyond Turkey. The EU's energy policy*, a publication of Friedrich Ebert Stiftung, pp. 25–28, available at: library.fes.de/pdf-files/id/07553.pdf, accessed 15 February 2014.

Belyi, Andrei V. (2008) 'EU external energy policies: a paradox of integration' in Jan Orbie (ed) *Europe's global role: external policies of the European Union* (Aldershot: Ashgate), pp. 203–215.

Benford, Robert D. and David A. Snow (2000) 'Framing processes and social movements: an overview and assessment', *Annual Review of Sociology*, 26, pp. 611–639.

Betsill, Michele and Elisabeth Corell (2001) 'NGO influence in international environmental negotiations: a framework for analysis', *Global Environmental Politics*, 1:4, pp. 65–85.

Beyers, Jan (2004) 'Voice and access: political practices of European interest associations', *European Union Politics*, 5:2, pp. 211–240.

Boersma, Tim and Corey Johnson (2012) 'The shale gas revolution: U.S. and EU policy and research agendas', *Review of Policy Research*, 29:4, pp. 570–576.

Bolton, Paul, Donna Gore and Ruth Winstone (2007) *Energy security*, House of Commons Library, Research Paper 07/42, available at: http://researchbriefings.parliament.uk/ResearchBriefing/Summary/RP07-42, accessed 15 May 2013.

Bomberg, Elizabeth (1998) 'Issue networks and the environment: explaining European Union environmental policy' in David Marsh (ed) *Comparing policy networks* (Buckingham: Open University Press), pp. 167–184.

Bomberg, Elizabeth (2017) 'Fracking and framing in transatlantic perspective: a comparison of shale politics in the US and European Union', *Journal of Transatlantic Studies*, 15:2, pp. 101–120.

Börzel, Tanja (1997) 'What's so special about policy networks? An exploration of the concept and its usefulness in studying European governance', *European Integration online Papers (EIoP)*, 1:16, available at: http://eiop.or.at/eiop/texte/1997-016a.htm, accessed 15 November 2014.

Börzel, Tanja (1998) 'Organizing Babylon: on the different conceptions of policy networks', *Public Administration*, 76:2, pp. 253–273.

Bourdieu, Pierre (1986) 'The forms of social capital' in John G. Richardson (ed) *Handbook for theory and research in the sociology of education* (Westport: Greenwood Press).

Bourdieu, Pierre and Loïc Wacquant (1992) *An invitation to reflexive sociology* (Chicago: University of Chicago Press).

Bouwen, Pieter (2002) 'Corporate lobbying in the European Union: the logic of access', *Journal of European Public Policy*, 9:3, pp. 365–390.

Bouwen, Pieter (2004a) 'The logic of access to the European Parliament', *Journal of Common Market Studies*, 42:3, pp. 473–495.

Bouwen, Pieter (2004b) 'Exchanging access good for access. A comparative study of business lobbying in the EU institutions', *European Journal of Political Research*, 43:3, pp. 337–369.

Bouwen, Pieter and Margaret McCown (2007) 'Lobbying versus litigation: political and legal strategies of interest representation in the European Union', *Journal of European Public Policy*, 14:3, pp. 422–443.

Braun, Jan (2011) 'EU energy policy under the Treaty of Lisbon rules: between a new policy and business as usual', European Policy Institutes Network Working Paper 31, available at: http://papers.ssrn.com/sol3/papers.cfm?abstract_id=2001357, accessed 3 July 2015.

Broscheid, Andreas and David Coen (2007) 'Lobbying activity and fora creation in the EU: empirically exploring the nature of the policy good', *Journal of European Public Policy*, 14:3, pp. 346–365.

Brubaker, Rogers and Frederick Cooper (2000) 'Beyond "identity" ', *Theory and Society*, 29:1, pp. 1–47.

Buchan, David (2009) *Energy and climate change: Europe at the crossroads* (Oxford: Oxford University Press for the Oxford Institute for Energy Studies).

Buchan, David (2010) 'Energy policy' in Helen Wallace, Mark A. Pollack and Alasdair R. Young (eds) *Policy-making in the European Union*, 6th edition (Oxford: Oxford University Press), pp. 357–379.

Burnham, Peter, Karin Gillard Lutz, Wyn Grant and Zig Layton-Henry (2008) *Research methods in politics*, 2nd edition (Houndmills, Basingstoke: Palgrave Macmillan).

Burns, Charlotte and Neil Carter (2012) 'Environmental policy' in Erik Jones, Anand Menon, and Stephen Weatherill (eds) *The Oxford handbook of the European Union*, 1st edition (Oxford: Oxford University Press), pp. 511–525.

Buzan, Barry, Ole Waever and Jaap de Wilde (1998) *Security: a new framework for analysis* (Boulder, Colorado: Lynne Rienner Publishers).

Büthe, Tim and Walter Mattli (2010) 'International standards and standard-setting bodies' in David Coen, Graham Wilson and Wyn Grant (eds) *Oxford handbook of business and government* (Oxford: Oxford University Press), pp. 440–471.

Carley, Kathleen M. (2006) 'Destabilization of covert networks', *Computational and Mathematical Organization Theory*, 12:1, pp. 51–66.

Carpenter, Charli R. (2011) 'Vetting the advocacy agenda: network centrality and the paradox of weapons norms', *International Organization*, 65:1, pp. 69–102.

Carroll, William K. and R. S. Ratner (1996) 'Master framing and cross-movement networking in contemporary social movements', *The Sociological Quarterly*, 37:4, pp. 601–625.

Castells, Manuel (1996) *The information age: economy, society and culture*, vol. I, *The rise of the network society* (Malden, Mass.: Blackwell).

Chalmers, Adam William (2012) 'Interests, influence and information: comparing the influence of interest groups in the European Union' in Michèle Knodt, Christine Quittkat and Justin Greenwood (eds) *Functional and territorial interest representation in the EU* (Oxford: Routledge), pp. 123–138.

Chilvers, Jason (2008) 'Environmental risk, uncertainty, and participation: mapping an emergent epistemic community', *Environment and Planning A*, 40:12, pp. 2990–3008.

Christiansen, Thomas and Mathias Dobbels (2013) 'Delegated powers and inter-institutional relations in the EU after Lisbon: A normative assessment', *West European Politics*, 36:6, pp. 1159–1177.

Coen, David (2007) *Lobbying in the European Union* (Briefing paper) (Brussels: European Parliament, Directorate General Internal Policies of the Union), PE 393.266.

Cress, Daniel and David Snow (1998) 'Mobilization at the margins: organizing by the homeless' in Anne Costain and Andrew McFarland (eds) *Social movements and American political institutions* (Lanham, Md: Rowman & Littlefield Publishers), pp. 73–98.

Crombez, Christophe (2002) 'Information, lobbying and the legislative process in the European Union', *European Union Politics*, 3:1, pp. 7–32.

Cross, Mai'a K. Davis (2013) 'Rethinking epistemic communities twenty years later', *Review of International Studies*, 39:1, pp. 137–160.

Daojiong, Zha (2006) 'China's energy security: domestic and international issues', *Survival*, 48:1, pp. 179–190.

De Graaff, Naná (2011) 'A global energy network? The expansion and integration of non-triad national oil companies', *Global Networks*, 11:2, pp.262–283.

De Jong, Sijbren, Jan Wouters and Steven Sterkx (2010) 'The 2009 Russian-Ukrainian gas dispute: lessons for European energy crisis management after Lisbon', *European Foreign Affairs Review*, 15:4, pp. 511–538.

Dekker, Anthony (2002) 'Applying social network analysis concepts to military C4ISR architectures', *Connections*, 24:3, pp. 93–103.

Diani, Mario (2003) 'Leaders or brokers? Positions and influence in social movement networks' in Mario Diani and Doug McAdam (eds) *Social movements and networks: relational approaches to collective action* (Oxford: Oxford University Press), pp. 105–122.

Dinan, Desmond (2014) 'Governance and institutions: the unrelenting rise of the European Parliament', *Journal of Common Market Studies*, 52:S1, pp. 109–124.

Dudley, Geoffrey and Jeremy Richardson (1998) 'Arenas without rules and the policy change process: outsider groups and British roads policy', *Political Studies*, 46:4, pp. 727–747.

Dudley, Geoffrey and Jeremy Richardson (1999) 'Competing advocacy coalitions and the process of "frame reflection": a longitudinal analysis of EU steel policy', *Journal of European Public Policy*, 6:2, pp. 225–248.

Duffield, John S. and Vicki L. Birchfield (2011) 'The recent upheaval in EU energy policy' in Vicki L. Birchfield and John S. Duffield (eds) *Towards a common European Union energy policy* (Palgrave Macmillan: Houndmills, Basingstoke), pp. 1–9.

Dür, Andreas (2008) 'Interest groups in the European Union: how powerful are they?', *West European Politics*, 31:6, pp. 1212–1230.

Dür, Andreas and Gemma Mateo (2012) 'Who lobbies the European Union? National interest groups in a multilevel polity', *Journal of European Public Policy*, 19:7, pp. 969–987.

Durão Barroso, José Manuel (2009) Remarks by Commission President José Manuel Barroso upon the signature of the Nabucco intergovernmental agreement, SPEECH/09/339, available at: http://europa.eu/rapid/press-release_SPEECH-09-339_en.htm, accessed 10 May 2013.

Durão Barroso, José Manuel (2011) Joint Declaration on the Southern Gas Corridor of José Manuel Durão Barroso (President of the European Commission) and Ilham Aliyev (President of the Republic of Azerbaijan), 13 January 2011, Baku, the Republic of Azerbaijan, available at: http://ec.europa.eu/energy/infrastructure/strategy/doc/2011_01_13_joint_declaration_southern_corridor.pdf, accessed 8 May 2013.

Eberlein, Burkand and Abraham Newman (2009) 'Tackling the regulatory dilemma: the rise of incorporated transgovernmental networks' in Ingeborg Tömmel and Amy Verdun (eds) Innovative governance in the European Union (Boulder, Colorado: Lynne Rienner Publishers), pp.237–254.

Eikeland, Per Ove (2011) 'The Third Internal Energy Market Package : new power relations among Member States, EU institutions and non-state actors?', *Journal of Common Market Studies*, 49:2, pp. 243–263.

Eising, Rainer (2007) 'Institutional context, organizational resources and strategic choices: explaining interest group access in the European Union', *European Union Politics*, 8:3, pp. 329–362.

Eising, Rainer (2009) *The political economy of state-business relations in Europe: interest mediation, capitalism and EU policy-making* (New York: Routledge).

Eising, Rainer and Beate Kohler-Koch (1999) 'Introduction: network governance in the European Union' in Beate Kohler-Koch and Rainer Eising (eds) *The transformation of governance in the European Union* (London: Routledge), pp. 1–12.

Emirbayer, Mustafa and Jeff Goodwin (1994) 'Network analysis, culture, and the problem of agency', *American Journal of Sociology*, 99:6, pp. 1411–1454.

Enders, Walter and Xuejuan Su (2007) 'Rational terrorists and optimal network structure', *Journal of Conflict Resolution*, 51:1, pp. 33–57.

Eng, Gary (2003) 'Energy security initiative: some aspects of oil security', a publication of the Asia Pacific Energy Research Centre, available at: http://aperc.ieej.or.jp/file/2010/9/26/Energy_Security_Initiative_2003.pdf, accessed 5 January 2013.

Entman, Robert M. (1993) 'Framing: towards clarification of a fractured paradigm', *Journal of Communication*, 43:4, pp. 51–58.

Ernst, Rose (2009) 'Working expectations: frame diagnosis and the welfare rights movement', *Social Movement Studies*, 8:3, pp. 185–201.

Esakova, Nataliya (2012) 'European Energy Security: analyzing the EU-Russia energy security regime in terms of interdependence theory' (Frankfurt: Springer VS).

Escribano, Gonzalo (2012) 'The Europeanization of energy corridors to the EU' in José María Marín-Quemada, Javier García Escribano (eds) *Energy security for the EU in the 21st century: markets, geopolitics and corridors* (New York: Routledge), pp. 276–293.

Escribano, Gonzalo and Javier García-Verdugo (2012) 'Energy security, energy corridors and the geopolitical context: a conceptual approach' in José María Marín-Quemada, Javier García Escribano (eds) *Energy security for the EU in the 21st century: markets, geopolitics and corridors* (New York: Routledge), pp. 26–36.

Fabbrini, Sergio (2015) 'The European Union and the puzzle of parliamentary government', *Journal of European Integration*, 37:5, pp. 571–586.

Faul, Moira (2013) *Power and partnerships for international development: the case of the education Millennium Development Goals*, PhD Dissertation, University of Cambridge.

Faust, Katherine and John Skvoretz (2008) 'Comparing networks across space and time, size and species' in Linton C. Freeman (ed) *Social network analysis*, volume 1 (United Kingdom, London: SAGE Publications Ltd.), pp. 191–219.

Feindt, Peter H. (2010) 'Policy-learning and environmental policy integration in the Common Agricultural Policy, 1973–2003', *Public Administration*, 88:2, pp. 296–314.

Finon, Dominique and Catherine Locatelli (2006) 'L'interdépendance gazière de la Russie et de l'Union européenne : quel équilibre entre le marché et la géopolitique ?'. Cahier de recherche LEPII, série EPE; nr. 41, available at: https://halshs.archives-ouvertes.fr/file/index/docid/119602/filename/Cahier41.pdf, accessed 3 July 2015.

Fortin, Isabelle (2015) ' "Never waste a good crisis": energy securitization inside the EU after the 2009 gas crisis between Russia and Ukraine', Paper presented at the ISA Annual Convention, New Orleans, 18–21 February 2015, on file with the author.

Freeman, Linton C. (1979) 'Centrality in social networks: conceptual clarification', *Social networks*, 1:3, pp. 215–239.

Gahan, Peter and Andreas Pekarek (2013) 'Social movement theory, collective action frames and union theory: a critique and extension', *British Journal of Industrial Relations*, 51:4, pp. 754–776.

Garvin, Theresa and John Eyles (1997) 'The sun safety metanarrative: translating science into public health discourse', *Policy Sciences*, 30:2, pp. 47–70.

Gerber, Elisabeth R. (1999) *The populist paradox: interest group influence and the promise of direct legislation* (Princeton, NJ: Princeton University Press).

Gerring, John (2007) *Case study research: principles and practices* (Cambridge, New York: Cambridge University Press).

Gény, Florence (2010) 'Can unconventional gas be a game changer in European gas markets?', a publication of the Oxford Institute for Energy Studies, NG 46, available at: http://www.oxfordenergy.org/wpcms/wp-content/uploads/2011/01/NG46-CanUnconventionalGasbeaGameChangerinEuropeanGasMarkets-FlorenceGeny-2010.pdf, accessed 15 January 2013.

Glaser, Barney G. and Anselm L. Strauss (1967) *The discovery of grounded theory; strategies for qualitative research* (Chicago: Aldine).

Glockner, Iris and Berthold Rittberger (2012) 'The European Coal and Steele Community (ECSC) and European Defence Community (EDC) Treaties' in Finn Laursen (ed) *Designing the European Union: from Paris to Lisbon* (Houndmills, Basingstoke, Hampshire: Palgrave Macmillan), pp. 16–47.

Goddard, Stacie (2009) 'Brokering change: networks and entrepreneurs in International Politics', *International Theory*, 1:2, pp. 249–281.

Goffman, Erving (1974) *Frame analysis* (Cambridge: Harvard University Press).

Goldthau, Andreas and Nick Sitter (2015) *A liberal actor in a realist world: the European Union regulatory state and the Global Political Economy of Energy* (Oxford: Oxford University Press).

Goodman, Leo A. (1961) 'Snowball sampling', *Annals of Mathematical Statistics*, 32:2, pp. 148–170.

Greenwood, Justin (2007) 'Organized civil society and democratic legitimacy in the European Union', *British Journal of Political Science*, 37:2, pp. 333–357.

Gross, Catherine (2007) 'Community perspectives of wind energy in Australia: the application of a justice and community fairness framework to increase social acceptance', *Energy Policy*, Vol.35, pp. 2727–2736.

Gulati, Ranjay, Dania A. Dialdin and Lihua Wang (2002) 'Organizational networks' in Joel A.C. Baum (ed) *The Blackwell companion to organizations* (Oxford: Blackwell), pp. 281–303.

Gusterson, Hugh (2008) 'Ethnographic research' in Audie Klotz and Deepa Prakash (eds) *Qualitative methods in International Relations: a pluralist guide* (Houndmills, Basingstoke: Palgrave Macmillan), pp. 93–113.

Haas, Ernst B. (1958) *The uniting of Europe; political, social, and economic forces, 1950–1957* (Stanford, Calif.: Stanford University Press).

Haas, Peter M. (1992a) 'Introduction: epistemic communities and international policy coordination', *International Organization*, 46:1, *Knowledge, Power, and International Policy Coordination*, pp. 1–35.

Haas, Peter M. (1992b) 'Banning chlorofluorocarbons: epistemic community efforts to protect stratospheric ozone', *International Organization*, 46:1, *Knowledge, Power, and International Policy Coordination*, pp. 187–224.

Hafner-Burton, Emilie and Alexander Montgomery (2009) 'Globalisation and the social power politics of international economic networks' in Miles Kahler (ed) *Networked politics: agency, power and governance* (Ithaca, New York: Cornell University Press), pp. 23–42.

Hafner-Burton, Emilie, Miles Kahler and Alexander Montgomery (2009) 'Network analysis for International Relations', *International Organization*, 63:3, pp. 559–592.

Hall, Richard L. and Alan Deardorff (2006) 'Lobbying as legislative subsidy', *American Political Science Review*, 100:1, pp. 69–84.

Hänggli, Regula and Hanspeter Kriesi (2012) 'Frame construction and frame promotion (strategic framing choices)', *American Behavioral Scientist*, 56:3, pp. 260–278.

Helm, Dieter R. (2012) 'European energy policy' in Erik Jones, Anand Menon, and Stephen Weatherill (eds) *The Oxford handbook of the European Union*, 1st edition (Oxford: Oxford University Press), pp. 556–569.

Henderson, P. D. (1977) 'Two British errors: their probable size and some possible lessons', *Oxford Economic Papers*, 29:2, pp. 159–205.

Hewson, Claire (2007) 'Gathering data on the Internet: qualitative approaches and possibilities for mixed methods and research' in Adam N. Joinson, Katelyn McKenna, Tom Postmes and Ulf-Dietrich Reips (eds) *Oxford handbook of Internet psychology* (Oxford: Oxford University Press), pp. 405–428.

Hix, Simon (1998) 'The study of the European Union II: the "new governance" agenda and its rival', *Journal of European Public Policy*, 5:1, pp. 38–65.

Hix, Simon (1999) *The political system of the European Union* (New York: St Martin's Press).

Hollis, Simon (2010) 'The necessity of protection: transgovernmental networks and EU security governance', *Cooperation and Conflict*, 45:3, pp. 312–330.

Honoré, Anouk (2010) *European gas demand, supply and pricing: cycles, seasons and the impact of LNG price arbitrage* (Oxford: Oxford University Press for the Oxford Institute for Energy Studies).

Immergut, Ellen M. (1992) *Health politics: interests and institutions in Western Europe* (Cambridge: Cambridge University Press).

Ingold, Karin, Manuel Fischer and Paul Cairney (2017) 'Drivers for policy agreement in nascent subsystems: an application of the advocacy coalition framework to fracking policy in Switzerland and the UK', *Policy Studies Journal*, 45:3, pp. 442–63.

Jaffe, Amy, Mark Hayes and David Victor (2006) 'Conclusions' in David Victor, Amy Jaffe and Mark Hayes (eds) *Natural gas and geopolitics: from 1970 to 2040* (Cambridge: Cambridge University Press), pp. 467–483.

Jenkins, Gareth (2012) 'Turkey, Central Asia and energy: dreams and realities' in Elĕbieta Stadtmüller and Klaus Bachmann (eds) *The EU's shifting borders: theoretical approaches and policy implications in the new neighbourhood* (London: Routledge), pp. 182–199.

Jenkins-Smith, Hank (1990) *Democratic politics and policy analysis* (Pacific Grove, CA: Brooks/Cole Publishing).

Jenkins-Smith, Hank and Gilbert St. Clair (1993) 'The politics of offshore energy: empirically testing the advocacy coalition framework' in P. Sabatier and H. Jenkins-Smith (eds) *Policy change and learning* (Boulder, CO: Westview Press), pp. 149–176.

Jenkins-Smith, Hank and Paul Sabatier (1994) 'Evaluating the Advocacy Coalition Framework', *Journal of Public Policy*, 14:2, pp. 175–203.

John, Peter and Alistair Cole (1998) 'Sociometric mapping techniques and the comparison of policy networks: economic decision making in Leeds and Lille' in David Marsh (ed) *Comparing policy networks* (Buckingham: Open University Press), pp. 132–146.

Kahler, Miles (2009a) 'Collective action and clandestine networks: the case of al Qaeda' in Miles Kahler (ed) *Networked politics: agency, power and governance* (Ithaca, New York: Cornell University Press), pp. 103–124.

Kahler, Miles (ed) (2009b) *Networked politics: agency, power and governance* (Ithaca, New York: Cornell University Press).

Kanellakis, Marinos, Georgios Martinopoulos and Theodoros Zachariadis (2013) 'European energy policy—A review', *Energy Policy*, 62, pp. 1020–1030.

Kaysi, Hakan (2011) 'Energy security of the European Union and Turkey's role', *Ankara Review of European Studies*, 10:2, pp. 63–82.

Keck, Margaret and Kathryn Sikkink (1998) *Activists beyond borders: advocacy networks in international politics* (Ithaca: Cornell University Press).

Kenis, Patrick and Volker Schneider (1991) 'Policy networks and policy analysis: scrutinizing a new analytical toolbox' in Bernd Marin and Renate Mayntz (eds)

Policy network: empirical evidence and theoretical considerations (Frankfurt: Campus Verlag), pp. 25–59.

Kenney, Michael (2009) 'Turning to the "dark side": coordination, exchange and learning in criminal networks' in Miles Kahler (ed) *Networked politics: agency, power and governance* (Ithaca, New York: Cornell University Press), pp. 79–102.

Kenney, Michael, John Horgan, Cale Horne et al. (2012) 'Organisational adaptation in an activist network: social networks, leadership, and change in al-Muhajiroun', *Applied Ergonomics*, 44:5, pp. 1–9.

Keukeleire, Stephan and Jennifer MacNaughtan (2008) *The Foreign Policy of the European Union* (Houndmills, Basingstoke: Palgrave Macmillan).

Kilduff, Martin and David Krackhardt (2008) *Interpersonal networks in organizations: cognition, personality, dynamics and culture* (Cambridge: Cambridge University Press).

King, Nigel and Christine Horrocks (2010) *Interviews in qualitative research* (Los Angeles, London: SAGE).

Kinsey, Christopher, Stig Hansen and George Franklin (2009) 'The impact of private security companies on Somalia's governance networks', *Cambridge Review of International Affairs*, 22:1, pp. 147–161.

Kirchner, Emil (2006) 'The challenge of European Union security governance', *Journal of Common Market Studies*, 44:5, pp. 947–968.

Kirchner, Emil (2007) 'Regional and global security: changing threats and institutional responses' in Emil Kirchner and James Sperling (eds) *Global security governance: competing perceptions of security in the 21st century* (London: Routledge), pp. 3–22.

Klüver, Heike (2013) *Lobbying in the European Union: interest groups, lobbying coalitions, and policy change* (Oxford: Oxford University Press).

Knoke, David (1990) *Organizing for collective action: the political economies of associations* (Hawthorne, NY: Aldine de Gruyter).

Knott, Jack and Gary Miller (1987) *Reforming bureaucracy: the politics of institutional choice* (Englewood Cliffs, NJ: Prentice-Hall).

Kohler-Koch, Beate (1994) 'Changing patterns of interest intermediation in the European Union', *Government and Opposition*, 29:2, pp. 166–180.

Kohler-Koch, Beate (1997) 'Organised interests in the EC and the European Parliament' *European Integration online Papers (EIoP)*, 1:9, pp. 1–9, available at: eiop.or.at/eiop/pdf/1997-009.pdf, accessed 10 May 2014.

Krackhardt, David (1990) 'Assessing the political landscape: structure, cognition, and power in organizations', *Administrative Science Quarterly*, 35:2, pp. 342–369.

Krahmann, Elke (2003a) 'Conceptualizing security governance', *Cooperation and Conflict*, 38:5, pp. 5–26.

Krahmann, Elke (2003b) *Multilevel networks in European Foreign Policy* (Aldershot: Ashgate).

Krahmann, Elke (2005) 'Security governance and networks: new theoretical perspectives in transatlantic security', *Cambridge Review of International Affairs*, 18:1, pp. 15–30.

Krahmann, Elke (2010) *State, citizens and the privatization of security* (Cambridge: Cambridge University Press).

Krebs, Valdis (2002) 'Mapping terrorist networks', *Connections*, 24:3, pp. 43–52.

Kreutler, Maren (2014) *Interest group coalitions in the European Union: an analysis of (in)formal initiatives to influence European energy policy* (Baden-Baden: Nomos).

Lake, David and Wendy Wong (2009) 'The politics of networks: interests, power and human rights norms' in Miles Kahler (ed) *Networked politics: agency, power and governance* (Ithaca, New York: Cornell University Press), pp. 127–150.

Leal-Arcas, Rafael (2018) 'Natural gas, US shale dynamics and energy security: a view from the European Union' in Slawomir Raszewski (ed) *The International Political Economy of Oil and Gas* (Cham, Switzerland: Palgrave Macmillan), pp. 73–85.

Lindberg, Leon N. (1963) *The political dynamics of European economic integration* (Stanford, California: Stanford University Press).

Lofland, John and Lyn Lofland (1984) *Analyzing social settings: a guide to qualitative observation and analysis* (Belmont, California: Wadsworth Publishing).

Mahoney, Christine (2008) *Brussels versus the Beltway: advocacy in the United States and the European Union* (Washington, D.C.: Georgetown University Press).

Maltby, Tomas (2013) 'European Union energy policy integration: a case of European Commission policy entrepreneurship and increasing supranationalism', *Energy Policy*, 55, pp. 435–444.

Maoz, Zeev (2012) 'How network analysis can inform the study of International Relations?', *Conflict Management and Peace Science*, 29:3, pp. 247–256.

Marín-Quemada, José María, Carlos Velasco and Beatriz Muñoz (2012) 'Energy security of supply and EU energy policy' in José María Marín-Quemada, Javier García Escribano (eds) *Energy security for the EU in the 21st century: markets, geopolitics and corridors* (New York: Routledge), pp. 195–209.

Martin, Stephen (2006) 'Building on coal and steel: European integration in the 1950s and the 1960s' in Desmond Dinan (ed) *Origins and evolution of the European Union* (Oxford: Oxford University Press), pp. 126–140.

Marx Ferree, Myra, and David A. Merrill (2000) 'Hot movements, cold cognition: thinking about social movements in gendered frames', *Contemporary Sociology*, 29:3, pp. 454–462.

Matthews, John and Elizabeth Cramer (2008) 'Using technology to enhance qualitative research with hidden populations', *Qualitative Report*, 13:2, pp. 301–315.

Mays, Nicholas and Catherine Pope (2000) 'Qualitative research in health care: assessing quality in qualitative research', *British Medical Journal*, 320:7226, pp. 50–52.

Mazey, Sonia and Jeremy Richardson (2001) 'Institutionalizing promiscuity: Commission interest group relations in the European Union' in Alec Stone Sweet, Wayne Sandholtz and Neil Fligstein (eds) *The institutionalization of Europe* (Oxford: Oxford University Press), pp. 71–93.

Mazey, Sonia and Jeremy Richardson (2006) 'Interest groups and EU policy-making: organizational logic and venue shopping' in Jeremy Richardson (ed) *European Union: power and policy-making* (Oxford: Routledge), pp. 247–349.

McPherson, J. Miller and Lynn Smith-Lovin (1987) 'Homophily in voluntary organizations: status distance and the composition of face-to-face groups', *American Sociological Review*, 52:3, pp. 370–379.

Mérand, Frédéric, Stéphanie C. Hofmann and Bastien Irondelle (2011) 'Governance and state power: a network analysis of European Security', *Journal of Common Market Studies*, 49:1, pp. 121–147.

Mikhelidze, Nona (2013) 'The winner is TAP: the EU's failed policy in the South Caucasus', IAI Working Papers 13 | 25, July 2013, pp. 1–7, available at: https://www.files.ethz.ch/isn/167732/iaiwp1325.pdf, accessed 17 February 2020.

Neframi, Eleftheria (2012) 'Panorama des relations extérieures de l'Union Européenne en matière énergétique' in Claude Blumann (ed) *Vers une politique européenne de l'énergie* (Bruxelles: Bruylant/LGDJ), pp. 155–179.

Nilsson, Måns, Lars J. Nilsson and Karin Ericsson (2009) 'The rise and fall of GO trading in European renewable energy policy: the role of advocacy and policy framing', *Energy Policy*, 37: 11, pp. 4454–4462.

Oliver, Pamela E. and Hank Johnston (1999) 'What a good idea! Frames and ideologies in social movement research', Paper presented at the annual meeting of the American Sociological Association, August 8, Chicago, IL; available at: www.ssc.wisc.edu/~oliver/PROTESTS/ArticleCopies/Frames.2.29.00.pdf, accessed 5 December 2014.

Peters, B. Guy and Jon Pierre (2010) 'Governance approaches' in Antje Wiener and Thomas Diez (eds) *European integration theory*, 2nd edition (Oxford: Oxford University Press), pp. 91–104.

Peterson, John (2010) 'Policy networks' in Antje Wiener and Thomas Diez (eds) *European integration theory*, 2nd edition (Oxford: Oxford University Press), pp. 105–124.

Pirani, Simon, Jonathan Stern and Katja Yafimava (2009) 'The Russo-Ukrainian gas dispute of January 2009: a comprehensive assessment', a publication of the Oxford Institute for Energy Studies, NG 27, pp. 1–66, available at: http://www.oxfordenergy.org/wpcms/wp-content/uploads/2010/11/NG27-The

RussoUkrainianGasDisputeofJanuary2009AComprehensiveAssessment-JonathanSternSimonPiraniKatjaYafimava-2009.pdf, accessed 10 May 2013.

Podolny, Joel M. and Karen L. Page (1998) 'Network forms of organization', *Annual Review of Sociology*, 241:1, pp. 57–76.

Pollack, Mark (2010) 'Theorizing EU policy-making' in Helen Wallace, Mark A. Pollack and Alasdair R. Young (eds) *Policy-making in the European Union*, 6th edition (Oxford: Oxford University Press), pp. 15–44.

Powell, Walter W. (1990) 'Neither market nor hierarchy: network forms of organization', *Research in Organizational Behaviour*, 12, pp. 295–336.

Primack, Joel and Frank von Hippel (1974) *Advice and dissent: scientists and the political arena* (New York: Basic Books).

Princen, Sebastiaan (2011) 'Agenda-setting strategies in EU policy processes', *Journal of European Public Policy*, 18:7, pp. 927–943.

Proedrou, Filippos (2012) *EU energy security in the gas sector: evolving dynamics, policy dilemmas and prospects* (Ashgate: Farnham).

Qingyi, Wang (2006) 'Energy conservation as security', *China Security*, Summer Issue, pp. 89–105.

Radaelli, Claudio M. (1999) 'Harmful tax competition in the EU: policy narratives and advocacy Coalitions', *Journal of Common Market Studies*, 37:4, pp. 661–682.

Raszewski, Slawomir (2018) 'Conclusion: transitioning from the 'old' to the 'new' political economy of oil and gas' in Slawomir Raszewski (ed) *The International Political Economy of Oil and Gas* (Cham, Switzerland: Palgrave Macmillan), pp. 279–284.

Rein, Martin and Donald Schön (1993) 'Reframing policy discourse' in Frank Fisher and John Forester (eds) *The argumentative turn in policy analysis and planning* (Durham: Duke University Press), pp. 145–166.

Rhodes, Rod A. W. (1997) *Understanding governance: policy networks, governance, reflexivity and accountability* (Buckingham: Open University Press).

Rogers, Everett M and George M. Beal (2008) 'The importance of personal influence in the adoption of technological changes' in Linton C. Freeman (ed) *Social network analysis*, volume 4 (United Kingdom, London: SAGE Publications Ltd.), pp. 159–168.

Ronit, Karsten (2011) 'Transnational corporations and the regulation of businesses at the global level' in Bob Reinalda (ed) *The Ashgate research companion to non-state actors* (Ashgate: Farnham), pp. 75–88.

Rosamond, Ben (2000) *Theories of European integration* (New York: St Martin's Press).

Rose, Richard (2000) 'Policy networks in globalization: from local to cosmopolitan networking', NIRA Review 5–9, available at: http://www.nira.or.jp/past//publ/review/2000winter/02rose.pdf, accessed 15 January 2015.

Rozbicka, Patrycja (2013) 'Advocacy coalitions: influencing the policy process in the EU', *Journal of European Public Policy*, 20:6, pp. 838–853.

Rubin, Herbert J. and Irene S. Rubin (2005) *Qualitative interviewing: the art of hearing data*, 2nd edition (London: SAGE).

Ryan, Charlotte (1991) *Prime time activism: media strategies for grassroots organizing* (Boston, MA: South End Press).

Sabatier, Paul (1987) 'Knowledge, policy-oriented learning, and policy change: an advocacy coalition framework', *Knowledge: creation, diffusion, utilisation*, 8:4, pp. 649–692.

Sabatier, Paul (1988) 'An advocacy coalition framework of policy change and the role of policy-oriented learning therein', *Policy Sciences*, 21:2–3, pp. 129–168.

Sabatier, Paul (1998) 'The advocacy coalition framework: revisions and relevance for Europe', *Journal of European Public Policy*, 5:1, pp. 98–130.

Sabatier, Paul and Anne Brasher (1993) 'From vague consensus to clearly differentiated coalitions: environmental policy at Lake Tahoe, 1964–1985' in Paul Sabatier and Hank Jenkins-Smith (eds) *Policy change and learning: an advocacy coalition approach* (Boulder, Co: Westview Press), pp. 149–176.

Sartori, Nicolò (2011) 'The Southern Gas Corridor: needs, opportunities and constraints', IAI Working Papers 11 | 06, June 2011, pp. 1–16, available at: www.iai.it/sites/default/files/iai1108.pdf, accessed 15 February 2014.

Sartori, Nicolò (2012) 'The European Commission's Policy Towards the Southern Gas Corridor: between national interests and economic fundamentals', IAI Working Papers 12 | 01—January 2012, pp. 1–17, available on file with the author.

Schlager, Edella and William Blomquist (1996) 'A comparison of three emerging theories of the policy process', *Political Research Quarterly*, 49:3, pp. 651–672.

Schmidt-Felzmann, Anke (2008) 'All for One? EU Member States and the Union's common policy towards the Russian Federation', *Journal of Contemporary European Studies*, 16:2, pp. 169–187.

Scott, John (1988) 'Trend report: social network analysis', *Sociology*, 22:1, pp. 109–127.

Scott, John (1991) *Social network analysis: a handbook* (London; Newbury Park, California: SAGE Publications, 1991).

Siddi, Marco (2019) 'The EU's botched geopolitical approach to external energy policy: the case of the Southern Gas Corridor', *Geopolitics*, 24:1, pp. 124–144.

Simonet, Loïc (2012) 'Les institutions paneuropéennnes en matière d'énergie et les projects de gazoducs transeuropéens' in Claude Blumann (ed) *Vers une politique européenne de l'énergie* (Bruxelles: Bruylant/LGDJ), pp. 225–238.

Snow, David A., E. Burke Rochford, Jr., Steven K. Worden and Robert D. Benford (1986) 'Frame alignment processes, micromobilization, and movement participation', *American Sociological Review*, 51:4, pp. 464–481.

Sovacool, Benjamin and Michael Dworkin (2014) *Global energy justice: problems, principles and practices* (Cambridge: Cambridge University Press).
Stern, Jonathan (2006) 'Natural gas security problems in Europe: the Russian-Ukrainian crisis of 2006', *Asia-Pacific Review*, 13:1, pp. 32–59.
Stokes, Elen (2014) 'New EU policy on shale gas', *Environmental Law Review*, 16:1, pp. 42–49.
Tawonezvi, Joseph (2017) 'The legal and regulatory framework for the EU's shale gas exploration and production regulating public health and environmental impacts', *Energy, Ecology and Environment*, 2:1, pp. 1–28.
Tenbücken, Marc (2002) *Corporate lobbying in the European Union: strategies of multinational companies* (Frankfurt am Main: Peter Lang).
Triandafyllidou, Anna and Anastasios Fotiou (1998) 'Sustainability and modernity in the European Union: a frame theory approach to policy-making', *Sociological Research Online*, 3:1, available at: http://www.socresonline.org.uk/3/1/2.html, accessed 15 November 2014.
van Aartsen, Jozias, European Coordinator (2009) Activity report: project of European interest n° NG 3, available at: http://ec.europa.eu/energy/infrastructure/tent_e/doc/axis/2009_axis_linking_activity_report_2007_2009.pdf, accessed 20 October 2013.
Vicari, Stefania (2010) 'Measuring collective action frames: a linguistic approach to frame analysis', *Journal of Empirical Research on Culture, the Media and the Arts*, 38:5, pp. 504–525.
Vliegenthart, Rens and Liesbet van Zoonen (2011) 'Power to the frame: bringing sociology back to frame analysis', *European Journal of Communication*, 26:2, pp. 101–115.
Walker, Gordon and Rosie Day (2012) 'Fuel poverty as injustice: integrating distribution, recognition and procedure in the struggle for affordable warmth', *Energy Policy*, Vol.49, pp. 69–75.
Wasserman, Stanley and Katherine Faust (1994) *Social network analysis: methods and applications* (New York: Cambridge University Press).
Watts, Duncan J. (2003) *Six degrees: the science of a connected age* (London: Heinemann).
Webber, Mark, Stuart Croft, Jolyon Howorth, Terry Terriff and Elke Krahmann (2004) 'The governance of European security', *Review of International Studies*, 30:1, pp. 3–26.
Weible, Christopher M. and Paul A. Sabatier (2007) 'A guide to the advocacy coalition framework' in Frank Fischer and Gerald J. Miller (eds) *Handbook of public policy analysis: theory, politics, and methods*, 1st edition (Boca Raton: CRC Press), pp. 123–136.
Weible, Christopher M., Paul A. Sabatier and Kelly McQueen (2009) 'Themes and variations: taking stock of the advocacy coalition framework', *The Policy Studies Journal*, 37:1, pp. 121–140.

Wengraf, Tom (2001) *Qualitative research interviewing: biographic narrative and semi-structured methods* (London: SAGE).
Wyciszkiewicz, Ernest (2013) 'European institutions in the debate on shale gas' in Cecile Musialski, Matthias Altmann, Stefan Lechtenbohmer, Werner Zittel (eds) *Shale gas in Europe: a multidisciplinary analysis with a focus on European specificities* (Deventer, Netherlands; Leuven, Belgium: Claeys and Casteels Law Publishers).
Yafimava, Katja (2011) *The transit dimension of EU energy security: Russian gas transit across Ukraine, Belarus and Moldova* (Oxford: Oxford University Press for the Oxford Institute for Energy Studies).
Young, Alasdair R. (2010) 'The European policy process in comparative perspective' in Helen Wallace, Mark A. Pollack, Alasdair R. Young (eds) *Policy-making in the European Union*, 6th edition (Oxford: Oxford University Press), pp. 45–68.
Youngs, Richard (2009) *Energy security: Europe's new Foreign Policy challenge* (London: Routledge).
Zafonte, Matthew and Paul Sabatier (1998) 'Shared beliefs and imposed interdependencies as determinants of ally networks in overlapping subsystems', *Journal of Theoretical Politics*, 10:4, pp. 473–505.
Zito, Anthony R. (2001) 'Epistemic communities, collective entrepreneurship and European integration', *Journal of European Public Policy*, 8:4, pp. 585–603.
Zürn, Michael (1998) 'The rise of International Environmental Politics: a review of current research', *World Politics*, 50:4, pp. 617–649.

Index[1]

[1] Note: Page numbers followed by 'n' refer to notes.

A.-M. Bocse, *International Networks, Advocacy and EU Energy Policy-Making*, Palgrave Studies in European Union Politics,
https://doi.org/10.1007/978-3-030-49505-3

The manufacturer's authorised representative in the EU is Springer Nature Customer Service Centre GmbH, Europaplatz 3, 69115 Heidelberg, Germany. If you have any concerns regarding our products, please contact ProductSafety@springernature.com

Printed and bound by CPI Group (UK) Ltd, Croydon, CR0 4YY
05/10/2026
02228123-0003